Alexandrine

An Intimate Biography of Love, Heartbreak,
and Devotion

Marita Newton

Alexandrine: An Intimate Biography of Love, Heartbreak, and Devotion

Published by Wheatmark˚
2030 East Speedway Boulevard, Suite 106
Tucson, Arizona 85719 USA
www.wheatmark.com

ISBN: 978-1-62787-956-9 (paperback)
ISBN: 978-1-62787-957-6 (ebook)
LCCN: 2022903319

Bulk ordering discounts are available through Wheatmark, Inc. For more information, email orders@wheatmark.com or call 1-888-934-0888.

My soul is like the open sea, on which float memories of splendid storms, shipwrecks, and sunbeams.

—Alexandrine von Hedemann

This book is in memory of my father and my grand-mother, who inspired me to write it. I dedicate it to my children.

Contents

Contents

Part III: Count L

Preface

*A*lexandrine von Hedemann was a woman with strong desires, presence, and courage. Her exceptional beauty, her character, and her wayward spirit set her apart from others of her time. This is a story of her life and the man she loved, of success, lust, struggle, scandal, and sorrow.

In the mid-nineteenth century, the nobility in Germany was at its zenith. Alexandrine was born into such a life as Baroness von Hedemann. It was a life of luxury but oftentimes filled with despair and pain. By the time she was seventeen, she met her first love. Never again did she find such love until she met Prince Chlodwig.

Prince Chlodwig von Hohenlohe-Schillingsfürst was of a princely class, which provided him with wealth, properties, and position. He made his home in Schillingsfürst Castle, which he inherited as the seventh prince of Hohenlohe. As such, he was the hereditary member of the Upper House of the Bavarian government. This book includes a glimpse into his early years and his rise within the German government during his lifetime until his final appointment in 1894 by Kaiser Wil-

Preface

helm of Prussia as third chancellor of the German Empire. It provides an intimate look into this very public statesman, his private life, and the politics of Germany during this time. Prince Chlodwig was a venerated statesman when he and Alexandrine met in Munich in 1862. It was her beauty that first captured his attention. But it was her intellect, passion, and reckless nature that intrigued him the most, culminating in a love affair spanning thirty years.

The events and people depicted in this book are real. Some names were omitted or changed where it seemed appropriate.

Acknowledgments

This book could not have been written without the help of my father, Wolfgang Baron von Hornstein, whose own writings in *Wo Unsere Wurtzeln Sind* (*Where Our Roots Are*) gave me valuable insight into the von Hedemann family. Before his death in 2008, I had the opportunity to see photographs and other documents and to spend many hours talking about our ancestors. During that time, a small but almost forgotten history of the von Hedemann family came to life. One day, in a casual conversation with my father, the story of the incredible love story between Alexandrine and Prince Chlodwig von Hohenlohe captured my interest. It was a story that I wanted to tell, but the time was not yet right. Marriage, a career, and children came first. It wasn't until I retired and my children were grown that I found the time to give this story the care it deserved. Other information and stories referenced in this book were provided by my grandmother Gisela Karolina Anna Baroness von Hornstein. While my grandmother only met her grandmother Alexandrine a few times, she did, however, remember as a young girl visiting Schillingsfürst Castle,

where she met her grandfather Prince Chlodwig von Hohenlohe on at least two occasions.

A special thank-you to my husband, Geoff Newton, who
offered to do research into the political history of Germany for
the years this book portrays, as well as for his loving encour-
agement and understanding while I spent hours, weeks, and
months at the keyboard.

Prologue

In 1912, Alexandrine, in her eightieth year, decides to relieve herself of all her possessions and letters, which she divides among her friends and family until there is nothing left. It is then that she, still devout and committed to the Catholic Church, enters the convent at Frauenwörth Abbey to live out her remaining days in reflection and prayer. Whether she has done this to nurture her spiritual life or to atone for her sins is not known.

Here, she spends her days in solemn contemplation in the room assigned to her. Instead of looking through tall glass windows into carefully sculpted gardens of the great houses in which she once lived, she sits by the small paned window in her room, watching the nuns in their black habits bending over the convent gardens. They are carefully tending the vegetables that will later arrive on their table. The convent is a quiet and peaceful place, a sanctuary in her waning days. Her eyes no longer radiate with the fire of passion. Her hair, which once captivated the eyes of men, is no longer the color of chestnuts. It no longer shimmers and catches the sun. Still reaching her ankles, it is now streaked with strands of gray. To Alexandrine, none of that matters as she lives with her memories, as sharp and vivid as if time had not passed.

When the evening bell rings for vespers, calling her and the nuns to prayers, she slowly and with great effort stands up from the small wooden chair in her simple room. Taking her cane in her hand, she walks out into the hallway. The nuns, already on their way to evening prayers, pass her room. She falls in line with the silent parade as they walk down the familiar cold stone corridor to the chapel. She clutches her missal firmly to her breast. Within its pages is a letter yellowed with age, its edges worn from folding and refolding. She no longer needs to read it. Etched in her memory are the words she repeats as a prayer:

> *Whenever I am long parted from you, I miss you, as one misses the flowers in autumn, the sun and the warm, inspiring airs of spring. I droop, and grow bitter and sullen but sometimes your face comes to me in a dream.* —CS

Every evening in quiet contemplation and prayer, Alexandrine reflects on her remarkable life of the past thirty years with the man who saved her from her days of darkest despair with his boundless love for her. A man who awakened her heart.

Part I

Alexandrine

My past lies like a dream behind me; like a tale in which the Good Fairy made desires which seemed impossible to come true.

—Alexandrine von Hedemann

Baroness Alexandrine von Hedemann at age 20

1

Early Years

*O*n a cold and bitter March morning in 1833, Therese Luise Emilie Josephine Alexandrine von Hedemann-Heespen came into the world under unthinkable circumstances, destined for a life that would bring her heartbreak, turmoil, and disappointment. At the age of fifteen, her mother, Baroness Mathilde von Stephany,[1] married the young and dashing Baron Karl Friedrich Wilhelm Christian von Hedemann-Heespen, an ancestor of the Cossacks, who, in the sixteenth century, settled near the Don River. The wild and daring Cossacks produced legendary heroes and sometimes rebels. As accomplished riders, they raced across the Russian steppes with wild abandon. They were known to be dangerous, demonic, and passionately fierce fighters. The Cossack blood coursing through Karl's veins gave him the courage to organize the Silesian Rebellion in 1821 against the Carlsbad Decrees, which were designed to suppress liberal agitation against the conservative governments of the German states. As a result, he and

---

1   Mathilde was baptized Henriette Amalie Mathilde Caroline von Stephany. Some records show her name is spelled either Stephany or Stefanie.

others were sentenced by the Prussian government to remain prisoners for the rest of their lives. However, a few years later, he was pardoned by the king of Prussia partly because of his service as the king's head forester. After that, Karl settled quietly into running his estates in Bavaria and Silesia.

At twenty-four, tall with piercing blue eyes and a blond, well-trimmed beard, he stood with the bearing of an aristocrat in his Prussian Army uniform before the young and easily impressed Mathilde and proposed marriage. With his long, thin legs inside the sharply creased dark-gray pants, a saber with a silver hilt sheathed at his side, and his tall leather boots shined to perfection, he was holding a leather helmet with a glossy black finish and an ornamental plate containing the Prussian emblem of a large spread-winged eagle. All this made the young girl's heart leap with glowing joy.

"Yes!" she shouted. Embarrassed by her quick outburst, she quickly bowed her head and shyly said, "Yes, it would be my honor to be your wife. Of course, my father will have to agree to this marriage."

Her father, General Albert von Stephany, approved of the marriage, knowing the titled Baron von Hedemann had the good fortune to have been appointed the Prussian king's head forester, a prestigious and prosperous position. Mathilde, a tall bean of a girl with smooth skin the color of cream and lustrous red hair, seemed a good match for the handsome baron. Besides, Baron von Hedemann was rich and owned multiple properties in Bavaria and Silesia, which would bring wealth into her family.

Mathilde von Stephany's family was not in accord with the von Hedemanns' recklessness. However, there must have been adventure and romance somewhere in her blood. At sixteen, Mathilde's mother had a lover whom her family found unsuitable. She tried many times to elope with him until her father, seeing no marriageable future for his daughter and with a great deal of money in payment to the convent, entered her into the spiritual life. However, she could not reconcile herself to a pure and simple routine of daily prayer and reflection. She found ways to send her young lover letters pleading with him to rescue her. Not wanting to be separated from her, he appeared one day. Seeing him outside the convent garden, she climbed over the wall and leapt onto his waiting horse below. She loosened her wimple, letting it fly away in the wind. They rode off together as she held on to him with all her strength. The stories of what happened to her were numerous but not often true. All that is known is that Mathilde was born of this union.

The marriage ceremony, with a hundred guests of the most noble and titled persons in the region, was held at the von Hedemann castle in Nürnberg. No one expected the three-day affair would be anything but splendid. The first day of the celebration brought the guests together for a day of feasting on the expansive lawn, followed by a hunt for boar on the castle's property. While the men took to their mounts with their howling hounds in pursuit, the ladies gathered for a game of archery.

By midafternoon, three boars and six pheasants arrived in the kitchen. The cook and several kitchen maids dressed the pheasants while the castle butcher slaughtered the pigs. The kitchen was in an uproar of activity while several other dishes were prepared: consommé with liver dumplings, fresh sweet and sour kidneys, steamed fresh asparagus picked from the garden, and a six-tiered wedding cake complete with an elaborate ice sculpture of swans for the base. The dinner was served in the main hall, where one of the unfortunate boars was prepared and displayed on a large silver platter with an apple in its snout, sitting on a bed of fragrant pine boughs strewn with apples and sweet-smelling oranges fresh from Italy. Carafes of wine and sparkling champagne poured into crystal goblets in a never-ending cascade throughout the evening. At midnight, the guests were ushered into the ballroom, where a twenty-piece orchestra began to play. Mathilde, dressed in an elegant dress of dark-blue silk, took Karl's offered hand and entered the ballroom for the first dance. Soon after Mathilde and Karl made their turn around the floor, the other guests joined in for a night of dancing.

The wedding ceremony took place the next day in the castle's chapel. It was a plain affair with the priest administering the vows to the young couple. Only their parents were in attendance as witnesses to the religious consecration ritual. Another night of dinner, champagne, and wine followed. This night, actors, jugglers, and mimes performed for the guests. Later in the evening, fireworks were seen over the castle's turrets.

The next morning, a breakfast buffet with a variety of breads, sweet tarts, meats, fruits, poached eggs, and sweet cream was served for any remaining guests. The newly married couple was escorted to their waiting carriage with cheers and applause from the guests and servants. After a two-month voyage at sea, stopping off in Italy, Greece, and Turkey, they returned to Nürnberg. After only a few days, the couple, with their personal servants, traveled by train to the Hedemann family castle in Silesia, where they made their home and began their married life.

Their marriage, for a time, was a happy one, but it was destined for great unhappiness as sadness and grief prevailed over most of their lives together.

During the first six years of marriage, three children arrived rather quickly. Later in their lives, these three children would die. The eldest daughter, Maria Albertine, married a count but suddenly died on her wedding trip. Within two years of her death, the widowed count married her younger sister. She, unfortunately, took ill with a violent fever shortly after they married. In such despair, she took her own life. A son, Karl August, traveled to America during his middle years, after he lost the family fortune. Under circumstances unknown to anyone, he shot himself.

After the birth of each child, Mathilde grew increasingly despondent, having bouts of depression followed by hysteria. Her frequent angry outbursts with uncontrolled, incoherent babble led to a declaration of insanity by her doctors. As Mathilde was pregnant at the time with their fourth child, Karl was certain her behavior would only worsen after another child was born.

At the urging of her doctor, the baron made the difficult decision to have her admitted into an institution for the insane in Zabkowice, Silesia, close to Nysa,[2] where they lived. In those days, the conditions of these sanitariums made them nothing short of the most wretched of places, which made Karl's decision even harder. He was convinced it had to be done, and after many days of agony, he relented, and she was taken away from him and their children.

It was there, within the walls of the asylum, that Alexandrine was born. She was taken away by her father immediately

---

2   Nysa is often spelled Neisse.

after her birth to be raised by him in their home in Nysa. A wet nurse was found from one of his tenant farms to nourish the unfortunate child. Seeing no improvement in Mathilde's condition over the next couple of years, and with her doctor's declarations of no possibility of leaving the institution, Karl made another difficult decision to divorce her. Having three rampageous young children in the house, in addition to the still very young Alexandrine, he desperately needed not only a wife but a mother for his four children.

When Alexandrine was six years old, her father married Jenny von Malchow, a young, childless widow. Already showing signs of her wild Cossack blood inherited from her father, Alexandrine was a constant irritant to her stepmother. Jenny complained that Alexandrine was what she called "inconvenient" and an impediment to her happy life. Another decision was made. Alexandrine would be sent away to live with a distant and rich uncle in Augsburg until she was older and had hopefully outgrown her wild nature.

Heinrich von Schätzler had no children at the time, so he and his wife happily accepted Alexandrine into their home. He owned a magnificent castle on the outskirts of Augsburg. It was while she was living with her uncle that she found true happiness. She was the darling of her aunt and uncle, who provided her with everything and anything she desired. "You are our little princess," they would say. She could do no wrong, even when she caused trouble, which she was often wont to do.

This happy time came to an end when, after many years of trying to bring their own child into the world, a daughter was born. Adele, the new "princess," now took first place in their hearts, while Alexandrine was relegated to second place. No longer did Alexandrine sit on her uncle's lap while he read her stories; no longer did her aunt spend all day doting on her; there were no more walks together in the garden while picking flowers for the table. In fact, Alexandrine rarely saw her aunt as she spent most of her time doting on Adele in the nursery. Her aunt would reassure her niece by telling her she was loved and still a precious child. But now her aunt had a baby, who required much of her attention, which made their time together less and less.

When Alexandrine was ten years old, unhappiness visited her like a dark, sinister cloud. Her loving aunt suddenly died. Her uncle mourned his wife desperately, and in his grief, he shied away even more from his precocious niece. He did the only thing he could do. He hired a governess.

It was generally known that there was nothing more commonplace than the sadistic cruelty of a governess who was either given or took upon herself complete authority over her charges. The younger Adele was still too young for a governess and continued under the care of her nurse. Thus, the governess had only one charge: Alexandrine. The governess's mission was to make sure that she grew into a model child. More importantly, to drive out her wild and beastly nature, which the governess said was a result of her Cossack blood. Unbeknown to her uncle, she was often made to stay up until midnight to complete her lessons. The governess was relentless in making sure she behaved, going so far as to beat her with a stick on her backside if she complained or broke some rule. Alexandrine's fear of the governess's wrath was so great that she dared not complain. After another beating that drew blood, and with proof of the governess's cruelty toward her, Alexandrine gathered up her courage and confided in Adele's nurse. Without a moment's hesitation, the nurse let the young girl's uncle know the severity of what was being inflicted on her by the governess. Alexandrine was convinced her life was saved. However, instead of reprimanding the governess or sending her away, her uncle wrote to Alexandrine's father: "With regards to Alexandrine, it is in her best interest that she be returned to live with you." Karl had no choice but to send for his daughter.

Alexandrine, now twelve years old, was put on a train in Augsburg for the long journey to Silesia, where her father lived. Her uncle sent along the governess to accompany her and deliver her safely to her father. After several days through Germany and Austria, they reached the city of Kreuzburg on the border of the state of Silesia. The train could go no further. The governess sought out an inn where she and Alexandrine could stay until her father arrived. A courier was sent along with a letter of their arrival. After waiting several days for an answer, they found out that the courier had become stuck in a bog. A second courier was sent.

A few days later, Alexandrine saw two riders on horses arriving. She recognized her father immediately. Her sister, Albertine, was the other rider. Alexandrine stood speechless as she saw the small group riding out of the woods. Her sister appeared to her as an enchanted princess riding a white stallion. She was dressed in a loden-green gown spread out over the horse's rump, a small felt hat trimmed with pheasant feathers on her head. Her father, looking stately and dignified riding a black stallion, approached the inn where she and the governess were waiting. Alexandrine, overcome with joy, broke free of the governess's hand. She ran shrieking to her father, who pulled her up onto his saddle. Throughout her life, she would never forget that moment. They left the inn but not before they put the governess on a train back to Augsburg.

Riding through Nysa, Alexandrine was in awe of the numerous churches in the city. "Why are there so many churches here, Papa?" she asked.

"I'm not sure, child. I have heard it said they were built as a result of centuries of wars and invasions by the Russians or perhaps during the Napoleonic Wars. Both Protestants and Catholics built churches during those times. Thirty-one to be exact. Some say that Nysa is called the 'Silesian Rome' because of its many churches."

They rode on through the market square. Small wooden houses covered in ivy, with smoke rising into the light-blue sky, lined the streets. The smell of wood smoke was thick in the air. A road leading out of the village wound its way into the dark, thick woods of fir and spruce before it disappeared. They rode on. Leaving the forest, a meadow suddenly appeared. They raced the horses as Alexandrine screamed with excitement. Soon the one-story castle came into view. It stood on a small hill with a pretty view of the Nysa River winding its way through the valley. The Hedemann castle was not as great as others in the area, but the two towers on either end made it seem much larger than it was.

From her window, Alexandrine could see only a little of the village of Nysa in the distance as trees and bushes grew thickly in front of the windows. From the drawing room, she could see a little lake lying quietly at the foot of a small mountain not far away. A gravel path surrounded a large grassy park within the castle's outer walls. It was there that Alexandrine spent many afternoons happily playing with her sister.

Her heart was gladdened as nothing else before. Mornings were truly the most beautiful when the sun climbed up into the radiant blue sky. There was something so delicious in the crystalline air bringing with it the strong smell of pines. On her walks through the meadows, Alexandrine could hear the birds chirping as they fluttered from tree to tree. As she reached the forest, a deer peeked out from behind the trees to snatch a tuft of grass before leaping back in. *Wilderness and loveliness are united in this place*, she thought. Some days, she and her sister would hide among the trees and under bushes when hunters from the village came riding by. With stealth, they followed them through the woods. When gunshots broke the silence, they cried for the unlucky deer who had sacrificed its life for their sport.

Beyond the forests stood the steppes, the vast grasslands that cover most of lower Silesia and Russia. Alexandrine often wished she could go back in time, riding her horse to exhaustion across the steppes with the wild and daring Cossacks, her hair flying in the wind and breathless with excitement. "*Gallop on, my pony, quicker, farther! Away from my dreary memories,*" she would say to herself. In her dreams, her pony would take her farther and farther away in the dazzling sunlight through the scorched, arid steppes, where all around was only sky and land.

It was a dream she wished would come true. The closest she would come to her dream was on the days she and her father rode together through the forest and out into the plain. She often challenged him to a race, but her horse was no match for his superior stallion. Her father slowed his horse for her to catch up, claiming she was the better rider. Alexandrine only laughed.

She saw very few people during her stay in Nysa as her father never entertained. The only people who came to the castle were a few beggars in tattered clothes, standing outside the kitchen door, stretching out their bony fingers for a few morsels of food. She was not allowed in the kitchen, so did not see them either. But she was content. There was no governess, and living with her father and sister was everything she ever wanted. Even her stepmother was not there to remind her of her imperfections. Jenny and the other children were happily together in Nürnberg.

But for Alexandrine, no amount of happiness would last for long. Her father, having no further need to stay and oversee his coal-mining interests in Silesia, announced that it was time to return to Nürnberg. Alexandrine would once again be under the critical eye of her stepmother.

In only a few weeks after their arrival, her stepmother once again pleaded with her husband to send Alexandrine away as her free and undisciplined nature was too much for her.

"I cannot abide this willful child. She will be the death of me if you do not send her away," Jenny would cry.

Her father did not want to send Alexandrine away again but feared for his wife's health and his enjoyment of a happy home. Within a few days, Alexandrine was once again placed on a train to Augsburg to stay with her uncle Schätzler. To her dismay, she would be under the care of the dreaded governess, who was still living there. When she arrived in Augsburg, she was greeted at the train station by her uncle and taken directly to their castle. Stepping out of the carriage, Alexandrine was greeted fondly by Adele. The governess stood by her side, eyeing Alexandrine with the same cold gray eyes in the same dull gray dress that she remembered.

The governess, in her cool, thick Russian accent, said, "It is good to see you again, Fraulein Hedemann." Her voice sent shivers down Alexandrine's spine. She could see that this tall, thin, rigid woman had not changed.

2

Herrenhut

At the age of fourteen, Alexandrine needed more studies than her tutors could provide. Her father and uncle agreed that it was time for her to finish her education away from Augsburg. In addition to more advanced studies, it was time for her to learn proper manners as expected of a young lady of her station. To reach the top of society as the daughter of a baron, she would have to learn more than Latin and Greek. She needed to know how to handle herself with charm and grace. The correct deportment of a titled lady is essential for her success. It was decided that she be sent to the Herrenhut Institute in Gnadenfrei, Silesia.

"It is a matter of conducting yourself properly and studying very hard. You are still a little savage, and you must learn to comport yourself as the young woman you shall one day become," her uncle said, half-scolding her as he lifted her onto the step of the train car. He led her into the first-class compartment.

"I will accompany you as far as Dresden, where you will

change trains. From there it is not far." They both settled into the compartment seats for the long trip. She was relieved that he was with her. In Dresden, he made sure she found the train to Breslau. Before leaving her, he said, "The head mistress at the institute will meet you at the train station in Breslau. From there, she will accompany you to Herrenhut. You must behave yourself and be polite." He thought her obstinate but still young and somewhat malleable.

She cried bitterly all the while her uncle was trying to reassure her that this was for the best.

"I will not be happy here, Uncle. I will know no one and have no friends. Please do not leave me," she cried.

"You will not be alone, my dear girl. There will be many girls there just like yourself with whom you will become friends. It is an excellent school, and you must not distress yourself. In just a few short years, you will be well educated and a young woman with many prospects."

As the train pulled away from the station, her uncle waved to her from the platform. Alexandrine waved back as tears slid down her cheeks. The train sped through the farms and fields for what seemed to be endless hours. All she could think was that the world she knew was being left far behind. Too far. For the first time, she was frightened.

The train pulled into the station puffing and hissing, expelling clouds of black smoke and soot. The shrill whistle announced its coming. She collected her suitcases and stepped out onto a small wooden platform, not knowing what to expect. She looked around the platform but saw only a man in a black military-style coat with brass buttons and a cap embellished with a gold crest. She recognized him as the stationmaster. He was looking intently at his fob watch, holding a whistle in his other hand.

Peering down to the far end of the platform, she could see a woman approaching with quickened steps dressed in a long, black, well-fitted wool frock with a small white lace collar held together with what appeared to be a mosaic broach. The woman smiled warmly and asked, "Are you Alexandrine von Hedemann?"

Alexandrine curtsied and replied, "Yes, Madame, I am."

The woman looked at Alexandrine and said, "I am Frau Müller, head mistress at Herrenhut Institute for Young Ladies. I am most happy to meet you. We will proceed directly to Herrenhut as it is not far."

A porter placed her suitcases into the carriage, while Alexandrine and the head mistress took their seats inside the carriage. The porter, after taking his seat, gave the horses a quick tap with his reins as they drove away from the train station and into the countryside. After approximately an hour of their being jostled over dusty, rutted roads that coursed their way through forests and small villages, the large three-story school building came into view. It stood in the middle of a clearing. Beyond it was a thick, dark forest. From a distance, Alexandrine saw only peaks and chimneys. A lot of them. They looked frightening.

Sensing the girl's apprehensions, the school mistress said to her, "Do not be alarmed; the school is not as frightful as it seems. It is a very old manor house built in the thirteenth century, which was converted into the school sometime at the turn of the century. You will find it quite comfortable once you are inside."

The carriage entered through a stone arch on which the name "Herrenhut Institut" was chiseled in bold gothic letters. The road, now somewhat smoother and paved with small pebbles, wound its way through a green lawn. The road circled around an enormous sundial with its large brass pointer casting its shadow at an engraved number: IV. The late-afternoon sun was casting long shadows over them as they drove closer to the yellow plastered building with its many windows. Somehow, it was becoming less frightening to her.

Instead of the plain façades that adorned most old German buildings, the façade was decorated with flowers, coils of rope, and chevrons. Even though Alexandrine was no longer afraid of this new place, she could not assuage her fears of living away from her family. All she knew up until then were her uncles, nurse maids, governesses, and tutors. She often thought of herself as brave and not afraid of very much, but an overwhelming fear suddenly gripped her heart. Up to now, she was a captive princess, with only the paintings that hung on the walls to show her the world. She knew nothing of the real world beyond the gardens and the forests where she lived with her father or uncle. Her life had been mostly about parties, picnics, new clothes, gossiping, and walks in the gardens or sometimes exploring the woods and meadows around her.

As she entered the large imposing foyer of the great house, with its black-and-white marble floor and columns, she did what she always did when fate intervened: she summoned up her courage and looked to her future. Suddenly, she heard them. She was not prepared for the onslaught of young girls rushing to greet her with an excitement of giggles. Two of them quickly took her hand and led her into the grand parlor.

Questions bombarded her in rapid succession.

"Where are you from?"

"Why did you get sent here?"

"Do you have parents, and where are they?"

It was a cacophony of voices, giggles, and questions, leaving her no room to answer them.

One of the older girls finally said, "Please do sit down. Never mind these girls. I shall get you some tea."

The other girls quickly sat themselves at her feet, waiting for the answers to their questions.

"I will gladly answer your questions, but first you must tell me your names."

One by one, they blurted out their names. They looked up at her with such inquisitiveness that Alexandrine felt she could no longer wait to answer their many questions.

She started, "I live with my uncle in Augsburg."

One of the girls interrupted. "But where are your father and mother?"

Alexandrine answered, "My father lives in Nürnberg. I don't know where my mother is."

The girls, showing no satisfaction with her answer, wanted to know more and asked her to tell them why she did not know her mother.

"I can only tell you what I know," she said. "My father never spoke of my mother, and when he remarried, my stepmother would not allow him to tell me anything. Nor was I allowed to ask. I remember there was a painting of a beautiful woman with red hair on the stairway wall in my father's castle in Nürnberg. I suppose it was my mother, but no one would tell me."

There were a lot of sighs from the girls.

It was while she was telling the girls about herself that

they, in turn, told her the reasons they were at the school. Some were from broken homes with only one parent to care for them. Some could not conform to proprieties and needed structure. Many whose parents, like her own, thought their daughters were an inconvenience and would be better brought up by strangers. Some of the girls were quite young and depended on the older girls for comfort. Alexandrine was still only fourteen herself and naïve.

That night, in her strange new room, she was frightened by vague shapes and noises in the dark. The shapes she saw could only have been the thin lace curtains blown by the gentle country air through the open windows. The noises, she decided, were no more than the leaves rustling in the trees outside. She took comfort in knowing she was not alone. The other girls, like herself, also struggled with the darkness of their situations when they first arrived. While watching the same shadows and listening to the same sounds she was, the other girls were also waiting to be rescued.

Alexandrine resolved to make the best of it. Fear was not part of her nature, and somewhere deep within herself she found hope that her dreams would someday be fulfilled. She knew she was destined to be happy. Somewhere in the distance, she heard the gong of the hallway clock. At the stroke of twelve, she finally drifted off to sleep.

~

At Herrenhut, she heard more sounds from the large clock in the entry hall during the day. It rang with a great clang at every hour. With seven loud clangs, the girls were wakened from their sleep. A quick splash of cold water from the basin and then quickly dressing to run down to the little chapel for prayers began their day. When the clock tolled eight, it was time for breakfast. At nine, the classrooms filled with students. At four, classes ended. And so it was every day but Sunday. Sunday was a day of rest with tea parties and walks in the garden.

Alexandrine threw herself into her studies of French, Latin, history, geography, and, most of all, manners. She learned the proper use of tableware, how to fold her napkin, how to address persons of distinction, and how to do a perfect curtsy. She found laughter and friendship with her new friends. In her free times, there were playful games, explorations, and a few pranks played on the caretakers. They roamed the grounds and gardens in search of adventure, oftentimes getting a good scolding from the head mistress for their mischievousness. Alexandrine found these days filled with good memories. At last!

3

First Love

*I*t was at Herrenhut that an unexpected friendship developed that would determine Alexandrine's future and live with her as a ghost haunting her every step for years to come.

After three years at Herrenhut, she had occasion to spend some Sunday afternoons at the home of Baroness von Prittwitz, a friend of her father. As the baroness lived nearby, she often invited Alexandrine to her country home for coffee and cake. The baroness, a portly woman in her fifties, and her sister-in-law, Elise, who was much younger, lived together in the family's country house on the outskirts of Gnadenfrei. The baroness and Elise, both widows, shared a love of the arts and literature, often traveling together to foreign lands such as Egypt, Greece, and Turkey. It was their desire to visit the countries they read about in their vast library. Having just returned from the Greek islands, they were eager to invite Alexandrine to share their experiences. She came willingly to hear the many stories of lands far away that she had never seen and only read about.

Still too young for hoops and petticoats with layer

upon layer of silk to smother herself in the style of the day, Alexandrine wore simpler clothes. Her plain dresses were high-waisted with cap sleeves and showed only a hint of her blossoming breasts. The light cotton skirt swirled around her slender, youthful figure and hung lazily above her ankles. She usually wore a white silk ribbon loosely tied around her long chestnut hair, letting it cascade down her back. In many ways, she was still a child, but at seventeen, she was slowly developing into a woman.

On one of those warm spring afternoons, while having coffee and cake in the garden with her two friends, a fair-haired, tall young man walked across the lawn to where the little group was sitting. He introduced himself as Herr von Scheffer. Alexandrine's girlish heart could not keep still, and her eyes followed him without guile. She sensed that he had noticed her, too, as his eyes followed hers. They did not speak words, but she was sure their hearts had silently spoken to each other.

After he excused himself, Alexandrine asked, "Baroness von Prittwitz, what do you know about Herr von Scheffer?"

"My dear," she said, "Hermann is the only son of Baron von Scheffer and has been appointed as horse trainer to the duke of Mecklenburg, who owns stables in Gnadenfrei. He is a charming young man and comes often to see us to advise us on our stables."

After that happy first meeting, Sunday afternoon visits were never the same. Alexandrine looked forward to those days with joyful anticipation. The baroness, aware of the sprouting of young love, kept a watchful eye whenever the baron came on Sunday.

The lovestruck Alexandrine had only rare opportunities to see or speak with him, but she had the gay, confident expectation of any young girl that she wanted that to change. At first, it was a glance here and there. This soon led to a light secret touch on the hand. All her sensations rushed to her skin where he touched her ever so lightly. Such a little thing but such bliss. Would she even remember what they talked about when he touched her? She only knew her newfound passion lifted her up to new heights, giving way to a happiness that she had never imagined. All at once, her senses sharpened, colors brightened, and her heart raced whenever he was near.

In the following weeks, he somehow found ways to be just around a corner, behind a tree, or in the school garden. A brush on the lips. Quick and furtive. They dared not do more. They were both walking on air in the aura of young love. It was her first love. Her first real romance. She had never loved before so had no reason to deny herself the rich pleasure of it. Her days and nights were surrounded with thoughts of him. It was the awakening of a young girl's desire that filled her heart. She delighted in his company and the confidence of his love for her. She could hardly bear having him from her sight.

Alexandrine was not prepared for the flood of joy when he suddenly spoke of a betrothal. She was only half understanding what had just happened or what would happen.

"Oh, yes, Hermann," she cried out quickly as her heart pounded with excitement. It made her nearly faint.

He pulled her to him in an embrace. He held her firmly to him with his strong arms, kissing her tenderly. Then, with a new passion in his voice, he said, "I love you. I will go immediately to speak to your father."

"Yes, go at once," she said, barely able to breathe. "My father will gladly receive you and give us his blessing. He will not deny me this happiness, and once he sees you, he will, of course, say yes." She had the naïve belief that her father would not deny her.

Hermann did not delay. He took the first train to Nürnberg and was received in Baron von Hedemann's library. He, too, had the confidence of youth and was committed to his pursuit. He did not hesitate to approach the subject with Alexandrine's father. The baron listened to the impassioned speech without interruption. He regarded the young man highly and consented without questions, for he already knew much about Hermann von Scheffer through his association with the duke of Mecklenburg.

Scheffer returned to Herrenhut to tell his beloved Alexandrine that her father gave his consent most enthusiastically and without reservations—except for one. He said, "Your father requested only one thing."

"What did he request? Tell me quickly," Alexandrine asked, almost fearful of what it might be and what might hinder their engagement.

"He required only that we wait until you have finished your studies at Herrenhut before an announcement can take place."

"Oh, Hermann, I was afraid he would ask for more. In three months' time, my studies will be concluded."

She, of course, was overjoyed as in three months, her days at Herrenhut would end, and a new future beckoned. But in a month's time, her joy would be shattered.

Baron von Hedemann's financial circumstances, which were already on the margin, fell to an even more dangerous level. His coal reserves in Silesia had recently fallen to an all-time low. There was little return on his holdings and little hope for a better outcome in the future. He had hoped the young

Scheffer was in a higher financial position. Unfortunately, Karl found out that the elder Scheffer suffered from his own misfortunes. The marriage was called off. A better match had to be found for Alexandrine. The von Hedemann family had to be saved. She and Scheffer were forced to part.

"No!" she shouted at the letter she received from her father. "This cannot be. It is unfair. I will marry no other. I will die rather than be forced into marriage with someone else."

She had known love, and with her father's uncompromising words, her heart was broken forever. Scheffer was gone, cast from her with one mighty word. Her misery found no solace. She was living in an emotional desert with sleepless nights, tossing and turning. When sleep finally came, she dreamed of never finding true love again. She woke with tears streaming down her face. It was a nightly torment.

4

The Making of a Baroness

Upon leaving Herrenhut, Alexandrine was sufficiently educated and could assume her responsibilities in society. Her education was uncommon, her mind enriched, her manner polished. She understood her place within her class and was ready to be received in society. In time, her father reassured her, she would make a suitable match with a wealthy nobleman.

"Once you are married, you will take up your position as a mother and wife and in the management of a great house worthy of your station," he told her.

She did not answer. She could not fathom how she could ever be happy in an arranged marriage.

The day she left Herrenhut, she wept. She wept for the happy times she had with her classmates because she would miss them. She wept for the memory of one of the unhappiest and most tragic times of her young life when she found love and it was taken away from her.

Returning to her father's house, she found things changed. Alexandrine, at first welcomed by her stepmother, soon found herself as a governess to the children born to her father and his wife while she was at Herrenhut. As her father's financial condition still suffered, there were fewer and fewer servants. Some of those chores were now relegated to Alexandrine. In the midst of her days filled with sewing or minding the children, her Cossack spirit still called to her.

Sitting in front of the window in her room, Alexandrine looked dreamily out upon the lawns and gardens that surrounded the house. She remembered roaming through the romantic forests, fields, and pastures of Silesia. She could no longer ride freely across the steppes spurring her horse on tirelessly until, frothing at the mouth, it could go no further. Those carefree days would never be again. New dreams took their place. She dreamed that her young handsome lover would come to free her from her grim existence. "Where are you? Why do you not come?" she asked, looking out the window.

When her father received a letter from his brother General August George von Hedemann,[3] her dreary and unhappy time came to an end. "Alex, come quickly," her father called. "Your uncle has invited you to stay with him and your great-uncle, Alexander von Humboldt,[4] at Castle Tegel."

"I do not wish to leave you, Papa," she said, barely able to

---

3   August Georg Friederich Magnus Baron von Hedemann was a general in the Prussian Cavalry from 1799 until the end of his life in 1859. He married the daughter of Wilhelm von Humboldt, Aurora Raffaele Adelheid von Humboldt. This marriage combined the von Hedemann and von Humboldt lineages.

4   Friedrich Wilhelm Heinrich Alexander Baron von Humboldt was a German polymath, geographer, naturalist, explorer, philosopher, and scientist. He was the younger brother of Wilhelm von Humboldt. Both brothers were born and raised at Castle Tegel, outside Berlin. They continued to live there together after Wilhelm's marriage to Caroline von Dacheröden and the birth of their eight children.

hide the real explosion of happiness inside her that she was feeling. "But if you desire it, I will welcome the opportunity to live at Castle Tegel."

That evening, in her room, she could hardly believe her good fortune. She summoned her chambermaid to help pack her gowns and riding clothes for the trip. She was hopeful that it would be a long stay at Tegel.

She had never met her great-uncle, Alexander. She knew only a little of his long and illustrious career as a famous naturalist, geographer, and explorer. She knew that he was her namesake and godfather and felt fortunate to be named after such a famous person.

Alexandrine arrived at Tegel, a large and imposing castle a few kilometers outside Berlin. She was full of hope and longing for a better life. The carriage drove down the long stone drive toward the house where she would spend several glorious months. As the carriage proceeded closer to the castle, on both sides of the road leading to the courtyard lay splendid gardens filled with flowers in myriad colors. There were walkways through flowering trees and sculptured yews. Woods surrounding the house beyond gave it a country feel. At last, the palatial castle, built in 1558 of brilliant white stone in the Renaissance style, came into view. Its white sandstone façade included four three-story towers rising as sentinels on all corners of the castle. She was in awe of its beauty as she came closer. The carriage came to a halt in the courtyard below the steps of the grand entrance. A footman opened the door of the carriage, lowered the step, and led her into the main entry hall.

Entering the house, she could see through to the back. The large windows caught the glint of the sun and opened to yet a second garden. From where she stood, long marbled halls stretched down either side from east to west. In the west wing, there was a drawing room, two small and one grand dining rooms, the flower room, a smoking room, and the estate office. In the east wing, there was another drawing room, a gun room, a library, a game room, and yet another dining room, which was used for breakfast. Around a corner, beyond the west wing, there was a conglomeration of kitchens, pantries, laundry, and ironing rooms. The ballroom, with walls of mirrors and crystal chandeliers hanging from an elaborately painted ceiling, was on the second floor. Twenty guest and family rooms also occupied the floor. The third floor housed the servants. Above that was a miscellany of towers, turrets, hidden doors to hidden rooms, and attics.

Alexandrine was warmly welcomed by her great-uncle, Alexander, who was already well advanced in years but still handsome in his old age. She curtsied. He took her hand and said, "Welcome, my dear niece. I hope your journey was not too tedious?"

"My trip was pleasant and uneventful, thank you, Uncle. I am very happy to see you and to find you well."

"Your rooms have been prepared."

Next to him stood the estate's housekeeper. Alexander introduced her as Frau Baumann. She was tall, thin, and plainly dressed, her hair neatly tucked into a bun. She had an air of authority about her.

Frau Baumann bowed and said, "I will take you to your rooms, Baroness."

Before leaving, Alexander said, "After you have rested and changed, please join me in the yellow dining room for supper. A small dinner has been prepared for us as we are the only ones here tonight. Your aunt Louise is resting in her bedchamber tonight. You will meet her tomorrow. Your uncle August will also arrive tomorrow. He will be home on leave for only a short period of time but is anxious to see you. Your aunt Gabriele and your other uncles are unfortunately abroad."

Alexandrine's room, as formal as anything she had yet seen, was rich with decorations and furniture painted in gold. The tall, narrow windows had an unobstructed view of the garden, which pleased her. The walls, covered in large flowered wallpaper, were embellished with narrow wood lattice. Seeing the splendid carved four-poster bed, with its fine embroidered linens, she threw herself on it, delighting in the luxurious feel of the silk coverlets. *Here is where I belong,* she thought.

Anna, the chambermaid, slight of build, no more than eighteen, and dressed in a simple black dress with a white starched apron and a small white lace head covering, entered the room carrying two large buckets of hot water to warm the bath. She helped Alexandrine disrobe and held a towel over her as she stepped into the soothing warm bathwater. Anna sponged her with scented soap. After dressing Alexandrine, Anna rang the house bell that hung on the wall to call for the footman, who would take her to the small dining room where her uncle waited for her.

He was already seated at the head of the table. When Alexandrine entered, he rose, took her hand, and led her to her seat next to him, which the footman held out for her. Alexander's white hair, receding a little, framed a still-youthful face with few lines. His bushy eyebrows almost obscured his eyes, but Alexandrine could see the twinkle in his eyes as he smiled warmly at her. He had a rakish kind of laugh, which delighted her. They spent the evening in small talk. He was interested in her life and encouraged her to speak freely. He instilled in her a confidence she had not felt before.

"But, Uncle, I want to hear of your journeys."

"My dear niece, I would not know where to begin. I have spent my life on every continent and seen much. To me, however, it is still not enough. There is so much more of the world to explore." He laughed heartily at the thought as he was already eighty-two years of age. "I should spend my life in quiet reflection here within these walls, but there is still more I wish to do. Perhaps a little slower now as my old age is grinding on me like a millstone around my shoulders."

"I cannot see you, Uncle, in such a state. You are much too young to sit idly by while the world spins under your feet without trying to stop it long enough for you to get on it."

Alexander took her hand and said, "You are the sweetest child. I should travel only if you will come with me." They both laughed, and Alexandrine thought how nice it felt to laugh again.

A light supper of cold meats, potato salad, a variety of cheeses, and warm bread was brought in by the kitchen staff and served by footmen. Both of their wine glasses were quickly refilled once emptied by another footman poised and ready with a decanter of red wine from the estate's own vineyard.

Alexandrine, still in awe of her uncle's accomplishments, wanted to know more. "In my studies, I have heard so much about your travels, especially into the Americas. At Herrenhut, we studied geography, and your name was included in many of the texts on explorations. I think you must have seen all there is in the world."

"Yes, I have, my child. I have yearned to explore the world

since I was a child. But botany is my most fervent passion, which has taken me to places where no man has yet been. It has been a most rewarding life. But now I wish to retire as the evening is spent. We can talk some more as I hope your stay here will be a long one."

"Of course, Uncle. I look forward to many days with you, your books, and the stories of your adventures that I hope you will share with me."

That night, Alexandrine wrapped herself in the warmth of her heavenly feather bed. With thoughts of the generous hospitality of this learned and famous uncle, she fell into a deep and restful sleep.

In the morning, Anna came into her bedchamber to pull back the heavy drapes, welcoming a sunny morning. Alexandrine saw the trees caught in the shimmering rays of the first light. When the sun hid itself behind an errant cloud, the trees shaded the lawn with a cool softness. After dressing for the day, she went down to the breakfast room, where she joined her great-uncle. She was surprised to see her uncle General von Hedemann, who arrived early that morning. Alexandrine helped herself to some China tea, toast, and marmalade. Later, eggs, sausage, and bacon were brought in.

General von Hedemann addressed Alexandrine. "I am delighted that you consented to visit us and hope you will find your stay enjoyable and, perhaps, even enlightening."

"I most certainly will, Uncle," she said, looking at both of her uncles with great affection in her eyes.

After breakfast, Alexander and the general excused themselves. They explained they had to attend to some estate business.

Alexandrine took the time to inspect the garden. She

passed sweet, scent-filled rose bushes, rhododendrons, and azaleas. Beyond lay a well-tended lawn dotted with trees: willows, linden, pines, and oaks. Sculpted yews laid out in precise patterns, with paths leading through them, led to a charming vine-covered cottage. She imagined this cottage to be hidden there as a place for a tryst. It stirred her imagination. Thrush twittering in the trees and the gentle hum of bees buzzing around the roses filled her with a new happiness. The past was fading quickly in this luxurious and most welcoming place.

As she didn't see very much of her uncles during the day, she spent those days exploring the castle's many rooms. The library intrigued her the most with its walls of oak bookcases, which held hundreds of old leather-bound books smelling strongly of must, many with broken spines due to their age. Large wingback leather chairs sat randomly around the room. But her favorite place to sit was under the large sunlit window on the plush brocade-covered cushions of the window seat. In another part of the library, there were several tables surrounded by straight-back chairs, places where guests could seat themselves after dinner for games of piquet or whist. She spent several hours every day in the library reading from the many books there.

At Tegel, with her uncles, she was surrounded by a life of luxury, culture, and companionship. Talk at dinner was spirited and involved philosophy, science, and theories but all with the lightest touch. Other times, conversations drifted to lighter topics such as the theater, plays, poets, and essayists. Her thirst for knowledge was satisfied, as well as her desire for a noble kind of life, the kind of life her station as a baroness demanded. Watching the other ladies who came to parties at Tegel, Alexandrine learned that a woman had to have something special—charm, style, culture, and a certain flair—in order to hold the imagination of others in her class. Without that, nothing could be gained. Among the young ladies, many conversations led to talk of marriage. The subject of a marriage in one's class was always in the forefront. A good and profitable marriage was sought after with great zeal. One's status in society depended on it.

~

After three months, Alexandrine's stay at Tegel ended. By the time she left, she was full of happy memories, a lust for life, and enough art and culture to nourish her mind and soul. After Tegel, she had no desire to return to her father's house in Nürnberg. It did not have the same comforts, elegance, or intellectually stimulating conformity of Tegel. The thought of again living with her uncaring stepmother was, to her, beyond endurance. She decided instead to return to her uncle in Augsburg.

5

Marriage

*A*rriving at her uncle Schätzler's house, she found nothing had changed except, to her relief, the hated governess was gone. Her uncle welcomed her with open arms. The coachman who had driven her to the train to where she would ultimately live at Herrenhut and the nurse who so tenderly comforted her and cared for her were still there. The nurse was so overcome with joy at seeing Alexandrine that she embraced her with tears of overflowing joy. Her cousin Adele ran from the doorway to embrace her, overwhelming her with kisses. The childhood jealousy she once bore the baby Adele, as the better-loved child protected under parental love, was washed away with those embraces.

A round of parties and balls began. Those days appeared to be a never-ending whirlwind of excitement. Alexandrine found herself living in an enchanted world of parties, dances, ball gowns, and flirtations. She received one extravagant gown after another, each more embellished with pearls and gemstones than the last. She lacked for nothing. At the balls, she was noticeably the most beautiful young woman there, admired by every man, young and old. Many a suitor offered to walk with her on the terrace in the hopes of gazing into her violet eyes and professing an instant and undying love for her. It was a glorious time for her. One that she did not wish to end. But, of course, end it would. She was now twenty-four and still unmarried. She was approaching the age when she would soon be considered past her prime.

One day, her uncle, with great excitement, called for Alexandrine and Adele with what he described as astonishing news. She and Adele eagerly joined him in the drawing room. They were full of anticipation of what news could make him so happy.

He stated boldly, "Adele has not one but two suitors who have asked for her hand in marriage. One is the Baron H, and the other is the banker Hermann Erzberger. Both are wealthy men and therefore considered suitable matches."

Adele, still quite young, did not see this as happy news. In fact, she did not like it at all. "The baron is such a bore, and Herr Erzberger is too old. I shall have neither," she blurted out.

"Be still, Adele, you will consider these proposals," her father snapped back at her.

With the hope of making a match with the young Adele, the baron came to her father's house frequently on one pretext or another. As Adele would not walk with him alone, he accompanied both Adele and Alexandrine on their walks through the gardens and to the lake for picnics. The young baron, frequently ignoring Adele, maneuvered himself closer to Alexandrine during their walks. Adele, not caring at all, was glad he had no interest in her and often conveniently disappeared, leaving the baron and Alexandrine alone. One day after a short walk around the lake, they sat on the grass for their picnic, which was brought from the house by a footman. Having quickly finished a bottle of wine, the baron stood up, brushed the grass from his pants, adjusted his waistcoat, reached down to take Alexandrine's hand, and led her away from Adele.

He bent close to her, asking somewhat timidly, "Will you do me the greatest honor, my dearest Alex, to become my wife?"

Alexandrine, not expecting his proposal, found herself unable to speak. To him, she seemed to be carefully choosing her words. She did so, however, to spare him. Had he not also proposed to Adele?

After returning to the castle, Adele ran to her father with excitement: "He proposed to her!"

"Who did?" her father asked.

"Baron von *Boring*, of course. Can you imagine, Father?"

Entering the room, Alexandrine said, "It's true, Uncle. He proposed to me most ardently. I did not give him an answer."

Her uncle was not at all surprised as the baron, who had made frequent visits, seemed more taken with Alexandrine than his daughter. He, however, was disappointed it was not Adele the baron chose. Baron H was worth a great deal in property and wealth, which would increase his own fortune, too, should he marry Adele. A wealthy baron was always desirable, he thought. But if he chose Alexandrine, so be it. There was still the wealthy banker.

"My dear niece, you must give him an answer quickly. We will announce the engagement at the next ball, which will be held in two weeks."

Alexandrine searched her heart. Her first love, Scheffer, still dwelt there with all the passion she remembered and which she still felt for him. But she knew he could never again be to her what he once was. Even so, she could not come to a decision. The baron was polite, educated, and wealthy. She would surely have a comfortable life, but she did not love him, nor did he stir any passion in her heart.

Her uncle, trying very hard to explain his reasoning to her while reassuring her that she would be making a good decision, said, "Give him time, Alex. Love grows within a marriage, and you will learn to love him. He is a decent and honorable man who will bring you happiness."

The young baron continued to come every day and stayed well into the evening. He and his soon-to-be betrothed usually went for a stroll before dinner, and when Alexandrine came in after one of those walks, her cheeks were pink. Adele, ever mindful of what her cousin was doing, was sure he had kissed her. Alexandrine would not disclose anything to Adele for fear she would go running to her father to tell him what happened. That would surely inspire him to start making plans for her wedding, even before the engagement was announced. That just would not do!

Adele was right. Alexandrine allowed the young baron to kiss her. It was not a passionate kiss, which she expected, but a light touch on her lips. *He may not stir my passion*, she thought, *but he could provide other things*. His properties were numerous, and his status in society was secure. She predicted that her life with him would be filled with luxuries in a house of expansive proportions with servants and comfort. "*Is it enough that he loves me and offers me a life of privilege? Will that satisfy me?*" she asked herself.

The next few days floated by pleasantly until the day of the ball. Adele was beside herself with joy as this ball would also be the day of her coming out into society. She could not wait to see the look on everyone's faces when her father announced Alexandrine's engagement.

Then the awful news arrived. The day of the ball, the young baron went for a ride, not on his usual horse but a new one full of spirit, which he had just purchased. At some time during the ride, the horse stumbled on a tree root that was protruding aboveground on the path. Unable to control his horse, he fell to the ground with a thud, breaking his leg. The horse ran off. The young baron lay on the ground crying out in pain, which caught the attention of another rider. Together with his groomsman, they carried the poor ailing baron back to his castle. A doctor was called to set his broken leg. A message for Alexandrine arrived shortly thereafter: "Forgive me, my dearest lady, but it is with sincere regret that I cannot attend the ball. However, I will await your answer at home. Your humble servant, H."

The ball, the last of the season, would be well attended with all the notables throughout the region. On the day of the ball, there was a flurry of excitement. Dresses had to be cleaned and prepared, petticoats stiffened, corsets re-laced. The ladies were put to bed early in the afternoon for naps so they would be refreshed for a night of dancing that usually started at midnight and went until four in the morning. Upon their arising, baths with scented oils were drawn.

Standing naked in front of the mirror, Alexandrine admired her well-formed body. She was no longer the skinny girl of a few years ago. She had ample curves with the breasts of a young and desirable woman. Stepping into her bath, she was content with what she saw. Her maid was sponging her with lavender soap when Adele burst into Alexandrine's room. She was in her robe, still wet from her bath and full of enthusiasm and excitement.

"I cannot wait for tonight to come, cousin," she said. "It is my first ball and also my last as the season has ended. It will be so exciting to see everyone in their fine clothes. I hope I will dance every dance."

Alexandrine, seeing how happy her young cousin was, said, "Of course you will, Adele. Your dance card will be filled. The young men will not be able to resist how beautiful you look."

"Oh, no. It is not I but you at whom they will be looking. You will charm the eligible men, and I will be left with no one."

"Adele, do not talk such nonsense. Go! Get ready. There is so little time."

After they were dressed, bejeweled, coiffed, and powdered, it was time to go downstairs to the dining hall for supper. Her uncle and several of his friends joined them. The talk at the table was spent discussing who would be at the ball and where everyone would spend the summer that year. Almost everyone of means who lived in the cities found refuge in the mountains during the sweltering summer heat. They would return in time for another season of balls, concerts, operas, dinner parties, and hunting trips.

After dinner, they drifted into other rooms to admire the stately paintings or find an out-of-the-way corner to gather for gossip. The men retired to the smoking room for cigars and brandy. Later, the small party gathered in the music room, where one of the ladies played the piano and another sang.

Close to midnight, carriages arrived to take them to the ball, which this year was held at Castle Wellenburg. Once announced, they marched two by two into the ballroom to secure their places, either on chairs or against a pillar, where they could be seen or have an advantage to look over who was in attendance. It was the last opportunity for young ladies and gentlemen to meet each other in order to perhaps form an alliance. If not, then they would likely have to wait for the next year's round of balls.

Because it was the last of the big parties, everyone dressed in their utmost finest. The men looked dashingly handsome in full evening dress with tails, white ties, and waistcoats. The ladies, with wasp-thin waists held in by corsets tied so tight they could barely breathe, were dressed in yards of satin or taffeta with low-cut bodices embellished with glittering gemstones, showing off their bulging breasts. Everyone floated about the room, going out of their way to be pleasant and to show an interest in one another. The younger girls smiled coquettishly behind their fans. When the music started, it was the signal for the dancing to commence. Couples stood in a line in order of their place in the social hierarchy. The most highly regarded couples danced first before the others could join in.

After the first dance, Alexandrine seated herself next to her uncle. He was discussing the unfortunate accident that befell the young baron when the banker Hermann Erzberger approached them. He begged Alexandrine for a dance. She looked at her uncle, who only nodded his head in permission. She took Hermann's arm, walking out onto the dance floor for a waltz. She was happily surprised that he was a good dancer. She continued to dance with him for two more rounds. As the couple joyously glided over the dance floor, all eyes were on them. Former and would-be suitors looked at the banker with envy.

After the third dance, Alexandrine's eyes fell on the lonesome Adele sitting on one of the velvet tufted chairs along the wall, seated like a delicate figurine on display. She had not been asked for even one dance. Adele, somewhat plain with a rather distinctive straight nose, a square chin, and thick dark hair was still young but certainly eligible for a successful union. Alexandrine sat beside her and put her arms around her shoulders, in hopes of reassuring her.

Looking at Adele's sad face, she said, "Don't be discouraged, cousin. They will sweep you away next year. They are not smart enough this year to see your goodness and charm."

Every young man who came to speak with them, which they did in great number, only had eyes for Alexandrine, asking for a dance and leaving poor Adele sitting alone. Little did these young men know that Adele would grow into a beautiful woman, much like the story of the ugly duckling that turned into a swan. She would someday no longer be ignored and put aside by would-be suitors. In the end, Adele would make a successful match, to the great relief of her father.

Toward the end of the evening, the banker again approached Alexandrine. Without a word, he took her by the hand and led her out onto the balcony, which overlooked the garden. The spring air was fresh and sweet with the perfume of flowers and was a pleasant respite from the air in the ballroom full of sweaty bodies hopping around in the mad confusion of a quadrille, which was popular in England and was recently brought to Germany.

Erzberger, in a black evening coat and a white ascot-style cravat of the latest fashion, slightly puffed at the neck and held in place by a silver pin with a small round diamond in the center, looked quite handsome and distinguished. He was not tall but had an air of sophistication. The slight touch of silver in his hair and mustache did not in any way take away from his good looks. His eyes sparkled, full of passion toward Alexandrine, as he looked at her. He took her hand, never letting his eyes fall from hers. He kissed it tenderly as if it were a delicate treasure. It was then that he surprised her by asking for her hand in marriage. Two proposals in one season!

Alexandrine did not give him the answer he wanted. She could not. "My good sir," she said. "I cannot give you an answer, for I have another proposal. I will think most sincerely on your request for my hand in marriage."

Erzberger, bowing over her hand and giving it a soft kiss, said, "I shall await your decision, fair lady, in the hope that you will make me the happiest of all men."

With that, they went inside and danced into the early hours of the morning. When the sun was beginning to show its morning face, everyone was finally exhausted and went home.

Some days after the ball, Alexandrine told her uncle that Erzberger, too, had asked for her hand. Her uncle was astonished as this presented a new dilemma. He said to her, "You must go immediately to your father. It is up to him to decide who is the better match."

Her uncle arranged for a carriage to bring her directly to the train station. The trip from Augsburg to Nürnberg seemed agonizingly long. But it gave her time to reflect on the current course of events that would decide her life. Did she not have the right to say whom she should marry? Had she not found someone to love and been denied it? Would she now have to marry someone she did not love? "I would rather be alone the rest of my life than to marry without love," she told herself.

When she arrived, her father was deep in thought in his estate office, going over his accounts. He looked up and was pleased to see his daughter standing there. When she told him of the recent proposals, he was surprised.

He took a minute to compose himself and then asked, "I have not heard of this. I thought Baron H and Erzberger were suitors intended for Adele?"

"That seems to be what everyone thought," explained Alexandrine. "Both Baron H and the banker had a change of heart. I have not accepted either proposal, Father. Uncle bade me to come to you for a decision, although you must know I am not at all happy with either choice."

Her father spent several days contemplating the choices. Would it be the wealthy banker or the also wealthy and noble-birthed baron? Which would be more suitable for this daughter? He struggled with a decision until he came to the conclusion that he could not choose. The thought of his daughter of high birth marrying a man without a title was not what he hoped for. However, the banker was wealthy, which could be an advantage. In the end, he reasoned that either man would be a suitable match for his daughter.

After a week of waiting for an answer, the banker suddenly appeared. He wooed Alexandrine so extravagantly, and with such devotion, that her father consented at once to the marriage.

Alexandrine, of course, still remembering how her father spurned Scheffer, raged against him. "You denied me the love of a man who would have made me happy, and now you want me to marry a man I do not love!" She threw the words at him.

She could not possibly feel toward Erzberger what she felt for Scheffer. The impossibly unhappy and unlucky girl kept to her most determined efforts, but she could do little with her father.

He looked at her sternly and spat out the words: "You must marry. You are approaching an age when no man will have you. You are well past a marketable age. You have no means of support. The question is settled."

Some days later, her mind spoke to her on the reality of her life and future. She knew her father was right. She would soon be past marriageable age. Her first love was gone and could never be by her side. She understood her position well. It was a deadly risk to remain unmarried, finally being forced to accept whoever would have her. She might have to settle for a fat old duke, twice widowed, with foul breath and a dozen children. Or, even worse, be forced into a convent to spend the rest of her life as a nun. In the end, she agreed, saying to herself, "Perhaps it is enough that he loves me and can offer me a comfortable life."

The marriage day was set for July 25, 1857. Since the day of his proposal and engagement, there was nothing to add to her happiness.

In the meantime, the unlucky young baron, disappointed over his loss of the beautiful Alexandrine, now took a renewed interest in her cousin Adele. He quickly pursued her, regularly visiting her and inviting her for walks. Her father, knowing that Adele was no great beauty and that her chances of landing another baron of the realm were slim, offered a large dowry to the young man. Having great wealth already, the baron could not be tempted by the dowry. He was more interested in getting the sweet young Adele into his bed. He was already thinking of untying her bodice, lifting up her skirts, and touching her soft thighs and pert young breasts when he proposed marriage. He knelt on the grass, took her hand, kissed it politely, and said, "My dearest lady, I have loved you these many months and would be in the greatest distress if you would not marry me. I offer you my most humble devotion. Please marry me."

Adele took a deep breath and replied sweetly, "Good sir, I do not love you, and I will never marry you."

With those words, she turned around, pulled up her hoop skirt, and ran out of the garden toward the house, her dress billowing up behind her like a great balloon.

~

Because her uncle had no wife to advise Alexandrine of her future responsibilities, he took her aside a few days before her wedding to prepare her for her new life and her role as a dutiful wife.

He sat next to her and, in the most loving way, said, "Marriage is a natural part of a woman's life. If you do not love him now, you will find love over time. Your life is to be with your husband and children first and then society. Without a husband, children, and the duties they entail, together with the management of a home or estate, everything else will pall."

Adele, too, offered her advice when Alexandrine asked her what she was supposed to do after she was married. "You do nothing," Adele said. "You go to parties, stay in country houses, and have babies."

The day soon arrived. Alexandrine's maids dressed her in a gown with several layers of the finest cream-colored silk and lace. Seed pearls were carefully sewn around embroidered flowers. She needed no jewels. Even the crinolines could not disguise her still-youthful slender but curvaceous figure. Her auburn hair, fashioned in braids, was carefully pinned around her head, with tendrils of curls cascading down, framing her face. Upon her head, the maid carefully pinned a crown of fresh flowers. A long lace train hung down, spreading out several feet behind her. A short veil hung over her face, concealing her sad eyes. Nevertheless, with a regal bearing and a gentle tilt of her head, she emerged from her bedchamber.

Waiting outside were her maids of honor, several servants, and footmen. They stared at her with awe. It was her true loveliness that caused everyone to break out into applause. She proceeded to walk slowly down the great staircase to the grand entrance below. Her father, waiting there to receive her, was magnificently dressed in a black velvet tailcoat, a white shirt with a high collar, and a silk ascot, which framed his handsome face. As she approached him, he smiled at her with overwhelming pride. For a fleeting moment, he saw Mathilde with her red hair standing before him on his wedding day, so many years before. He took his daughter by the hand and led her to the waiting carriage.

The coachman and a footman stood at attention on either side of the coach door, while another footman lowered the step of the coach that would take her to the church. Adele, her first maid of honor, helped her arrange her train inside the coach and whispered, "Be strong."

Her father entered from the other side and sat next to her. "You seem quite composed, my dear," he remarked. "This should be a happy day, and yet I have not seen you smile."

Alexandrine did not answer.

The rest of the wedding party stepped into other coaches as the servants waved them off. The little procession arrived at the church in Augsburg. Everyone was thankful it was a sunny day. They were sure it would bring good luck to the bride and groom.

However, alighting from the carriage at the church door, Alexandrine had the misfortune to step on a thorn. Her foot bled, which ruined her white slipper. She was sure it was an omen. Suddenly, all the tragedies, all the sorrows, all the disappointments that she had endured over the past years erupted in a deluge of memories. How could this not be an omen? She was entering into a marriage with a man twenty-four years older than she was. A man she did not love. She knew that a bourgeois life in middle-class Augsburg lay ahead. There would be no more culture, learning, riding, or balls. She would bear children and raise them herself, most likely with only a few servants to help. There would surely be more thorns.

She stood in front of the two massive wooden doors of the thousand-year-old church, wanting to run away, when, suddenly, two footmen swung the doors open. Her father entered first and waited for her to step inside. The congregation of family and friends of her uncle stood up, turning toward the open church door as a beam of light threaded through and onto the figure of a girl, casting her as an angel floating into the church. The groom, standing at the altar, blinked in disbelief as this lovely creature in white caught all the light in the church. He could not believe that this girl, loveliest in all the world, would be his forever.

Alexandrine's father took her by the arm. Adele and the other maids of honor took their places at the front of the church. As flower girls strewed rose petals at Alexandrine's feet, the little party marched in slow, even steps toward the altar to the sound of Johann Pachelbel's "Canon in D." Alexandrine and Hermann knelt before an altar as they exchanged their vows. It was done. She could no longer run away.

A short trip into the Austrian mountains followed. Hermann, as chief financial investor for the Deutsche Bank in Augsburg, was impatient to return to work. He had a fine old house in the city center and settled Alexandrine within its historic walls. The house had been in the Erzberger family for generations. His widowed mother and two of his unmarried sisters occupied the first floor, while the newly married couple moved into the second floor.

~

As the years passed, Alexandrine found more thorns. From the time of their marriage, she noticed the differences between them. His steadfastness, adherence to rule and order, and calm and weak nature did not match her wayward spirit or her thirst for life. The chasm between them could be measured no less than from one side of the ocean to the other. The passion and imagination that were ever present in her blood could not be stirred in him as he saw no importance in anything but his work. Their nights together were unremarkable and unfulfilled. She soon found herself lonely and despairing of any future happiness as she was feeling less and less for the man she married. As Hermann found rest in heavy slumber besides her, she lay awake in silence. A deathly loneliness enveloped her like a dark, grim mantle. She knew she could not escape. In her dreams, a voice told her, "A life without feeling is another kind of death."

In the beginning of her marriage, she tried to make herself into the bourgeois housewife she was to become. Endless tea parties with the ladies of Augsburg did nothing to lift her spirits. She found nothing illuminating in sipping tea while they talked endlessly about such trivial things as the latest in fashion or where to buy the best floss for their cross-stitch. When winter came and the skies were heavy with endless gloom, she was glad there were no more tea parties. She knew she had sacrificed her own happiness to the ideal of duty. It was now her punishment to live in an unhappy marriage.

At last, her lonely days ended, and happiness came to her. She became a mother. The birth of her children filled her with a new kind of love and hope for a fulfilled life. Her loneliness was displaced by her devotion to them.

Late in April of 1859, a messenger arrived. A letter addressed to her from her brother told of her father's ill health and requested she come immediately to Nysa. She wrote back that her present circumstances would not allow her to travel. Her children were too young to be left at home without her there to oversee their care. When another telegram arrived begging Alexandrine to come at once as her father was surely on his deathbed and could not leave this earth without purging his heart of the guilt he'd suffered all these years, she prepared for the journey to Silesia.

She made the three-day journey through Bavaria and Austria, and from Vienna, north to Nysa. November brought snow and ice, which in Silesia would not melt until spring. The stinging bitter wind, frozen rivers and lakes, and tufts of frozen grass greeted her as her carriage made its way through the village to the castle. She found the house cold as fires were neglected by a dwindling staff of servants; some time ago, the rest had deserted the old baron for better stations.

Kneeling beside her father's bed, she wept as she remembered their times together in the forests among the great trees, galloping through the meadows with primroses along the paths. She thought of the tender young trees with bright new leaves bursting out in spring that beckoned them to seek new adventures in the valleys of Nysa. It was while racing with her father across the steppes that they both embraced their wilder side in its purest form.

He spoke in a hoarse whisper, asking her to come closer. His eyes, red and swollen with pain, looked at his daughter as he said, "I am saddened that I cast you into a loveless marriage, my daughter. I cannot leave this earth knowing I have harmed you. Before I die, I beg you to forgive me."

"Father, there is nothing to forgive." Alexandrine spoke the words tenderly. "You helped me see how desolate my life would have been without a marriage, children, and a home. You saw how my life was wasting away with endless parties, being wooed by every man who was still able to walk, until my youth was spent. You helped me see that there could be a happy life with a man so caring and gentle as Hermann. It is not your fault that my Cossack spirit could not be tamed. It is I who is to blame."

At breakfast the next morning, she learned her father had died in his sleep overnight.

Funeral preparations took up most of the next day. Her only remaining brother, as the heir, took charge. Distant aunts, uncles, and cousins were notified. Alexandrine and her brother felt the loss of their two sisters, who tragically died some years before.

The assembled family, all sitting with their own painful thoughts, was a mute community filled with wretchedness. On the day of the funeral, a cold, bitter November wind blew. Soon it began to snow. It was a dark and melancholy walk to the gravesite where Karl Friedrich Wilhelm Christian von Hedemann-Heespen was laid to rest next to his illustrious Cossack ancestors.

After the funeral, Alexandrine's brother returned to the house to look over the finances in his father's office. In his last years, Karl had taken no interest in looking after his tenant accounts in Bavaria, or the receipts from his coal mines in Silesia. Her brother faced a mountain of bills. As heir, he had the duty to assume the responsibility and management of the estate and the vast von Hedemann properties. The continuation of the Hedemann line depended on him.

Her father's death left a deep void in Alexandrine. During the funeral and afterward, she mourned him deeply. Even though she still had her uncles, they were no comfort to her. To add to her total misery, her brother had cut her inheritance to a mere pittance as the family fortune was in ruins. A few years later, her brother took a steamship to America, hoping to invest in the country's growing railroad wealth. However, news of her brother's death reached Alexandrine some years later. He had shot himself.

As her life took on a new purpose with her children, she doted on them as a means of expressing her love. However, in time, even the love she felt for her children would not be enough to still the tempest in her. She continued to hope for something she knew would never be there. Then, one day, fate intervened in her darkest hour to lift her up into heights never before imagined. It was as if the sun suddenly poured all its warmth and light onto her and her alone. What she had so long desired was within her reach.

6

The Affair

*B*aron von Scheffer was now a first lieutenant in the Bavarian Army and stationed at the garrison in Augsburg. Alexandrine's first love was within her orbit! Some higher power had intervened in her darkest moments to bring him to her. It was only a matter of days before he found her. A letter arrived. A meeting was arranged. The joyful reunion was to take place at a small hotel far to the south of Augsburg, in a small village away from prying eyes. Scheffer was now a handsome man, tall in stature, mature, and with financial means, unlike the young boy who sought Alexandrine's hand so many years ago.

On the day she knew her husband would be away on business, Alexandrine ordered a coach. Her heart spilled over with joy as she waited for it to arrive. She hurried the driver as she thought her heart would surely burst before getting to the hotel. After what seemed an eternity, the coach arrived at the hotel. As she went inside, she saw him at the top of the stairs, waiting for her. She could already feel his arms around her as her feet flew, as if on wings, up the stairs. Scheffer overwhelmed her with caresses and passionate kisses. They did not talk. They could not. He pulled her from the floor and carried her into the room. There, he placed her eagerly on the bed. Their youthful passion, denied to them so many years ago, at last released, exploded, and could not be restrained.

When his arms enfolded her, she trembled at his touch. When he so tenderly touched her breasts, caressed the curves of her waist, felt the softness of her inner thigh, his surge of longing for fulfillment was met with her desire. Her mind ceased to function, and she floated away on a cloud of breathless joy. Once their passion was spent, they lay together looking at each other so dearly. They were filled with happiness. He uttered the words "I love you," which he had no right to speak, but she did not protest. She outlined his lips with her finger as he said the words again.

Several more visits to the hotel did not diminish their passion but enflamed it even more. The desire to feel each other's warm bodies against their own, and the awareness of it, could not be tamed. On those nights after being with her lover, Alexandrine found no sleep. Watching her husband asleep next to her, she could not assuage her guilt for having betrayed him. She reproached herself, *He tried to show me kindness and love, and this is how I rewarded his loyalty.*

Even though she often found herself tortured by her conscience, her dreams spoke a different story. They repeated the love she shared with Scheffer, feeling his arms around her, kissing her with a tenderness she had never found before, loving her with unrestrained passion. She did not want it to end. However, it was not long before it did.

The small population of the city of Augsburg found something newsworthy to share among themselves. Even Scheffer's commander, who was also his friend, was not immune to the gossip. He encouraged the young lieutenant to break off the affair. "It will come to no good end," he said.

Even still, Alexandrine and Scheffer pursued their passion, deceiving themselves that their days of lovemaking and forbidden joy could not be destroyed by idle gossip.

As it happened, the gossip, no longer held secret among a few, finally reached her husband's ears. Alexandrine's guilty conscience could no longer be cast aside, and so she confessed to him. He said nothing. Perhaps he closed his eyes and ears and, being a weak man, did not confront his wife. They did not talk together as before and circled around the subject, drawing away from it as if it were a poisoned spring. If only there might be a way to restore the spring to health. That evening at dinner, Hermann watched his dearest and lovely Alexandrine through new eyes. He laid down his fork and looked at her in the candlelight casting its soft glow on her lovely face. It suddenly came to him. She cared for someone else and cared no more for him. As he followed her upstairs to their bedchamber, he was suddenly overcome with a dormant feeling of anger. He could never have believed he could be angry at her. But he was. He lashed out at her, admonishing her for her recklessness, her deceit, her unfaithfulness. She stood in front of him taking the assaults, saying nothing. She knew she deserved his anger.

As the days passed, he came to understand that she had escaped him. But he still loved her. Even when there was definite proof of her infidelity by way of her pregnancy, he chose to overlook it. He had spent all his anger and now only felt the pain of it.

Apologies were in vain as her guilt was plain. If it were possible to give him back the joys of the past months, her heart could not let her do that. In spite of the pain she caused her husband, she could not, in all truth, say she regretted any of it. Were it not for his outraged relatives, he might have let the affair go on and play itself out. Hermann's mother and sister, having heard the gossip, rallied to his side, proclaiming his status in society was clearly in peril as a result of his wife's adulterous behavior. They continued to barrage him with pleas to rid himself of her hold on him and divorce her. Erzberger, not wishing to divorce her, was nevertheless powerless against his mother and sister's hatred for Alexandrine. Having no impact on her son's devotion to his wife, his mother took it upon herself to pursue Alexandrine with a renewed relentless and vengeful passion. With their heartless attacks on his wife, he could no longer bear the constant pressure from his mother. Their only mission was to convince Hermann to rid himself of the woman whose selfish and reckless behavior brought shame and disgrace to the family.

With a heavy heart, he at last capitulated and said to Alexandrine, "I feel no other option than to grant my relatives' wishes and seek a divorce. You have caused me and my family much harm, and there is no other way."

What was also settled was the fate of their three children. They would stay with their father and be raised by him and his family. This was an unexpected blow to Alexandrine from which she would never recover as she loved her children dearly. There was nothing she could do. She had been declared guilty of adultery, and her actions had consequences. She was forced to leave her children with their father and leave Augsburg, having no longer any status in society there and no hope for a quiet life as a divorced woman. This final act would leave a never-ending wound in her heart. She took one look back and thought, *He has his happiness for the rest of his life. I will only have memories.*

As she left her home, she begged her husband, "Let us not be estranged or enemies." He did not answer her but turned and went inside the house. With that, the marriage ended.

7

A New Beginning

On the day she left Augsburg, Alexandrine, in despair of not knowing what her fate would bring, stood outside the train station checking the schedules. She was not sure where she would go. No longer welcomed at her uncle's house or her father's, she decided to take the train to Munich. At least there would be no one there who knew her and no one who could malign her further. As she watched the countryside pass by from the train window, her memories sped backward to her careless love and her husband's ill treatment, which, in her mind, she earned with her sinful lust. But the guilt she suffered during that long, dark journey to Munich was nothing compared to the anguish that pierced her heart at having had her children taken from her.

Arriving in Munich, she stood outside Scheffer's parents' door; her heart beating violently, for she did not know how they would receive her. Had Scheffer told them everything? Had he been honest about her shame? When at last she had the courage to ring the bell, no one came. After several more minutes, the door finally opened. To her surprise, the Scheffers were delighted to see her. She was not only welcomed but doted on as if she were a long-lost daughter. But, as comfortable as it was in this warm and loving home, she thought it would be best for her to find her own lodgings. She stayed with the Scheffers for a couple of weeks before she found a small apartment near Maximiliansplatz that suited her. She was now well into her pregnancy. This child of her sin would soon be born. Even though she could no longer embrace the children who were taken from her, this child conceived in love could not be harmed by Erzberger's family.

After the divorce, Erzberger's mother was still not satisfied. They continued to persecute Alexandrine in the hope of annihilating her completely. The lawyer who had been her representative in the divorce proceedings was lured away by the Erzberger family and persuaded through a generous payment to compose a document of accusations against her and Scheffer. It was damning and completely evil. They intended that all of society's doors be closed to her, wherever she might be. The document was circulated within her social contacts and finally found its way into the Cabinet of the Imperial Council and Embassies. No stone was left unturned to complete her total ruin.

None of that could deter Alexandrine from the joy that was presented to her when her son was born. Scheffer's son! This child, the culmination of their love, she named Hermann, after his father. To her, he was undoubtedly the most exceptionally beautiful child. His complexion, blond hair, and blue eyes were his father's. She poured out all the love onto him that she did not receive as a child herself, as well as all the love she was denied giving to her other children.

Scheffer returned to Munich to be with Alexandrine and Hermann whenever he was granted leave. It was as though nothing had happened since they said their goodbyes in Augsburg. Her love for him flooded through her as passionate as it was when they spent those early days in Augsburg. They found a much larger house on Karlstrasse within walking distance of the Ring and Marienplatz. There, they lived together as Hermann thrived and grew into a happy child. It was during this time that the subject of marriage was approached. Hermann wanted his son to be legitimate and to carry on the von Scheffer family name and title.

Once more, fate intervened to complete the ruinous circle. To both of their dismay, a marriage between the two of them could not be. One of the obstacles was his military duties, which often took him far away for lengthy periods. But above all else were the inflexible hinderances of the Church. The divorced Alexandrine was considered immoral and unworthy. At one time, Scheffer took his pistol and pointed it at the church bishop to force his permission to marry her. Even with the threat of being shot, the bishop did not concede. The unhappy couple continued on as before until his military obligations took him farther and farther away. Their love for each other during those long absences finally melted away like a winter's thaw until there was nothing left.

Living alone in Munich in the house she once shared so lovingly with Scheffer, Alexandrine became a burden. The money he sent provided little and, in time, stopped altogether. It wasn't long before Erzberger's mother, through her relentless pursuit to destroy Alexandrine, found out about the birth of her illegitimate son. Relishing anything that would further discredit her former daughter-in-law in her son's eyes, she made this bit of news known to him. As a result, he cut off what meager allowance he had bestowed on Alexandrine as a divorce settlement.

The Scheffer family spared what little they could. By all means, Alexandrine was living a poor and meager existence. With whatever little food she had, she made sure baby Hermann did not suffer. In all her years living within the luxuries of her father and uncle's homes, she never expected to be living a dreary and lonely existence ever on the brink of disaster.

One day, she called her cook and maid to her. "I am sorry, but I can no longer keep you. I haven't enough money to pay your wages," she told them in all honesty.

They could hear the sadness in her voice but seemed not to be deterred. Maria said, "My lady, I have no wish to leave you. Your good fortune will return, and all will be as it was."

Lisel, the cook, chimed in. "I will not leave you. I have a small inheritance, which I will happily use for our food. Do not concern yourself any longer."

Alexandrine was overwhelmed by their generosity. With tears welling up in her eyes, she said, "Thank you, my dear Maria and Lisel. You will be repaid for your loyalty. You will always have a home here. Of that you can be assured."

She would have sunk into an abyss of total despair except for her friend and cousin Countess Ida von Hahn-Hahn, a writer who took the sad and unlucky Alexandrine under her wing. Ida, a few years older than Alexandrine, had known her from her days at her uncle's house in Augsburg. She was a frequent visitor at the castle, who also became a close friend and confidant. After moving to Munich, Alexandrine sought out her old friend. It was then that Ida, seeing Alexandrine fall deeper and deeper into darkness, approached her with a gift. She arranged for Alexandrine to accompany her on a trip to the Holy Land. Alexandrine, still on good terms with the Scheffers, placed young Hermann with them.

8

A Pilgrimage

Alexandrine and Ida boarded the train in Munich, traveling through Switzerland and then to Italy. They stopped off in Milan to rest and refresh themselves before reboarding for the trip to Genoa. A large steam-powered ship was waiting in the port of the Italian city to take them to the Holy Land. After several hours spent loading goods for transport to cities along the Mediterranean, as well as supplies for the crew and passengers for the journey, the ship slowly left port. Alexandrine stayed on deck to watch the shoreline disappear. This was her first sea voyage on such a large ship. Everything on it fascinated her. There was not only a large stack that released a cloud of steam, but there were two great masts with sails. As the screw engine growled and they moved slowly out into the sea, Alexandrine looked toward the horizon and thought about the new adventure that awaited her.

They were not the only passengers. A group of twelve nuns from France was making the same pilgrimage to the Holy Land. Once the women were settled in their berths, one of the captain's officers knocked on Ida and Alexandrine's door to ask if they had need of anything. He also said the captain would be honored by their presence at dinner in his quarters. The invitation was also extended to the nuns, who, however, were already quite indisposed. Seasickness had overcome them. Every evening thereafter, Alexandrine and Ida were the captain's only guests.

The trip was not unpleasant as the sea was relatively calm. The nuns, however, spent their days vomiting. Ida and Alexandrine helped them the best they could, even emptying out their buckets. On the third day, one of the nuns, whom Alexandrine thought to be no more than sixteen, came out of her room and ventured into the dining room, still pale and somewhat weak, not having eaten in three days.

"I am Sister Maria Louise du Rennes."

As the captain stood up to welcome her, he said, "Please join us, Sister. We are happy to see you have not succumbed to the seasickness."

The nun, not understanding, looked at him shyly. It was apparent to Alexandrine that she did not comprehend what the captain said. She took the nun's hand and led her to a seat at the table. She felt she knew enough of her schooled French to communicate sufficiently with the sister. After dinner, when everyone had departed, Alexandrine asked Sister Louise how she became a nun as she was yet so young.

She began by telling of her family in France. "My family comes from a very old line of the French aristocracy and, I'm sure, is considered wealthy by most standards. I have five brothers and six sisters," she said. "In France, women are not in the line of inheritance."

"It is the same in Germany," Alexandrine interjected.

The nun went on. "The most advantaged families are able

to provide money or properties for a dowry for their daughters, thus marrying them off to men of property and wealth. This also ensures the girl's family even more prosperity and position through an auspicious match. Did you not find that true where you are from?" she asked.

This opened a wound for Alexandrine as she knew all too well how important it is for families to marry off their daughters for the wealth and lands she could bring them by making a successful marriage.

Sister Maria Louise continued. "After my six sisters were married, there was no more money for another dowry. I was fourteen when it was decided that I should enter religious life. There were no other opportunities for a daughter who had no prospect of a suitable marriage than to become a nun. And so here I am."

Alexandrine, looking at the young nun, who seemed so sad, said, "It seems to be the same everywhere. In Germany, many a noble house went bankrupt over the cost of substantial dowries for their daughters. Often, more than one daughter in the household was sent off to the nunnery."

Alexandrine and Sister Louise spent the rest of the journey in each other's company. Alexandrine learned a great deal about life in France; the current emperor, Napoleon III; and the many turbulent years in the country since the Revolution of 1789. Sister Louise explained, "You would love Paris. The emperor has made many changes. My father says that he has brought Paris back to glory, rebuilding many of the old buildings destroyed during the revolution. In addition, he has promoted industry and tourism. Paris is a beautiful city, and you absolutely must visit." She talked with such fever and love about Paris that Alexandrine was compelled to say, "I should be happy to someday go to Paris and see all that you have told me."

On the deck of the ship, Alexandrine noticed an increasing wetness in the air, causing a stifling heat as they came closer to their destination. Her hair took on a curly look, and her skin was damp and oily in appearance, which she felt compelled to blot with her handkerchief every few minutes. Looking at Ida, who seemed calm and composed, Alexandrine asked, "How are you able to stand it? The air is too hot and humid for me."

"I think about the cold, dark, and dreary winters in Munich," she retorted. "Enjoy the sun. You'll be back in Munich soon enough, dreaming about the sea and the sun."

After several stops along the way to pick up more passengers, food, and supplies, the ship finally docked in Haifa. The sea breeze was blowing briskly in port, and the sun seemed even stronger as they disembarked. Waiting for them was an open carriage and a guide who was ready to take them to their hotel. Alexandrine opened her parasol as she did not like the hot sun on her face.

Once Alexandrine and Ida arrived at the hotel, the porter, overburdened with their multiple suitcases, led them up a grand staircase to the second floor and to their suite. The room was spacious enough, with two beds, a settee, and a writing desk. A small table with two chairs faced the French door, which opened to a balcony filled with flowering potted plants and floral vines cascading over the metal railing. From the balcony, they were happy to have an unobstructed view of the blue waters of the Mediterranean Sea. Even the breeze blowing in from the sea did nothing to cool the air. A maid arrived to unpack their suitcases, and after a cooling bath, Alexandrine and Ida dressed for dinner. Alexandrine was glad she remembered to pack a few cotton dresses.

The hotel dining room was on the main floor with a large terrace overlooking the sea. Tables were set with white linen tablecloths and a bouquet of fresh flowers in the center. Hotel guests were already seated for dinner. The maître-d' showed them to a table at the edge of the terrace, which was already occupied by two portly middle-aged women who introduced themselves as Caroline and Mabel Noyes from Norwich in County Norfolk, England. Alexandrine and Ida could speak a little English, and the two women could speak a little German, so between them a somewhat disjointed conversation took place.

"Don't you find it dreadfully hot here?" Caroline lamented, fanning herself.

"We English cannot abide the heat, but it is better than the gloomy days in England. My sister and I arrived two weeks ago, but we have another week before our return." Looking at Alexandrine, Mabel asked, "How long are you staying here?"

Alexandrine answered, "We just arrived today and plan to stay only a few days in Haifa. From here, we will travel throughout the Holy Land for a month before returning to Germany."

"Oh, my dears, you must let us show you around Haifa. We have become quite expert at what you must absolutely see in this ancient city," Caroline interjected. Mabel added, "Yes, you must let us come with you. It would be such fun."

After dinner, they were enjoying coffee and desert when a young man dressed in a lightweight linen suit arrived and asked, "May I join you ladies?"

Mabel's eyes brightened at the sight of the handsome young man. "Of course, Sir William, please do. You look quite dapper this evening."

She introduced him to her newfound friends.

Viscount William Smithson arrived in Haifa at the same time as the Noyes sisters and obviously had already made their acquaintance. William took Alexandrine's hand and bowed over it with a light kiss. "*Enchanté*, mademoiselle." He walked over to where Ida was sitting and did the same. He snared a seat from an adjoining table and placed it between Alexandrine and Mabel. After seating himself, he signaled the waiter for a cup of coffee.

Mabel said, "We're taking them to see the sights of Haifa. Won't you join us, Sir William?"

"That is kind of you, Mabel, but I am soon to depart for England."

Quietly listening to the plans being made on her behalf, Ida broke into the conversation. "You are most kind, Miss Caroline and Miss Mabel, but we have just this afternoon arrived. We can make no plans yet as we must first recover our land legs."

Mabel looking disappointed and said, "I understand, my dear. I had so hoped to accompany you. I wish you a pleasant stay in Haifa and beyond."

Ida stood up and placed herself behind her chair. Seeing Ida standing up, William, too, stood up. Ida announced, "Please excuse me as I am very tired from our long journey. I must regrettably bid you all goodnight."

"Goodnight, then. It was lovely to meet you, and I'm sure we will see you at breakfast," Mabel said hopefully.

Alexandrine also bade her farewell. William bowed as they left the room.

The two women were both glad to be on their own again. Reaching the stairs to their room, they both let out a silent sigh of relief that they had averted being corralled by these two English ladies. In their room, they found it no cooler, even with the fan noisily turning above their beds. Neither of them slept. They tossed and turned most of the night, listening to the constant whirr of the fan. The next morning, they ordered a breakfast of eggs and toast and a pot of coffee brought to their room. Neither of them was in the mood for the cheerful Misses Mabel and Caroline.

After breakfast, they both dressed in the lightest clothes they could find. Alexandrine's dress was a pale-pink cotton, which hung loosely over her youthful figure, catching any slight breeze. She put on a wide-brimmed straw hat and grabbed her parasol before she and Ida went down to the hotel lobby. Stepping into the streets of Haifa, they both felt the heat of the sun on their skin. The burning sun bore down on them unmercifully with only a few wisps of clouds to tease them as they walked down the street. Palm trees, moving ever so slightly in the hot breeze, cast only a sliver of real shade. People were bustling about in the midday sun, seeming not to mind the blistering heat at all. At last, a café came into view. Seating themselves at a small table under the awning was a welcome relief from the sun. They were grateful for whatever shade the awning provided.

When a waiter finally approached them, he spoke Arabic, which neither Ida nor Alexandrine understood. In sign language, Ida indicated she wanted to see a menu. In a very distinct accent, the waiter said, "Menu" as he pointed to a board on the wall of the building. It was written in Arabic. The puzzled look on their faces prompted the waiter to say in the best way he could, "Feesh, only feesh."

Ida and Alexandrine tried hard not to laugh and said, "Thank you, we'll have the feesh."

They lunched on heavily seasoned perch, wild rice, and fresh fruit. Alexandrine yearned for a glass of sherry to soothe her mouth from the over-seasoned fish, but there was none to be had in this Muslim city. She had to be content with a cup of hot tea.

On the way back to the hotel, William approached them. As he tipped his hat, he asked, "Good afternoon, ladies. How did you find Haifa today?"

"Good afternoon, Sir William. We have yet to see much of the city, but we had a delightful luncheon at a very quaint little restaurant not far from here," answered Alexandrine.

"Ah, I know it well. Did you have the fish?"

"Yes, it was quite good," Alexandrine answered, barely able to control herself any longer. Both she and Ida broke out in uncontrollable laughter remembering the *feesh*.

"If you will permit me, I would very much like to invite you to an even better restaurant this evening. That is, of course, unless you have other plans."

"We would be delighted. Wouldn't we, Ida?"

Ida nodded reluctantly.

"Superb. I shall meet you in the lobby at eight this evening," he said as he tipped his hat and walked away. Suddenly, he turned around and addressed both. "I should like to remind you lovely ladies that Haifa is mostly Arab, so women do not enjoy the same freedoms here. Walking unescorted is not permitted. I would not like it if you were set upon for your immodesty."

"Thank you, Sir William. We shall certainly not want to be immodest or be set upon, as you say." They both laughed quietly as he turned back.

When they were back in their room, Ida scolded Alexandrine. "Why did you agree to have dinner with Mr. Smithson so quickly? We don't know him."

"Oh, but he is so handsome. And why not? We will have an adventure!"

As promised, William was waiting for them in the hotel lobby promptly at 8 p.m. He took both their arms and led them gallantly to a waiting taxi. He instructed the carriage driver to take them to the German Colony. After a quick ride through the city and somewhat outside its fortress, they stepped out of the taxi and walked a short distance to a small, white sandstone building. William asked the driver to wait. There was no sign on the building and only a number seven hand-painted on the old wooden door. William knocked. After a few minutes, a woman in a long, plain cotton frock and head covering answered the door. "*Bitte, kommen Sie herein,*" she welcomed them in German. Inside, there was one rather large, heavy-looking wooden table set with earthen bowls and goblets. A few men sat at one end of the table having a quiet conversation, looking up now and then at the newcomers. Alexandrine could not understand the language. She asked William what they were speaking.

"It is a version of German mixed with Hebrew. It is most difficult to understand unless you're born here."

The woman returned from the kitchen with a decanter of red wine, poured it quickly into the goblets, and then scurried back to the kitchen. When she returned, she placed several large, overfilled plates of smoked fish, herring, stuffed cabbages, boiled potatoes, and loaves of bread on the table. Alexandrine and Ida's eyes bulged out at the sight of such a bounty of food set before them.

"This is too much food for us," Ida complained. "How can we possibly eat all of this?"

"Not all of it is for you," William said. "See those men there?" He pointed to the men at the end of the table. "They will come and help themselves. This is how it's done here in a commune. Everyone shares."

And it was. The men moved closer and took whatever food they wanted and ate noisily. Ida thought their manners were boorish. Alexandrine looked at the men as if to study them. To her, they were interesting: dressed in what looked to her as night shirts over baggy trousers, their hands rough and dirty obviously from doing farm work; their speech sounded coarse. Alexandrine remembered she wanted an adventure. This certainly was that.

At the end of the evening, William paid handsomely for the meal. The taxi driver was still waiting for them to drive them back to the hotel.

Returning to the hotel, Alexandrine said, "Thank you for a most interesting and enjoyable evening, sir. The meal was excellent, just as you promised."

"It was my pleasure. Will you allow me to escort you around Haifa tomorrow?"

"That would be lovely," Alexandrine quickly answered.

"Then I shall be happy to do so. I bid you both a good night," William said as he took Alexandrine's hand and kissed it lightly.

~

During the next two days, William escorted Alexandrine and Ida around Haifa, telling them some of the history of the region from the arrival of the early Muslims to the Crusaders, followed by the Ottomans. He also spoke about Napoleon Bonaparte's conquest of Haifa and the more recent Egyptian occupation. "But now we find ourselves in a major wave of Israelite immigrants who are arriving from Morocco along with another influx of Muslims."

"You have amazed me with your knowledge of this region, Mr. Smithson. How is it that you know so much?" Alexandrine asked.

"I have been a professor of Eastern history studies at Oxford for the past nine years. I come here every year on sabbatical," he answered.

Alexandrine looked at him with admiration as she respected anyone with a resourceful mind and accomplishments. "I do wish to know more, Sir William, but we will sadly be leaving tomorrow on our tour."

"So am I," he reflected. "I must return to England."

"Then we shall say goodbye. Or, as in Germany, *auf Wiedersehen*. It means 'until we meet again.'"

"Yes, we shall meet again," William responded with a bow and a kiss on Alexandrine's hand. To her, it felt like an invitation.

A Pilgrimage

The following morning, William left his calling card and a message for Alexandrine and Ida:

> *You have been the most enjoyable companions, and I send you my most fervent wish that you find inspiration in your journey. Should you ever have the opportunity to visit England, it would be my utmost pleasure to accompany you further.*
> *Most sincerely, William*

After William left, Alexandrine and Ida departed for Jaffa, Jerusalem, Nazareth, and Mount Carmel. Alexandrine experienced no solace in these places as she had long ago found no comfort in religion. She was raised Evangelical and did not know much about Catholicism or the beliefs of the early Jews who settled there. She did, however, feed her soul with all the historical sites, art, and beauty of the land. After a month, she was ready to return home to Karlstrasse. She was still impoverished but physically fully nourished in both mind and spirit.

9

Crown Prince Ludwig of Bavaria

After returning to Munich, the cold, damp, gray skies that Alexandrine remembered would have seemed unendurable except for her newfound accord. She was no longer unhappily sitting by the window watching carriages go by with ladies dressed in their finest, adorned with hats in the latest fashion. Nor was she envious of women walking arm in arm with their husbands passing by her window. Memories of her travels to the Holy Land gave her a renewal of life. In a few months, the days would be warm and lovely again. Trees would soon be unfolding with virginal young leaves and delicate blossoms giving up their sweet fragrances.

On one of spring's first bright and cheerful sunlit days, she called to her devoted maid. "Maria, we are going out. Bring Hermann and prepare the *Kinderwagen*. Dress him warmly, for I wish to go into the city," she shouted as she hastened up the stairs.

Alexandrine put on a high-neck white blouse and a dark-green wool skirt and jacket. She put a shawl that she purchased in Jerusalem over her shoulders and placed a small hat decorated with feathers and ribbons over her red hair. *That should do*, she thought. Poverty did not diminish her desire to be fashionable and present herself as befitting her station. She was, after all, still a baroness. Even in the unhappiest of times, she kept her demeanor at its highest.

With Maria pushing the pram over the cobblestone streets, they walked the short distance down Karlstrasse to Maximilianplatz. In the course of the day, Alexandrine found herself wandering around the Inner Ring of the city. She stopped and pointed to one of the buildings and said, "Look, Hermann, there is the Bavarian Parliament. Perhaps someday you will become the minister of Bavaria."

She had hoped that little Hermann would grow to be a statesman and not choose a career in the military like his father. She and Maria continued walking around Marienplatz. Shopkeepers dressed in traditional Bavarian loden jackets and leather knee breeches welcomed Alexandrine inside. She greeted them cordially and went on. In the *Konditerrei*, she bought two pieces of strudel—one for her and one for Maria. She broke off a piece for Hermann and fed it to him. He laughed and giggled and clapped his hands for more.

Walking by the Hofbräuhaus, the pungent smell of stale beer assaulted them. Alexandrine heard the brass band playing, beer steins clinking, men shouting in unison: *"Eins, zwei, drei, skufa!"* She saw people sitting together at long tables singing, arms linked together, swaying back and forth with the music, lifting up their steins of beer. Large-breasted, stout barmaids in *Dirndls* carrying eight steins in their large hands placed them heavily on the tables, spilling a good deal of beer.

No one seemed to notice. Alexandrine wanted to go inside but decided this would not be the time as she wanted to enjoy the city as long as the sunshine lasted.

Standing in front of the Frauenkirche's great door, she contemplated going inside. She was not Catholic but was curious what she would find inside the cathedral. As she entered through the great wooden doors with their massive iron hinges, the smell of incense and burning candle wax overwhelmed her senses. What she saw in the cathedral was a wonder to behold: tall marble columns and large, colorful stained-glass windows with picture of saints and angels, telling stories in silence. Throughout the church, in every niche and on every pedestal, were statues of saints. In the most prominent sections stood delicate marble statues of Mary, Jesus, and Joseph. The wooden pews stretching toward the altar were bathed in an unearthly light from the windows. There in the front stood a large, carved wooden altar covered with a white cloth. A small gold cabinet with two doors stood on it, which Maria said contained the chalice that held the communion hosts. Above the altar, there hung a large silver cross with a likeness of Jesus nailed to it. A few women with scarves on their heads were kneeling in pews, praying with rosaries in their hands. As they prayed, they held a bead on the rosary and then moved to the next one while they recited:

Hail Mary, full of Grace
The Lord is with thee.
Blessed are thou amongst women
And blessed is the fruit of thy womb, Jesus.
Holy Mary, Mother of God,
Pray for us sinners

Now and in the hour of our death.
Amen.

The words were spoken by each of the women as if in a round. One beginning, one ending. Alexandrine did not know what the words meant. She saw a few men and women standing at the sides of the church in front of a carving on the wall. They prayed and then moved on to the next one. She asked Maria what they were doing.

"My lady, those carvings are called the Way of the Cross. There are fourteen stations, each depicting Christ's condemnation, his walk to be crucified, and then his death on the cross for our sins. Before each station, prayers are said before moving on to the next until the fourteenth one, where Jesus is laid in the tomb. People do this in honor of the Passion of Jesus Christ."

"How do you know so much about this?" Alexandrine asked.

"I was raised Catholic. However, circumstances in my early youth caused me to lose faith."

"What circumstances could cause you to lose your faith?"

"It's a difficult story, my lady."

"You do not need to tell me, Maria, if it brings you shame."

"No, it's not that. It has been many years, and I have long forgotten the pain of it. When I was a young girl, I fell in love with a young boy. We did not know much about adult feelings and certainly not of their consequences. I became pregnant. I was thirteen at the time, much too young to understand what I had done or how it happened. All I knew is that one has to be married to have babies. That's what the other girls told me. They also said that a baby grows inside your stomach, and when it's big enough, it comes out your bottom. The thought of that frightened me, and I cried for weeks. My parents felt the shame of what I had done and brought me to the convent in the town where I lived. The nuns took care of me, and when the baby was born, they took it away. It was then I lost my faith as I wondered how God could let me have a baby and then take it away from me. I never knew what happened to the baby, but I know it was a girl."

Alexandrine's heart almost broke while Maria told the story, and she wept when she heard the baby was taken from her. She knew all too well the pain of losing one's beloved child.

Suddenly, the church's large pipe organ came to life. The long, deep chord exploded across the empty cathedral. On a balcony at the rear of the church, it began playing George Friederich Handel's "Messiah" in preparation for Easter Sunday Mass, while a chorus rehearsed. The large brass pipes of the organ extended in glory to the church's ceiling. Its deep resonant sounds reverberating throughout the church moved Alexandrine. She and Maria decided to stay a little longer listening to the rich sounds of the magnificent organ. The choir of nuns' voices sounded like angels floating through this magnificent church.

On the way out, Alexandrine looked down on the stone floor. "Look, Maria, at the stone under your foot. It looks like the devil's footprint."

Hermann was too young to understand, but she wanted to know more about it. Maria said, "I heard someone once tell me the story. This is where it was thought the devil stood while the cathedral was being built. The devil made a deal with the builder. He would finance the construction on one condition: the cathedral could have no windows. However, the clever builder, wanting beautiful stained-glass windows depicting holy images, tricked the devil. He positioned the marble columns so that the windows were not visible from the spot where the devil stood. By the time the devil discovered the treachery, the church had already been consecrated. He could only stand in the front of the church and stamp his foot in anger. This left the footprint that you see at the entrance."

Alexandrine laughed and said, "That's a wonderful story, Maria."

After a delightful day touring Munich, Alexandrine returned home with a full and happy heart. But her future was still uncertain.

~

She continued to walk around Munich as a diversion. One day while having coffee and cake in one of the outdoor coffeehouses in Marienplatz, Alexandrine found herself glancing across the open marketplace at Crown Prince Ludwig looking out of his gold-encrusted carriage. He, too, had seen her. She knew he admired beautiful women, but she quickly decided it was her hair he admired. That day she wore it loosely braided under a small felt hat, allowing the thick braids to cascade down her back. He smiled at her, and she rather shyly smiled back.

The next morning, a messenger arrived. Maria answered the door and, racing up the stairs, handed the note with its royal seal to Alexandrine in her bedchamber. "A footman is waiting outside for your reply." Alexandrine unfolded the cream-colored bond paper with the crown prince's royal crest and read, "My dear Baroness, may I call upon you this evening? I shall await your reply with the greatest anticipation."

Alexandrine quickly wrote, "As you wish, your Royal Highness. I shall await you this evening. Your humble servant, Alexandrine von Hedemann."

Maria hurried down the stairs to hand the note to the waiting messenger. She returned upstairs out of breath and full of excitement.

"My lady, we must prepare you for the crown prince's visit. I will lay out your favorite gown and bathe you in lavender-scented water."

That evening, Alexandrine waited for the crown prince's arrival. The hours passed slowly. The clock on the mantle chimed eight times, then nine, then ten. Still, she waited. At midnight, she heard hoofbeats on the cobblestones outside her house and the unmistakable clatter of a carriage. An unmarked, closed carriage drawn by two elegant matching horses stopped at her front steps, and the crown prince stepped out. A footman escorted him to the door and then returned to wait in the carriage. Maria opened the door and bowed low in front of the prince, who quickly stepped inside. She led him into the sitting room, where Alexandrine stood waiting for him.

"Your Royal Highness, I am honored that you should come this evening." She curtsied. He took her hand and led her to the settee, where he seated himself next to her.

He looks so young, Alexandrine thought. Ludwig had just celebrated his seventeenth birthday. His father, Maximilian II, was crowned king of Bavaria after his father, Ludwig I, abdicated. Ludwig, who would become Ludwig II, would, in a short two years, be crowned king of Bavaria. It would come at the unexpected illness and death of his father. Ludwig was not prepared to become king so suddenly.

Maria brought in tea and cakes. At first, it seemed awkward for both of them until the crown prince opened the conversation by saying, "If it pleases you, Baroness, I would like you to call me by my given name, Ludwig, and I shall address you as Alex."

Alexandrine was more than happy to forget the formalities as she found him most charming and relaxed there in her modest house. She was wondering why and how he came to know her.

"Tell me, Ludwig," she asked, somewhat timid about calling him by his given name, "how do you come to know me?"

"I saw you the other day sitting alone in a café in downtown Munich. I thought you most enchanting. It's not often I see a woman with such grace and dignity outside the court. I sent out inquiries, and here I am. I hope you will not think me bold."

"Not at all, your Royal Highness. I mean to say *Ludwig*," she apologized.

"Tell me," Ludwig asked, "I know only a little about you and would like to know more."

Alexandrine, not wanting to explain away all her past indiscretions, avoided the question and said, "My life is much too mundane to talk about. I would much rather know how a young prince such as yourself finds amusement at court and to hear your political views. I believe there is talk of Bavaria's involvement in the German Confederation."

He replied, "I find politics quite boring and have no interest in it. My real interest lies in art, music, and architecture. I have studied the architecture of France, Italy, and Greece and hope to someday bring these ideas to Bavaria."

"And do you find art and music equally interesting?" she asked.

"Yes, indeed. I have just recently summoned the composer Richard Wagner to court. I find him most interesting, and his talent is beyond compare. We have become good friends, and I feel a particular accord with him."

Alexandrine, having seen Wagner before at a small gathering at Ida Hahn's house, remembered him looking at her with an odd smile. To her, he looked tragic and alone as if he were deposed royalty. She thought he had a strange face consistent with a strange man, having an enormous head, a long nose that turned downward, and eyes hard and narrow. She did not like Wagner or his music, which she thought was heavy and dull. She agreed with many of his critics who called him egotistical and ungrateful.

She did not tell the young crown prince that but instead said, "Forgive me, Ludwig, I have heard much about the composer but nothing so enthralling. I have heard he is quite rude at times and critical of his contemporaries. Some say he is a political radical and a philanderer."

"That is doubtless true. A true genius is often misunderstood," he said. "When I was fifteen years of age, I had the privilege of seeing his opera *Lohengrin* and, later, *Tannhauser*. They filled me with such imagination that I dreamed my life should always be surrounded by such things."

Looking deep into Ludwig's eyes, Alexandrine saw a man with a gentle soul. She said softly, "You have a true artist's soul, Ludwig. You will always find beauty in all things and find ways to fulfill your need to express yourself. I understand such things as I am also an admirer of art, music, and poetry." He seemed happy to hear those words spoken of him.

Ludwig took his leave soon after but not before requesting another rendezvous.

From that day forward, she saw him often. He visited her from time to time for what she described as only the pleasure of talking with her. He found within her a kindred spirit and confidant, someone who did not judge or criticize. His only other confidant was his cousin Elisabeth, who ultimately married the Austrian emperor Franz Joseph. Until her death, Elisabeth communicated with him regularly and provided him with much-needed companionship during what he considered to be a lonely life as he was not inclined to partake in court gatherings, preferring to stay in his quarters.

On one of his many visits, Ludwig arrived unmistakably distressed. Alexandrine looked at his dear sweet face, so honest and sincere, and asked, "What is making you frown so?"

He said only that his life is in misery. Alexandrine held his hand and looked into his mournful eyes. "Tell me, my friend, what has happened."

"I am told to marry. I cannot marry," he blurted out.

Alexandrine urged him to tell her why he could not marry. She had long heard rumors of Ludwig's penchant toward homosexuality. Whether they were true or not, she did not know, nor did she care. Rumors also flourished around his relationship with Wagner. He had told her during their frequent evenings together about his feelings for the composer that went beyond his admiration for his craft. He often said how no one understood him like Wagner did and that their souls were united in that understanding. It seemed naturally perfect that Ludwig's love for Wagner's mind and art should develop into romantic love. He as much as admitted his love for Wagner, which was never returned. However, a pure and good friendship lasted until Wagner's death in 1883.

Ludwig, through much strain, confessed, "I have been

charged with producing an heir once I'm crowned king and am forced to engage myself to Duchess Sophie of Bavaria, my cousin, who is also the youngest sister of my dear, dear friend Empress Elisabeth. Even though I find her charming and we share our interest in the works of Wagner, I cannot reconcile myself to marry her. Our engagement has already been announced."

Some months later, it was reported that after several postponements, the wedding was finally canceled. Ludwig never married and never had any mistresses. He constantly fought his homosexual nature in order to remain true to his Catholic faith.

Over the next two years and until his coronation, Ludwig frequently visited Alexandrine in her little house on Karlstrasse. However, after his coronation, his visits ended. She understood the reasons he could no longer visit her. He was now king. Over the next years, she learned much about Ludwig's life. He spent most of his years not so much interested in public affairs as the king of Bavaria but more in designing and building palaces around Bavaria, each more extravagant than the last.

First, the "fairy tale" Neuschwanstein Castle near Füssen was built as a retreat and in honor of Richard Wagner, who continued to be a confidant and close friend. Later, Ludwig commissioned the building of the beautiful and excessively gilded Schloss Linderhof, with a grotto where he was rowed in a boat shaped like a seashell. The grotto was lit with red, green, and blue electric lights, a novelty at the time. His greatest achievement was to be Herrenchiemsee, built on the largest island in Lake Chiemsee in lower Bavaria. It was built as a replica of the palace and gardens at Versailles as a *homage* to the adored King Louis XIV. It was, however, not finished during his reign. Ludwig II's passion for his extravagant artistic and architectural projects in favor of the day-to-day affairs of state emptied the coffers. His continued project of building ever more castles throughout Bavaria, combined with his withdrawal from his duties as king, was finally used against him. In 1886, the "fairy tale king" was declared insane.

10

A Reversal of Circumstances

It was after her return from the Holy Land, that Alexandrine's loneliness for her children cost her the last pennies she had. She took a train to Augsburg, where she rented a room over a blacksmith's shop in a small conspiracy with the children's nursemaid. This allowed her a few minutes a day to see and hold her children. They clustered around her with happy cries when she gave them candy she brought with her from Munich. However, Alexandrine could not stay long. She did not want to encounter her ex-mother-in-law or her ex-husband, Hermann. Returning to Munich, she held the memory of those dear children close to her heart, for she did not know when she would see them again. In that melancholy moment, she asked herself, "Shall I never dress them in light summer frocks or little suits and woolen stockings in winter? Shall I never be able to teach them French, brush their hair, bathe them, or tell them to finish eating their meat so they will grow strong?"

A few days after returning to Munich, she found her situation still dire with no hope of improving. She thought of the king. She knew from her conversations with young Ludwig that his father, Maximilian, was a kind and generous ruler. She ordered a carriage to take her to the Munich Residence Palace, Nymphenburg. Happily, she was not hindered and was escorted to the king's apartment. He smiled and said, "Baroness, I am happy to see you as I have heard much about you and your kindness toward my son, Ludwig."

Curtsying low, she answered, "Thank you, Your Majesty. Your son has shared many an evening with me conversing about all the things he loves most, particularly the arts. He has a natural proclivity for beauty in all forms. In that we have much in common."

After a short exchange, she told him about her unfortunate circumstances and how grateful she would be if he would be so generous as to offer her a small loan.

"Of course, Baroness. In appreciation of your friendship with my son, I would be glad to be of service."

Without hesitation, he reached into a cupboard, took out a handful of Bavarian gulden, and handed them to her. "Here, take these. There is no need to repay me, for I am much indebted to you for your friendship with my son."

"I am most grateful to Your Majesty." She bowed and backed out of the room. Anyone who might have looked her way could not miss the happy smile on her face after she left.

Through the generosity of the king, Alexandrine was happily saved from total poverty. She immediately returned to Augsburg, paid off her debts from her last visit, and found a new place to stay closer to her children. When Erzberger found out she had borrowed money from the king to come to Augsburg, he was wrought with concern over her circumstance. As the mother of his children, he could not live with the knowledge that she had no income of her own and had to borrow money from strangers and, most embarrassingly, from King Maximillian himself. He immediately arranged, through his solicitor, to provide her with funds and promised a generous monthly allowance thereafter. However, this generosity did not come without a stipulation.

Erzberger, being a good man, was still torn between doing the right thing and appeasing his relatives. He required Alexandrine once more to leave Augsburg. He feared that she would undoubtedly be in more danger as his relatives had not forgotten her sins and the ruin she had caused her husband and children. In the end, Alexandrine returned to Munich in financial good health but once again saddened by the loss of her children.

Her newfound fortune made it possible for her to seek a housekeeper and a nursemaid for little Hermann. She also paid back wages to her loyal cook and her faithful maid, Maria. Alexandrine found her life suddenly improved, although the stigma of her past indiscretion, and the manner in which it was made public by her former husband's family, still prevented her from entering society.

It was in late August that year of 1862 when she had occasion to attend a new concerto by Franz Liszt in the Munich Opera House with her friend Ida. It had been a long time since she was able to enjoy a cultural event and nourish her soul with music and culture. As her gaze drifted around the opera house, she wondered how others could be so happily talking, smiling, and acting indifferent when she could not. She still suffered from the pangs of loneliness inflicted on her by her former in-law and her husband.

Returning from the concert, she asked the coachman to let her out several blocks from her home as she wanted to enjoy the evening air and walk the rest of the way. The crisp autumn air told of a summer gone and winter soon to come. It was, however, still a pleasant evening with a slight breeze lightly blowing the cape she wore over her blue dress.

The next afternoon, Alexandrine received a bouquet of flowers. There was no note and only a card signed "Count L." She did not recognize the handwriting, nor could she imagine who Count L was. In her circles, she knew several barons, counts, and dukes but could not guess who would be so bold as to send her such a large bouquet of flowers with only an initial. More flowers arrived the next day and the next. After a week of these daily deliveries, the air in her small house overflowed with sweet scents while the floors were covered with spent petals. Then, one day, a bouquet of lilies arrived. Folded neatly inside one of the petals was a small handwritten note. It simply said: "May I have the pleasure of calling on you, dear lady?" It was signed "Count L."

Part II

Prince Chlodwig

*With all philosophy, I should feel unhappy
if I had not nature.*

—Prince Chlodwig von Hohenlohe-
Schillingsfürst

Prince Chlodwig von Hohenlohe-Schillingsfürst circa 1860

11

A Restful Place

*A*fter finishing what he considered a successful meeting with Otto von Bismarck in Berlin, Chlodwig von Hohenlohe boarded the train to Munich. Once outside the city, he found tranquility in the passing landscape as it transformed from the city's row houses and cold stone pavements to green hills, meadows, and farms. Farmers were harvesting their grain, piling it into bushels ready for market. The verdant landscape sped by as the train made its way through Germany south to Munich. He never tired of the pretty German landscape of green fields and dainty houses with window boxes overflowing with flowers in neat little villages. It was in sharp contrast to traveling through Russia with its sparse population, its miserable villages and stunted forests. Not so long ago, he had crossed hundreds of miles in Russia during a bitter winter with deathly gray skies and biting winds. He did not care to do it again. No longer involved with constant meetings, people, and discussions about political views, he finally fell into a restful sleep.

As his train approached Nürnberg, he decided to switch

trains and take another one to Rothenburg; from there, a carriage would take him to Schillingsfürst. Although he grew up in Corvey, he considered Schillingsfürst his home. Even though he had inherited many other properties throughout Bavaria and Russia, Castle Schillingsfürst was the only place that enriched his mind and heart. It had an abundance of nature. The many large windows looking out onto forests and meadows let the summer sun bathe the rooms in the castle with bright and cheerful sunlight. Here, he could ride and hunt every day. Here, he found inspiration writing poetry or drawing in a scrapbook, often with his children on his lap looking on. Here, he spent many afternoons with one of his children seated on his knee while others looked over his shoulder as he drew portraits of them; his wife, Marie; the servants; and anything else he fancied. The children looked on in awe and delight when he finished one of the drawings.

Arriving at the castle, the coachman took the prince's valise and assisted him up the grand marble steps to the front door. The butler, having heard the coach drive noisily over the inner moat and through the courtyard, opened the door. He was surprised to see the prince standing there. "Your Royal Highness," he stated, bowing his head. "We had no news of your arrival. I shall make haste to have a small dinner prepared for you."

"There is no need to hurry, Josef. I wish first to see the princess and will go directly to her."

"Very well, sir."

His increasing duties called him away more frequently of late, and therefore he was not able to see his wife as often as he would like. Marie was already in her bedchamber resting in her bed, recovering from the birth of their twin sons.

She welcomed him home with outstretched arms. She was always happy when he came, even though it was late and unannounced.

Chlodwig had not yet seen his twin sons, who were born while he was in England on a visit to Queen Victoria. Marie called for the nurse to bring Moritz and Alexander down from the nursery. The nurse handed both of them to their father. He delighted in seeing his newborn sons, as he did all his children. The nurse then brought in the other children to see their father. The oldest daughter, Elizabeth, was already fifteen and would soon be of marriageable age. Stephanie, the next oldest, was eleven, Philipp nine, and Hermann five. The two girls curtsied, and the boys bowed to their father.

Their mother had retained the finest tutors to prepare them for their stations in life as royal princes and princesses. Proper manners were expected even from the youngest child. In time, suitable marriages would be sought for the boys to further the Schillingsfürst line and properties. The girls, through large dowries, would be married to nobles within their class so that they would lead respectable lives in the highest circles of society.

While at Schillingsfürst, Chlodwig spent several days hunting in the forests that surrounded the castle, often bringing down boars, which were brought to the kitchen, where they were salted and stored in the cellar. He considered himself a good shot. After a few more mild and sunny days riding and hunting there, he could stay no longer as he was needed in parliament. He had much to bring forth to the assembly after his recent meeting with the emperor of Bavaria, Wilhelm, and Otto von Bismarck. Before leaving, he asked after the accounts of his many estate holdings. His steward reported how his tenants were managing and that the summer harvest was as expected. However, he explained some of the tenants were complaining about what they thought was a poor price for hops that year. Chlodwig thought to himself that it was not unusual as prices fluctuated every year. He would leave the matter for his steward to handle. He told Marie he would be gone a length of time before returning as he had much business to attend to in Munich and another trip most likely to Frankfurt. She took that as a matter of course. She was well used to being alone. She had her own duties to occupy her days. And she had her children.

12

Munich

Chlodwig left Schillingsfürst, arriving in Munich by train early in the evening. He went to his club, where he enjoyed his favorite cigar and cognac. Several members of the Bavarian Parliament were already there in the smoke-filled room, arguing. He was not a man who liked confrontation and usually sat quietly listening to what he thought were wasteful conversations by men who had a mediocrity of understanding. Each one was intent on grinding down the other, with ever-increasing bullying, to their own point of view. He finished his drink, put out his cigar, and left the club. He had enough. There was ample arguing and bellowing in the House of Parliament. He did not want to listen to more of it when all he desired was to enjoy a few minutes with a good cigar.

He went straight to his friend Friedrich Bodenstedt's house. The butler greeted him, welcomed him inside, and took his coat, hat, gloves, and valise. Then he showed Chlodwig into the study.

"I will announce that you have arrived, your Royal Highness. Shall I pour you some brandy?"

"Yes, of course. And one of those cigars in the humidor."

"Right away, sir."

It was only a short minute before Friedrich arrived in the study. As always, he was more than happy to see his friend. He lived a somewhat quiet life in Munich so was glad to see Chlodwig for some bright and intelligent conversation. Although he was a professor of Slavonic studies in Munich, producing translations of Pushkin, Lemontov, and other Ukrainian poets, he was finding this vein exhausted and looked for other interests. He was well versed in the politics of the day, of which Chlodwig was a wellspring of knowledge.

"Tell me, my friend, has the situation with Denmark been settled? Or are we still pondering another war?" Friedrich asked.

During the evening and long into the night, he and Friedrich exchanged their opinions, not always in agreement with one another. However, it made for good conversation.

The following evening, Chlodwig, dressed in an elegant evening coat, a silk cravat tied around his neck, and a blue satin sash across his chest, left the house to spend the evening with friends at the Munich Opera House for a performance by Franz Liszt. As Liszt was a friend and frequent guest at his estate in Schillingsfürst, he never missed one of his piano concertos.

It was there that the prince first saw her.

She was seated in a box opposite his with an older woman and three younger men. Obvious suitors, he thought. He could not take his eyes off her. The drape of her blue dress with a low square neckline revealed the swell of her breasts. He watched her every move: the opera glasses she so delicately held to her face as she watched Liszt at the grand piano and as she so intently listened to the orchestra; the way she turned her head to speak to her friend; her radiant smile, which gave her face a new allurement. To him, the piano and orchestra continued in muted sounds as thoughts of her, this vision of loveliness, deafened his ears to the loudest crescendos.

After the concert, Chlodwig hailed a carriage to take him back to Bodenstedt's house. Before going in, he stood outside and lit a cigar to enjoy the cool evening when, to his surprise, he saw the lovely young woman he had seen at the Opera House walking slowly past the row of houses across the street. The white plastered houses along Karlstrasse, now gray with the city's soot, stood bound together side by side along the street. The tall curved windows and doorways exemplified the general character of the houses. The leaded windows on the first and second floors, which looked out onto the street, were covered with heavy velvet curtains. The third-floor windows were much smaller and well hidden behind lace curtains. They appeared likely to be the guest or servants' quarters.

In the autumn breeze, her dark-blue cloak, tied at her neck, blew gently, revealing her gown underneath. A quick puff of wind suddenly blew off her hood, revealing her chestnut-brown hair wound in thick plaits around her head, intertwined with pearls and gemstones. In the moonlight, it was as if small stars sprung out of her hair in the night. It suited her.

As Chlodwig stood in the shadows, not wishing to reveal himself, he secretly watched her. A disappearing plume of cigar smoke was the only evidence that he was there. It wasn't until she stopped in front of one of the houses and climbed the steps to the door that he realized this is where she lived. It was at that moment he decided he would send her flowers in the morning.

Chlodwig thought it was a chance of fate that the lovely young woman with the red hair lived across the street from his friend.

Inside Bodenstedt's spacious house, Chlodwig and Friedrich lit cigars, poured themselves a glass of cognac, and settled into their large, comfortable leather chairs by the fire. Friedrich got up from his chair when he noticed the fire in the large stone fireplace was dwindling. As he stirred the embers and added more wood, sparks flew up the chimney in wild confusion. The warmth of the fire was comforting after the cold of the night. The room reminded Chlodwig of a fashionable men's club. Red and gray wallpaper enveloped both the walls and ceilings. Large pastoral paintings of all sizes held by elaborate gilt frames covered the walls. The windows, draped in deep red velvet, were closed now to keep out the cold night air. Handwoven rugs from India covered the bare wooden floors. The room had the smell of leather and wool. It was clear that a bachelor lived there as there was not a single sign of a women's touch about the room.

Friedrich's manservant entered the room. He bowed his head toward the prince and then asked his master if he wished anything further this evening.

"Not tonight, Johann. You may retire."

"Thank you, sir. I bid you both a good night," he replied as he bowed and then silently left the room.

After Johann left and the doors to the drawing room were closed, Friedrich leaned close to Chlodwig and asked, "Don't you want to know more about her?"

He was taken aback by Friedrich's boldness as he thought no one could guess his infatuation with the enchanting woman he saw that night. He took a draw from his cigar and through a vaporous cloud of smoke asked, "What do you mean, my friend?"

"I only meant that you stood in front of my door for quite some time looking at her, obviously interested."

"Not at all, Friedrich," he denied. "It was a pleasant evening, and I thought to enjoy my cigar before coming inside."

He knew he could not fool his friend and admitted, "You know me well, my friend. Indeed, this vision of loveliness came into view, and I could not look away. I admit I was charmed by this lady."

Friedrich bent a little closer. "She is a rare beauty, and I've had my eye on her for some time ever since she moved into the house across the street."

Friedrich did not tell him about his frequent visits to her apartment, or the many evenings discussing politics, the arts, and other intellectual topics. She would pour him tea and offer him small sandwiches during their long evenings together. It was a friendship based on mutual admiration for each other. Not only was there a deep understanding of each other, but it was the convenience of living across from one another that made this intercourse so cordial.

To Alexandrine, Friedrich was the most intelligent man she had ever met. He never failed to impress her with the vast amount of knowledge that he brought back from the East. He turned those into literary accounts published in two books in 1848 and 1850. Not only did he have a thorough knowledge of Russia, but he also spoke the language fluently, having tutored the children of Prince Gallitzin in Moscow. To him, it was her beauty and her curious intellect that he admired. When he had a particular inspiration for another novel, he could not wait to tell her. With anticipation of her reaction, he would race up her steps, knock on her door, and rush in. She never tired of his visits.

"Come in, my muse. What have you brought me today?" she would ask. He would take his usual seat by the fire and wait for her to ask again.

"Tell me quickly, or I shall be bored," she teased.

Theirs was a relationship based on spontaneity, ideas, and good humor. Friedrich was not a particularly handsome man, but his eyes laughed when he told his stories, and his smile was genuine when he looked at her. They spent many evenings together in her sitting room, forming a friendship that would last decades. He, of course, fell in love with her but never contemplated telling her, nor would he reveal it to Chlodwig. Neither would he reveal that he spent many evenings watching her while standing on his balcony to catch a momentary glimpse of her.

Bodenstedt asked, "Don't you want to know her name?"

"I have the feeling you will tell me and even more."

In a half-whisper, Friedrich said her name: Baroness Alexandrine von Hedemann. "Does that satisfy you?"

Raising a thoughtful eyebrow, Chlodwig said, "A little."

"Oh, but you want more, don't you? I can sense it. There is a lot more, but I will not tell you tonight as I'm tired," he teased.

Chlodwig put out his cigar, finished his cognac, and stood up. "Goodnight, then, my clever friend. I will see what you have to tell me tomorrow."

He awoke early. The chambermaid opened the heavy velvet drapes in his bedchamber, but there was no sunshine that day. The sky was gray and felt like rain. She awoke the fire in the fireplace to a blaze of welcoming heat. Then she quickly left the room so as not to disturb him.

Chlodwig changed quickly into a dark-gray suit and vest with a white tie wrapped around the collar of a white shirt. He carefully brushed his thinning black hair and bushy mustache before he felt ready to greet the day. A good night's sleep had refreshed him for what he knew would be a strenuous day ahead in Frankfurt representing the Bavarian Parliament. Descending the stairs, he could hear the kitchen staff in the breakfast room placing the final dishes on the buffet at the far side of the room. He could smell the strong, delicious aroma of the coffee and hurried down the steps. Coffee first thing in the morning was one of his greatest pleasures. He also helped himself to a boiled egg, smoked salmon, sausages, and freshly baked rolls. In the mirror above the buffet, he could see Friedrich coming into the room. He came dressed in a robe and slippers as he had not yet dressed for the day.

"Good morning, my friend. I hope you had a good night's rest," Friedrich greeted him cheerfully.

"I did indeed," Chlodwig replied.

"Tell me your plans," Friedrich asked.

"Today I must take the train again to Frankfurt to sit on a committee of other statesmen to discuss Austria's position in Germany."

"Do you believe it is to be settled at the conference there?"

Chlodwig, understanding that Bodenstedt had a keen interest in politics, said, "No, Austria's aim to destroy Prussia and make herself sovereign of Europe is not quite in her power. Europe would never allow the destruction of Protestant Prussia. Austria's desire to reign supreme would, of course, depend on that destruction. As such, the whole matter is a fruitless agitation with possible dire consequences for Austria."

At age forty-three, as a hereditary member of the Upper House of the Bavarian *Reichsrat*, Chlodwig was keenly aware of the political climate in Prussia and, as a liberal, did not subscribe to the Prussian view of propagating enlightenment with a stick. He hesitated to speak further, not wanting to compromise his political views on the matter until returning from the conference.

As if sensing Chlodwig's hesitation to speak further, Friedrich interjected, "I have heard through rumors that should Austria proceed, there will surely be a war. I assure you nothing you say that could in any way compromise your position will go beyond these walls."

Chlodwig looked at his friend and knew he was right. He walked over to the buffet table, refilled his coffee cup, and then returned to the table. After sitting down, he said, "Let us not expound on the subject of war and treaties. I will hear enough of that when I return to Berlin." He sipped his coffee in silence.

Friedrich was not overly curious about what he had to say as he had already read everything he cared about in the newspapers. "And you, my friend, how goes your translation of the sonnets?" Chlodwig asked.

"I have completed all of Shakespeare's sonnets and will begin translations of his complete version of his plays."

"That's commendable, Friedrich. I will look for their publication," he responded.

Friedrich, not deterred by this obvious ploy to circumvent the subject of Alexandrine, said, "I know you are interested in my sonnets, but wouldn't you rather hear more of the beautiful Baroness Alexandrine?"

"Only if you wish." Chlodwig wanted to know everything, but he masked his impatience from Friedrich.

"Ah, my friend," he began. "She is a true romantic; she has the spirit and the soul of a gypsy. You may know her better as Mrs. Erzberger."

Chlodwig interjected, "Ah, yes, as a matter of fact I do. I recently came across a document that came to the attention of the Cabinet. It appeared to intentionally do her person and reputation harm. I gave it no mind as I could see someone was maliciously trying to ruin her for their own benefit."

"Yes, it was her mother-in-law and her husband's other relatives who initiated this persecution. After her scandalous divorce from Erzberger, a prominent Augsburg banker, his relatives began a crusade to tarnish her reputation throughout Germany, which, unfortunately, has followed her these many years. Shall I go on?"

"Yes, of course. There seems to be a bit more of the story you wish to share," he said with a look on his face that gave away his eagerness.

Alexandrine, having spent many evenings with Friedrich, cautiously shared a little of her life with her friend. Friedrich continued, "I know only a little as she is hesitant for anyone to know much about her life. I know she was born into luxury, privilege, and wealth. However, her life was fraught with sorrow and despair. Imagine a childhood home torn apart by the absence of a mother's love and a grieving father. The only happiness was found in short visits with her uncles before she was cast into a loveless and dreary marriage. Hermann Erzberger was a good and loving husband but had no inkling of his wife's inner spirit and longings. Alexandrine could not reconcile herself to the life of a bourgeois wife, a life without art or culture and devoid of adventure and romance. Then on some magical and mystical day, when she had lost all hope, an event presented itself. She found passionate love in the arms of a lover from her youth. As a result of this dalliance, she was a victim of her evil-minded mother-in-law. Even though Erzberger might have overlooked her indiscretions, his mother could not. As a result, he divorced her, and she lost the children she so dearly loved. She was more or less cast out of Augsburg society. And so she came to live in Munich on Karlstrasse."

Chlodwig listened to this story with spellbound attention, wanting more, but he said, "I would sit here all day pondering this elusive and rarest of ladies, but, my dear friend, I must get ready as my train leaves for Frankfurt in an hour. I thank you for your hospitality. I will return again in a week as I have further business in Munich."

"Of course, my dear friend. You are always welcome. Stay as long as you like. It gives me great pleasure to have someone to talk with."

Chlodwig welcomed this invitation as he had no regular home in Munich or in Berlin, having to travel back and forth regularly as his duties called. He returned to his room and rang the bell for Johann, who arrived within minutes.

"Your Royal Highness, how can I be of service?"

"I want you to arrange for a bouquet of flowers to be sent to Mrs. Erzberger at 15 Karlstrasse. Sign the card only as Count L. Thereafter, send the same bouquet every day in the same way until my return next week. I will leave the money in an envelope for you downstairs in the hall."

Johann bowed his head and said, "I will do as you requested, sir. I wish you a safe and pleasant journey."

"Thank you, Johann. I trust I can count on your discretion."

"Yes, your Royal Highness."

He left the house on Karlstrasse, not without taking one more glance at the house across the street, but saw no one. He then entered the waiting carriage for a short trip to the Munich station, where he would take the train straight to Frankfurt.

13

The Making of a Politician

Prince Chlodwig Carl Viktor von Hohenlohe-Schillingsfürst, in 1862, was already one of the most powerful men in Germany. He was viewed by his party as a future president-minister. As a prince of large estates in both Bavaria and Russia, he was respected by his servants, his tenants, and by all who knew him, holding him in the highest esteem.

His ascent within the political arena started early in life. What little is known of his younger years is by way of letters to his sister Princess Amalie, who was his emotional and spiritual confidant. She was a dreamy, sensitive young woman with whom he felt at ease, confiding in her his most delicate confidences. She, of all his siblings, knew him best. She tells of a story when he was very young and his tutor showed him a representation of the battle of Leipzig. The tutor pointed to certain figures and said that they represented the Allied powers. Chlodwig's response was "But I don't see any girls." Another time, he was asked to give the half of 10 and replied,

"Zero because the two figures could be divided by a stroke" (as in 1/0).

Chlodwig's six brothers and sisters enjoyed a privileged life growing up in Corvey, the family seat. The sons were brought up Roman Catholics, while the daughters were educated in the Protestant faith like their mother. Religious toleration was the foundation of their domestic happiness and the dominating motive that guided his political career. The brothers and sisters were bound together by a rare spiritual affinity. Their close relationship endured throughout their lives. When he and his brothers returned to Corvey on vacation from their studies in Heidelberg, the dreary castle came alive. In the evenings, Amalie would sit at the piano, while Chlodwig, in a fine baritone voice, would join one of his brothers in a duet. Other times, they would spend afternoons drawing. Philipp Ernst was particularly gifted in art.

During Chlodwig's schooling, his studies reflected his values. His certificate praised his high moral character, his talents and industry, his moral earnestness and good behavior. It goes on to say, "His attention and eager interest in every subject of instruction was a marked feature, as he uses his power of grasping the essential points of a subject, and then arranging them in logical order. He writes correctly and fluently, and his poetical essays show much life and imagination."

To complete his education, he and his brothers, Viktor and Philipp Ernst, traveled throughout Europe attending lectures and perfecting their French. French, of course, was considered the language of the nobility and high-born. He considered French the only language of conversation in society and thought it pleasurable to be able to speak it fluently.

For the princes, it was not all studies of feudal law, European international law, and constitutional and criminal law. There were parties. On one occasion, Chlodwig wrote in his diary, "I am looking forward to a ball which the Grand Duke Leopold of Baden is soon to give. One of my fancies is a growing preference for the society of large towns as against that of small, though the results in either case are the same. The evening parties sometimes given by Count Rantzau are in the first place, entertaining; and further, instead of the odious gossip and the médisances of scandal-mongers male and female, one can indulge in sensible conversation and avoid the horror of horrors, the affectations of a provincial tea party."[5]

It was on one of their trips to Italy that the brothers encountered Prince Albert of Coburg. It was this chance meeting that began a lifelong relationship with Albert and, later, Queen Victoria of England, whom Albert was soon to marry.

When, in 1834, Chlodwig's mother's brother-in-law Count Viktor Amadeus of Hesse-Rothenburg died, he left all of his estates to his nephews. In 1840, Chlodwig and his brothers were still at the University of Heidelberg when it was finally determined how the estates should be divided. In a twist of fate, Viktor Moritz Karl, the firstborn son, renounced his rights to the principality of Hohenlohe-Schillingsfürst and was made the duke of Ratibor, and Chlodwig became prince of Corvey. In January 1841, Chlodwig's father, Prince Franz Joseph, died. Chlodwig was now in line to succeed as the first prince of Hohenlohe-Schillingsfürst but renounced his rights to his third brother, Philipp Ernst, with the stipulation that it would revert to him should Philipp die.

Chlodwig was more interested in pursuing his political career than spending his time as a landowner. It was after a visit

5   Memoirs of Prince Chlodwig of Hohenlohe-Schillingsfürst, Vol. I, p. 12.

to his brother Viktor in Silesia, at his castle near Ratibor, that he decided to pursue relationships with people of the Prussian Ministry with the intension of securing admission into the Prussian diplomatic service. He went so far as to request the King of Prussia to excuse him from the prescribed preliminary service under the judicial and administrative authorities to obtain such a position. The longed-for decision from the king was delayed, and Chlodwig's impatience weighed heavily on him, so much so that he considered renouncing his hopes for a governmental position and living in Corvey as an independent nobleman. But his passion for politics was stronger, and he could not permanently abandon his original intent. He wrote to his mother:

> *My stay here [in Corvey] has shown me more clearly the impossibility of settling here indefinitely, which in its way is no bad thing. I am now setting forth homeless through the world, and must zealously pursue some prospect of entering a profession, and in this quest, homelessness is the best position to be in if I could only be certain of my future and settle my plans for the winter. If I cannot enter the Diplomatic Service, I shall try to enter the English military service and then join the Chinese expedition. But this plan is as yet quite vague. At the end of the year, as he had still not received an answer from the king, Chlodwig, with the influence of his aunt Princess Feodora of Hohenlohe-Langenburg, sought a position with the English Army. Feodora, as Queen Victoria's half-sister, was influential in obtaining commissions, particularly for one as astute as her nephew. She, of course, could not deny him and petitioned her half-sister on his*

behalf. This might have come to be except, before Queen Victoria could answer her sister's request, the long-awaited letter from King Friedrich Wilhelm arrived. The letter stated that he had taken Chlodwig's request to forego the obligatory preliminary training in judicial and administrative practice under consideration.

However, a second letter arrived not long afterward, which stated:

> *Your Highness, I hesitate to comply with your request . . . You cannot fail to see, as I see, that to grant the preference your Highness desires would be to place you in a position of some inferiority to those with whom the Diplomatic Service would bring you into association. In consequence, it will be a pleasure to me if your Highness will pursue your desire of beginning a diplomatic career in my service, by first complying with the general regulation existing upon your head. Your Highness's affectionate friend,*
> *Friedrich Wilhelm.*

Having given up the thought of obtaining a commission in the Queen's navy, Chlodwig, in the end, decided to enter the Prussian diplomatic service and follow the compulsory regulations as stipulated by the king. This was a minor position, but it was the catalyst that would ultimately launch his extraordinary and successful political career. These early years afforded him insight into the Prussian political system, learning much about Prussia's strengths and weaknesses. Unfortunately, he kept no regular diary in those early years, so little is known of those times.

In May of 1845, a shattering event took place: Prince Philipp Ernst died. The death of his beloved brother was unbearable for Chlodwig. He no longer had a confidant. Philipp was the youngest of the brothers, whom he most trusted with his most intimate thoughts. He languished for months over his death. He found no joy in anything and could not reconcile himself to finding another being so in tune with his feeling as Philipp was.

Chlodwig now succeeded as the seventh prince of Hohenlohe-Schillingsfürst. He left the family home in Corvey and moved to Schillingsfürst, where he spent his first winter. He described it as a terrible winter, which had its good side. It was where he found his voice in poetry. He loved nature as much as he loved art, and through his sense of mysticism and imagination, he brought this to his poetry. He was a poet in the true sense of the word. He did not see it as a pastime but rather a genuine need that his soul compelled him to undertake.

On one of those cold and dreary winters in Schillingsfürst, he wrote a poem to Amalie:

> *O'er the valleys and the hills*
> *I would be a wanderer bold;*
> *Though the cruel winter storms*
> *Thunder round our castle hold.*
>
> *I would be a mariner*
> *Boldly sail the waters dark.*
> *Though the fury of the wave*
> *Bode destruction to my lark.*

With the children of the South
Through the palm groves I would haste.
And upon an Arab steed
Scout the desert's burning waste.

With the sword for freedom's cause
I would smite the enemy
And the triumph of my land
With my dying gaze decry.

Anything were better than
Thus o'er musty deeds to frown,
Yawning, sharpening a pen,
Slipped into a dressing gown.

Another letter to Amalie stated:

I have just interrupted my restless nervous letter and looked out the window. Ah, how that calms the mind! It is a wonderfully beautiful moonlit night, beneath which wide valleys and mountains lie outspread. It is all quiet and peaceful and warm, and the spring breezes are blowing up here upon the mountain. The remembrance of the past fills my heart with silent sorrow, and from the past there too rise the good thoughts and actions of our life together with the remembrance of those who have passed away; nay, they rise in person. None the less, it is a consolation to think that this old home does not look out dead and desolate upon the lovely night, but belongs to a kind of third-rate poet who now and then looks out upon the moonlight himself. And it almost seems to me that the old stone barrack itself rejoices at the fact.

As a young man at Schillingsfürst, Chlodwig found a lonely life, with no human society. He occupied his time reading books and hunting. He believed that the pure air was the cause that retained his cheerfulness during that time. It was then that he took notice of the system of agriculture that was in vogue at the time and found it wrong. He eagerly took up another task: studying books about the subject. It was through this that he learned about better methods of agriculture and found an appreciation for the work done by the people who farmed his land.

14

Marriage to Princess Marie

It was Chlodwig's younger sister, Amalie, in whom he confided his newfound love for Princess Marie von Sayn-Wittgenstein. He was full of passion and praise, writing:

> I have been here [Frankfurt, where the wedding was to take place] for three days, and even if it were possible to tell you all what I am feeling, I should want time and peace and colossal talents. From the instant when waiting by the fire of the salon in the evening, I saw Marie hastening towards me, glad and radiant, while our joy prevented either of us from saying a word (fortunately we were alone)—ever since I have been seeing her and talking to her every day, while our intercourse never palls—since I have found her once more lovely, noble, candid all it is possible to be, I love her no more with a quiet admiration of her good qualities, no longer one might say, as her affianced husband, but I am c'est un expression un peu

triviale ... enamored, restless, feverish. And yet we have to
act a comedy a little longer, as the announcement cannot
be made for a few days.

Chlodwig and Princess Marie married in 1847. Her father, the son of Russian Field Marshal Ludwig Adolf Peter,
first prince of Sayn-Wittgenstein, also came from a long line of
aristocrats. As a result, the princess was the heiress to vast estates in Imperial Russia. Throughout their marriage, he added
her properties, and the management of Verkiai in Lithuania,
to his already extensive holdings in Bavaria and Silesia. One
of the estates they visited often was the renaissance castle Mir
in Russia, with its red façade and decorative turrets. It was a
favorite of his.

His sensitive nature and his need to be a close and loving
companion to a woman made his marriage to Princess Marie a
happy one. He was an attentive husband very much in love with
her. He often expressed to his sister Amalie that his greatest
joy was to have a woman by his side. He saw in Marie strength
of character, fidelity, patience, and, above all, love and caring
for him. He held love to be imperfect unless the lovers wholly
expressed themselves in that complete union. They enjoyed
much together, finding music, the arts, and poetry particularly
inspiring. Their affinity for those things in common never wavered throughout their long marriage. She traveled with him
when his burgeoning political career demanded he spend time
in Rome, Vienna, Paris, and London.

Within the first year of marriage, a daughter was born.
They named her Elisabeth Constanze Leonille Stephanie.
Over the course of their marriage, Marie bore him five more
children: Stephanie Marie Antonie; Philipp Ernst, who be-

came the eighth prince of Hohenlohe-Schillingsfürst; Albert; Moritz, who became the ninth prince of Hohenlohe-Schillingsfürst; and Alexander. The Schillingsfürst castle had the good fortune to be situated very near Langenburg, where his uncle Prince Ernst lived with his aunt Princess Feodora and their six children. Chlodwig and Marie's children spent many happy days visiting there. Close bonds between families of noble birth were common as they kept within their social class.

In Chlodwig's youth, he had a tendency toward reason and cold calculation, a worthy attribute for a statesman. But he also had another side as a sensitive soul who needed to live in close communion with a sympathetic listener who was also in harmony with his needs. These two contradicting tendencies were rare in a man with political and diplomatic abilities. Even after the marriage, he continued to depend on his sister Amalie and shared his most intimate feelings with her. At times, he lamented, "Why among the many hearts that can feel, should it not be possible to find one capable of understanding us because it tenderly loves us?"

As the seventh prince of Hohenlohe-Schillingsfürst, he had the hereditary right to enter the Upper House of the Bavarian government. In April of 1846, he entered the political arena in Bavaria and took part in its proceedings in Munich. It was at this time when he bought a residence in Munich and lived there with Marie and the children while parliament was in session. It took several months before he felt able to talk to people in a new dialect. He explained it as a dialect composed of Hohenlohe and Bavarian with a little mixture of French and German phrases.

Princess Elise, his youngest sister, joined them in the education of the children. Elise commented, "I so admire

Chlodwig when he takes little Elisabeth upon his knee. It is such a beautiful picture, his face full of tenderness bending over her curly little head while she strokes his cheek." Elise never ceased to admire her brother for his calmness, unselfishness, and patience in all his actions.

His political agendas took him into ever-widening circles. In Rome, he met with the pope; in England, with Queen Victoria and Prince Albert; in Vienna, with Emperor Franz Joseph I; in Russia, with Czar Nicholas; and in Paris, with Emperor Louis Napoleon Bonaparte III of France. On those frequent train trips, Chlodwig had ample free time to reflect on his career. *There is so much more to do,* he thought. It was his goal to get into an even more active role within the Bavarian government. His liberal idea of a united Germany continued to be a major part of that ambition during his early years and well into his long political career.

It was during this time that the First Schleswig War broke out in 1848. Danish and German nationalists both contributed to the war. The Danes living in Schleswig wanted it to be part of Denmark. The Germans living in Schleswig and in the duchy of Holstein, with the support of the Kingdom of Prussia, began an uprising to remain under German rule. Thus began the three-year war, which ultimately ended in 1851 with a victory for Denmark. Even after the war ended, Chlodwig's dream for a united Germany, bringing Schleswig back into the German confederacy, never wavered. He was not alone. It was commonly thought that the loss of the Schleswig territory and its German population would surely result in another war. It did some years later.

When Chlodwig and his wife had occasion to find rest and comfort, they returned to Schillingsfürst. Chlodwig's enjoyment of the peacefulness there was matched by Marie, who found her life there a quiet one. They both embraced their duties and found a useful life: she in the management of the estate and raising her children, while he continued his political career, spanning several decades. That is not to say they did not have time to entertain. Many artists, musicians, and composers, as well as dignitaries from all around the globe, were invited to Schillingsfürst.

As the years passed, Chlodwig found little time for anything else but his political career. Marie encouraged him to go to Russia to look after her estates. It was then that he decided to take a two-year absence from parliament. He and Marie left for Wittgenstein to spend two years in Russia to look after their estates. Even with a busy schedule of meetings with his tenants—discussing prices for their goods, the current market, or their agricultural methods—he found time for hunting trips.

On one such trip, Prince Peter of Sayn-Wittgenstein arranged for a shooting party that took them by carriage to the River Nieman, which they easily crossed. In the village, they took a peasant's cart to the woods until it could go no further. From there, they went by foot to a local farmstead and pitched a tent. The next day, after loading their guns and preparing their ammunition, they resumed their journey. Two local huntsmen led them through the woods in search of elk. The huntsmen blew their horns to entice the elk, which, although close at hand, stayed out of sight. Coming upon a swamp, the party of hunters tried to navigate it. It was full of trees and bushes, undergrowth, and reeds that seemed impossible to get through. They spent the better part of the day splashing, jostling each other, and jumping from any piece of firm ground to another. The day was lost, and the party returned to the tent. In the evening, they enjoyed a meal in the open air, discussing the experiences of the day in this "virgin" forest. Even though they did not secure their elk, they all relished the adventure.

The months in Wittgenstein passed quickly as Chlodwig had much to do with the management of the properties. Evenings were taken up with invitations to dinners or balls. One of the invitations arrived from Governor-General Nasimoff. A small man with bushy eyebrows and a stiff mustache, the governor-general was an insignificant but well-meaning person who presented himself to Chlodwig with what the latter thought of as exaggerated military airs. To him, the dinner was bad and the service inefficient. He also discovered that a prince has no official post or rank in Russia, so when dinner was announced, he was left to wait as the civil governors swooped up the ladies, and he and Prince Peter entered behind them. During the dinner, Chlodwig listened to the governor-general talk in the most nonsensical way about high politics. He only nodded and was glad when the dinner ended and he could leave.

Another evening, he was seated next to a lady of dubious class. His remarkable lack of interest in her gave Chlodwig time to run through and edit his next speech to parliament while half-listening to her prattle on about nothing of importance—except she was well informed about certain black and brown beetles that were prevalent in Russian households.

When Chlodwig and Marie returned to Schillingsfürst, they were happy to be back home and in the company of their children, where they found true joy. But like all his days, whether at home or abroad, there would come another duty.

15

Queen Victoria

*W*hen a letter arrived from Chlodwig's aunt Princess Feodora von Hohenlohe-Langenburg asking him to accompany her on her travels to England to visit her half-sister, Queen Victoria, he immediately answered. Feodora's husband, Prince Ernst von Hohenlohe-Langenburg, was ill, and so was her mother, Victoria, duchess of Kent. Even her sons were engaged in military duties and could not travel with her. As Feodora wanted a relative to accompany her on her travels, she contacted her nephew Chlodwig. He had long ago wanted to go to back to England. The last time he was there was in September of 1840, when he was invited to Windsor Castle by Prince Albert, whose marriage to Queen Victoria had been celebrated on February 10. He was more than happy to do as she wished.

He met Feodora in Mainz on June 21, 1859. From there, they traveled to Koblenz and down the Rhine to Köln, where they attended Mass in the cathedral. At the railway station in Ostend, Belgium, they were met by Captain Smith, who commanded the boat that had been sent over for them. He was an elderly but a striking man with long white whiskers. They did not board the boat that day as Feodora wanted a day of rest. Early the next morning, they boarded the *Friedrich Wilhelm*, a very new and fast steamship. A four-hour and twenty-minute trip brought them close to the white cliffs of Dover on the English coast.

At the harbor, a large military detachment waited to greet the princess and Chlodwig. The harbor master; an officer of the marines; and the general and his attaché in full military dress came aboard to pay their respects to the princess. With her arm resting on the general's arm, Princess Feodora walked through the crowd, which was held back by a line formed by his troops. The famous 32nd Infantry Regiment stood next to the train that she, Chlodwig, and their entourage boarded for the trip to London. As they entered their car, a band played "God Save the Queen." The train sped along past bright green pastures, cozy villages, and great country houses. They passed the Crystal Palace at Sydenham before entering the city. As the Crystal Palace was originally part of the Great Exhibition of 1851, which was the product of Prince Albert's effort to bring exhibitions of culture and industry to the people of Great Britain, Chlodwig wanted to stop there. But Feodora reminded him of her mission to see her sister, and she could not keep the Queen of England waiting. The fresh sea air and the warm clear air of the countryside gave way to the smoke-filled city streets. A royal carriage was waiting at the station to take them to Buckingham Palace, where they were met at the great doorway by Colonel Biddulph, Queen Victoria's master of the household.

Chlodwig would later describe the palace as quite modern with Corinthian columns and floors covered in the finest carpets. They were received by gentlemen-in-waiting in blue coats and black silk stockings. After they went up the wide carpeted stairs, Queen Victoria, with several of her ladies-in-waiting, walked down the corridor and greeted Feodora quite warmly. They were guided into a small room, where light talk was exchanged. Chlodwig was greeted most sincerely, after which Feodora followed the Queen to her rooms. A carriage was summoned to take him to the Brunswick Hotel as there were no vacant rooms in the palace. The hotel lacked any refinement, but it was nevertheless in close proximity and convenient.

Chlodwig spent the afternoon walking through Hyde Park, where he encountered a fashionable parade. He thought to himself, *There are no people as much a slave to manners and custom as the English.* The same afternoon, he wrote a letter to his sister:

> *This sheeplike imitation of each other is seen at its best in Hyde Park. Here is seen fashion in carriages, horses and dress. This season appears to be the summer for everything violet for both men and women even men's neckties and gloves. Everyone knows it's fashionable to ride at twelve noon and the afternoon is for people to drive or walk. Everyone moves mechanically up and down the small spaces for a couple of hours a day.*

He did not stay long in Hyde Park as the heat, the crowd, and the endless comings and goings of carriages, horses, and people made him very tired. Upon his return to his suite of rooms at the hotel, he had just enough time to dress for dinner at the palace. He put on his court dress: black coat, knee breeches, and silk stockings. He arrived a bit shy of 8 p.m., so he had time to look around the apartment where the royal family would assemble. The floor was covered with a crimson and gold carpet; empire-style furniture was upholstered in the same colors as the floor. There was a marble mantlepiece, and a large table stood in the center of the room. Two windows looked out into the garden with its well-kept park, lovely trees, and green lawn. He thought to himself, *It looks peaceful in the setting sun.*

Before long, guests starting coming. The first to arrive was Fourth Prince Ernst Leopold, captain of the British Royal Navy, in his military uniform with two rows of brass buttons, a row of medals from the Crimean War pinned to his chest, and a saber at his side. He cut an undeniably smart figure marching into the room with confidence. Behind him entered King Leopold of Belgium, a more relaxed figure obviously familiar with the palace and these kinds of affairs. With him was his second son, the count of Flanders, a tall, fair-haired, rather dull-looking young man. When Chlodwig arrived, Prince Albert walked up to him, greeting him in the usual way. Tired of greeting the guests as they came in, the prince took him aside and, in a most friendly way, asked to speak with him.

He knew Chlodwig loved music and the arts and was anxious to tell him of his recent visit to the Handel Festival at the Crystal Palace with its four thousand musicians before an audience of twenty-five thousand. Chlodwig was quite impressed and wished he could have witnessed it. "To me," Chlodwig said, "there is so much pleasure in music, and without it, man is but half complete."

To this, Prince Albert replied, "You are most correct, my dear friend. It is also my greatest wish to bring music to all classes."

Once all the guests arrived, the Queen entered. Beside her were her daughters, Princess Alice, and Feodora. As soon as the Queen appeared, there was a sudden clanking of swords as the men bowed and a great rustle of silk as every woman sank to the floor in a deep curtsy.

King Leopold broke away from the other guests to greet his niece, the Queen. After a short conversation, he held out his arm, on which Queen Victoria placed her hand. Walking together, King Leopold and the Queen moved into the reception room, where a number of other guests stood waiting. Along the wall there was an elegantly dressed buffet table with flowers, candles, and several silver tureens of soup, one with consommé, another with turtle soup, and a third with *pot-au-feu*. There were hot dishes in silver warming pans heated with small kerosene lamps containing veal, pork, ham from York, trout, and guinea hens. A dessert table with comfit, tarts, pudding, and a variety of cakes and other pastries completed the banquet. Servants in the scarlet and gold royal livery of the palace stood by, ready to serve the guests whatever they desired. After the Queen was seated, the guests took their appointed seats. The Queen was served first. After that, the guests were presented with their first course of soups. Meats followed, wine poured freely, and dessert and coffee ended the dinner. Everyone ate happily while lively conversations ensued. Most everyone spoke English, which Chlodwig had some difficulty understanding. Only Feodora and Prince Albert spoke to him from across the table in German. As expected, many of the conversations that he overheard were about the Austro-French War.

Albert spoke unfavorably of the emperor of Austria and his policy and maintained that Archduke Ferdinand Max had arrived at no better results in their war with Italy because he was hindered in all he tried to do. The conversation then shifted to the Jesuits as the cause of the present troubles. Chlodwig, who had a particular leaning against the Jesuits, stated that a sign of the decadence of human society is that its ablest members were under the influence of these organizations.

Prince Albert disputed this, saying, "Secret societies only existed when misgovernment called them into being. They made reform impossible and would do away altogether with popular freedom." Later in his career, he would have the opportunity to challenge the Jesuits and the secret societies in Parliament.

Their discussion came to an end as Queen Victoria stood up and, with her ladies-in-waiting, led the other guests into a large salon. It was a splendid room with mirrors, large paintings of past monarchs, and more columns. While the other guests were cornering themselves in small groups, talking about everything from religious doctrine to superficial topics of no interest to him, Chlodwig ventured over to the window. There, the Queen came to him, speaking in a very unaffected and natural way. She inquired after his family and with sympathetic understanding over the recent illness of one of his children. He was very glad for her show of concern and had heard many times of her kindness of heart. After some music and entertainment, the large mantle clock struck eleven. Everyone stood up all at once at the eleventh toll. Somehow, everyone knew that it was a signal that the evening had concluded. The Queen and Prince Albert, together with their little assemblage of ladies of the court, left first. Carriages with their respective footmen were already waiting outside the palace to take guests to their own residences.

The next evening was much the same except that the Queen took Chlodwig into her own chamber and spent a great deal of the evening talking with him about the latest political affairs in Germany. She expressed her concerns amid a fear that only half-measures would be taken in Berlin over Prussia's interests in the current tensions among Austria, France, and Germany. He agreed with her. She asked him to be her liaison with Prussia by providing her with regular reports of Prussia's political interests in foreign affairs particularly involving Austria. As he intended to leave the next day, he bowed to the Queen and reassured her he would do as she wished.

Before he could leave, Prince Albert approached him and said, "Chlodwig, my friend, do not leave England before seeing me tomorrow."

Prince Albert did not say anything further but made arrangements with his secretary for Chlodwig to arrive at the palace at ten in the morning. Arriving promptly the next morning, he found Prince Albert in his usual morning dress without uniform or Orders. He took Chlodwig into his library to an intricately carved bookcase with leaded glass doors, which looked to be made in Vienna. It was filled with a large assortment of historical and political books written in German. Albert took out a map showing the Austrian plan of war and expressed disapproval of the intended French invasion. Chlodwig offered advice on Austria's poorly designed military maneuvers and interjected his ideas on Austria's policies and his concerns over the ultimatum to France. At the end of his political observations, he mentioned the rumor going around that Napoleon III wanted to make peace proposals directly to the emperor of Austria. He gave Albert what advice he could and told the prince that he would take his personal views into account. With this, Prince Albert bade him farewell and wished him all success in the struggles with Germany.

Princess Feodora, deciding to stay in England with her sister, dismissed Chlodwig as her chaperone. He returned to Berlin, preparing to take on his position as adviser to Otto von Bismarck, the president-minister of Prussia, and briefing him on Prince Albert's concerns. Bismarck was appreciative of his years of public affairs and his perceptive insight into the Prussian system of government, and he valued Chlodwig as a supporter. It was his understanding of Prussia's weaknesses as well as its strengths that Bismarck saw as invaluable.

It had been an eventful week for Chlodwig, but it wasn't long before Parliament called him back to Munich.

When he returned, he went directly to his club, where the waiter, hunched over with old age, brought him a disagreeable dinner of overcooked veal and undercooked potatoes. After his half-eaten dinner, he settled into his favorite leather chair, lit a cigar, and sat back to consider his next speech to Parliament, which would undoubtedly not be received well as he would have to report on the new constitution that was under discussion. Under the new German Constitution, a directorate was to be formed of five members; Austria was to have one vote, Prussia one, and Bavaria one. The nobles would have a share in the legislative vote in the Council of Princes. There was already great opposition.

That evening, he returned to Bodenstedt's house. Friedrich poured him another brandy. They both sat back in their chairs next to the fireplace, slowly drawing on their cigars and leaving the smoke to drift through the room. Friedrich could sense that Chlodwig was troubled by his upcoming appearance before Parliament and, wanting to temper his mood, asked, "Have you called on the enchanting Mrs. Erzberger yet?"

"Not yet, my dear friend, but I believe it to be soon."

Part III

Count L

My heart sings when I see you; you give me light, the dreams of youth—you are my fairest world, my peace on earth.
—Prince Chlodwig von Hohenlohe-Schillingsfürst

Minister-President Prince Chlodwig von Hohenlohe-Schillingsfürst

16

A Welcome Caller

Late in the afternoon of the next day, after leaving the Munich Parliament House, Chlodwig pulled the bell at 15 Karlstrasse. The lady herself answered.

He bowed his head and said, "Pardon me, my lady, I am Count L. I have heard so much about you that my overwhelming desire to meet you compelled me to approach you today. However, if it is not your desire, I will withdraw."

Alexandrine would not let him withdraw, and there, at that moment, was forged a friendship that would last thirty years.

From that first meeting, he was a frequent visitor when his public duties allowed it. They spent many evenings sharing delightful conversations about those things they enjoyed most: art, literature, and the theater. While sitting on comfortably cushioned chairs before a warm fire, they talked late into the night. On other days, when Chlodwig's schedule permitted, they took walks around the city or shared dinner at a quiet little out-of-the-way restaurant.

After a busy day in Parliament, he would spend time at his club but even more frequently returned to Karlstrasse and

Alexandrine to spend a restful evening with her. During those early days of their friendship, they easily developed a deep rapport with each other.

At age forty-three, no one would describe Chlodwig as anything other than a small, almost delicate person. Alexandrine saw him as a man, not tall but very pleasant to see, with an attractive face, wonderful blue eyes, and a noble bearing. His short stature did not, however, diminish his superior intelligence, determination, and stamina. They were an odd couple. He was cautiously careful, discreet, and, above all, tactful; she, fourteen years younger, stormy and wayward, was driven to achieve a higher purpose, often giving in to passion at the blink of an eye. She prized his steadfastness and goodness, his intelligence, and his loving attention. He sought in her what he himself lacked: her unchecked recklessness, her uninhibited nature, her unconditional devotion, and her insatiable sense of adventure. During their years together, he was able to command enough strength and patience to calculate her nature and hold fast for the duration of their time together.

On one of their evenings together, he asked, "Dear lady, tell me how you came to Munich."

At first, Alexandrine was hesitant to tell him of her divorce, the loss of her children, and her disgrace. She looked into his kind eyes and found a sentimental soul and the invitation of understanding. With tears welling up in her eyes, she told him of her lonely marriage.

He leaned close to her and said, "Let me be your confessor. I will not reproach you as it is only my wish to comfort you."

With those words, she felt no more hesitation to bare her soul and went on. "Hermann Erzberger hid all of his qualities before our marriage except one: his charm. I was caught in a marriage without fulfillment of my inner longings with a man so dissimilar from my nature, so out of step with my needs and wants. My days were filled with despair of an empty life until one day my first love reappeared. It was the young boy who, in my youth, awakened within me all the passion of young love and desire. We were forbidden to marry, but I have carried him in my heart as a ghost who still haunts me. At a time when my life seemed forever without hope, he rescued me from my loneliness and brought out the passions that had been so long buried. We entered into a glorious and impossible love. The fruit of that love is our child, Hermann. The happiness with my lover was, however, short-lived."

Leaning back on the cushions, she continued. "This passion, although short and unfulfilled, brought about both of our ruins. My lover, being in the army, was sent far north to a new garrison and forbidden to return to Augsburg, where he might again seek me out. Although my husband, with all good intention, was willing to forgive my indiscretion, his family would not. They took it upon themselves to attack me with a vengeance that to this day has not ended. A deadly loneliness enveloped me. I was broken. I had sacrificed myself to an ideal, and it was my punishment to be alone with my failure."

Alexandrine's tears ran down her cheeks as she spoke. The pain of the resurrected past could not be held in check. Reaching into his vest pocket, Chlodwig pulled out a handkerchief and, with tenderness, wiped away her tears.

Sensing her dismay, he told her he had seen the document of which she spoke. "Please, dear lady, do not concern yourself. This maliciousness found no ears."

After several days, he returned to Berlin at the request

of Otto von Bismarck to provide his view of the Schleswig situation, which was now in the forefront again. The predominantly German population continued to debate their intent to remain in the German Confederation and sought independence from the Danish king. To compound matters, the king of Denmark, Fredrick VII, was in grave health and expected to die soon without an heir.

When Chlodwig arrived in Berlin, he wrote a letter to Alexandrine. He bade her to allow him again to visit her when he returned to Munich. He signed it "Count L."

Alexandrine received the letter with an open heart for the friendship that they had, a few weeks before, brought to life. Her thoughts brought her back to their last hour, and her heart swelled in the feeling of his true understanding of her nature.

"At last, a true friend," she spoke out loud to the walls, which had heard much in the past year.

When Alexandrine heard a carriage arrive and Chlodwig's footsteps outside her door, she flung it open. She was not prepared for the flood of joy she felt upon seeing him standing there with a bouquet of flowers in his hand. She had not felt so much happiness in all the months living in Munich.

After a small dinner, their conversation that night took on a political aspect as he had just returned from Berlin without a resolution to the Danish crisis. She listened to him with passionate interest in his political ideology and would have thought less of him if he did not want to express it to her.

He often said, "Nothing in political life is better or worse than the transition from doubt to firm conviction. It is a bad thing, because it wastes the inward life; a good thing, because it puts an end to the state of doubt."

He took pleasure in her company as he could tell that she

understood much about politics. He saw in her a willing participant in sharing his own interest and views of politics and reform.

The evening was still young, and they sought the comfort of the sofa while continuing their conversation. The glow and warmth of the fire stirred something inside him. It was almost beyond his strength not to kiss her tender lips and claim her as his own. But he did not. He had known his love for her, but he tried not to think of or hope for her to love him. Their conversation ceased. There was a contented silence between them as they sat together before the warm fire in the hearth. But the silence said everything.

He would attend to his business in the House of Parliament in Munich during the day and spend the evenings with her and then retire to his club or Bodenstedt's house. He often thought what charms she must have that could induce him to repeat his visits. He knew quite well. It was not just her beauty, her lovely figure, those radiant eyes, and the sound of her laughter. It was also her intelligence and her willingness to share his interests.

On the days when Chlodwig was gone, Alexandrine wandered around the house aimlessly, trying to will the days away before his return. She had known loneliness before, but it now lay before her as a great void. Worse yet were those solitary meals and the empty chair where he sat smoking his cigar with a glass of brandy in his hand, looking so lovingly into her eyes. She knelt down at the hearth, scraping a few pieces of coal from the coal scuttle onto the grate to rekindle the fire. She pulled a chair near, stretching her hands over the blaze to warm herself and take away the chill of her loneliness. As she watched the fire start to dim and the glow from the coals die in the hearth, a haze settled on her old memories, which she could now easily blow away, for she had new and happier ones.

She was hopeful, after all her sorrows, that perhaps new joy and love could be found. She asked herself, *"Did he alone lift the threatening clouds on my past life? Did they give way to my newfound serenity? What influences were brought to me to attain such peace? Perhaps it was my friendship with this man who came to me so suddenly."* Her mind was in confusion over her newly claimed joy. Did she deserve this? Falling back on the cushion on her chair, she passed into a light, dreamless sleep.

17

A Revelation

Alexandrine had known Chlodwig for several months and still did not know his name. She was content to know him as Count L and never asked more.

In the spring of 1863, she received an invitation from her friend Baroness Elisabeth, who lived in Salzburg, to attend a reception and dinner at her house. Finding herself alone for quite some time, as Chlodwig was traveling extensively, she accepted the invitation. She was eager to see her friend, whom she had not seen since her marriage to Erzberger. They had shared many happy days together as children at her uncle's castle in Augsburg.

Alexandrine took an afternoon train from Munich to Salzburg, arriving in the evening. She and her maid, Maria, settled themselves into a hotel near the train station. The next morning, she and Maria took a carriage ride through the city to look at the baroque architecture that was abundant in the old city and to stroll along the banks of the Salzach River.

That evening, Alexandrine called for a carriage for the short ride to her friend's house. At the gate outside the fine old baroque-style villa, the carriage fell in line with the others until it reached the steps. A footman accompanied her into the reception room, where she was announced as "Mrs. Erzberger." The reception room quickly filled with young and old, who seemed to be the bluest blood in Salzburg. The men, dressed in elegant evening wear, were no match for the women, who, even on this warm spring evening, dressed in multilayers of silks or heavy shimmering satin, their bare arms glistening from the warmth of the room, and their décolleté dripping with jewels heaving up under the strain of tight-laced bodices. Alexandrine felt somewhat lacking in the plain, unadorned gown she had chosen for the evening.

She had commissioned the gown from a French designer known for his forward designs. The dress was considered to be in the latest Paris fashion. It had not even reached the shores of England and certainly not yet been introduced in Germany or Austria. While the other ladies swished around the floor in their great billowing gowns, unable to stand close to anyone, Alexandrine's dress was fitted close to her figure, hugging it tightly with only a small bustle in the back, followed by a short train. The dress, baring her shoulders, was cut low enough to show only a hint of her breasts. She wore no jewelry. She needed no decorations as enhancement. She thought that appearing in such a gown outside of current convention would bring her no attention and perhaps even some disapproval. She was wrong. She was approached by a revolving army of men. As one left, more followed. Every one of them was full of admiration for this stunning young woman in this dress that showed off her remarkable hourglass figure. The women kept to themselves, sure this "Mrs. Erzberger" was not in their class and considerably jealous of the accumulation of attention she was getting from the men in the room.

The chatter in the room suddenly stilled. All eyes were on the entrance to the reception room as an announcement was made: "His Royal Highness, Prince Chlodwig von Hohenlohe-Schillingsfürst, and her Royal Highness, Princess Marie von Hohenlohe-Schillingsfürst." A line formed on either side of the doorway to allow the royal couple to enter the main room. Ladies curtsied, and men bowed.

Alexandrine looked toward the doorway to the salon in shocked amazement. It was his face, his form! Here he stood in his fine brocade evening suit with an elegant woman on his arm. She was only half understanding what she heard or what was happening. She retreated to the back of the room in silence to catch her breath. The minutes sped out of time over this revelation, dulling all her thoughts.

She was ready to bolt out of the house when it was announced that dinner was being served in the great dining salon. As if in a trance, she took an offered arm and walked into the dining room, taking her assigned seat. She did not notice the enormously long table in the salon, which was set with colorful flowers spilling out of copious silver urns and filling the room with their rich floral bouquet. The smell of burning candles set in dazzling silver candelabras sitting the full length of the table filled the air with the smell of hot wax. Three Austrian crystal wine glasses sat at each splendid place setting, one for each course. Once the whirlwind of names, titles, and faces settled and everyone was seated, lively conversations started anew between the guests. After the wine was poured and several toasts were made, a splendid dinner was served.

There were fifteen footmen dressed in the most elegant gold-trimmed uniforms serving each course. White-gloved hands appeared before each guest, placing gold-adorned plates filled with pâté, caviar, smoked salmon, and cucumbers followed by a bowl of gray velvet oyster soup. When these dishes were cleared from the table, they were replaced by a larger version of the plates removed. The white gloves appeared again with trays of fish and, finally, duck, pheasant, and pork, which guests served themselves to their liking. The wine glasses now made way for smaller tulip-shaped crystal glasses for the after-dinner wine. For the final course, an assortment of petit fours, small almond cakes, pudding, and fruit compote were served. None of this mattered to Alexandrine as the whirlwind of her thoughts could not be stilled.

Conversations and a few mild arguments continued throughout the dinner. Almost everyone spoke in French as it was considered the language of the educated and refined. Alexandrine thought of herself thoroughly educated in the French language, but she had to keep on her toes to keep up. During the dinner, many a young man and old aristocrat secretly glanced her way, making it clear she was admired. There was something so divinely sensual in her movements: dabbing her mouth with a napkin, holding a glass ever so delicately, or lifting a fork slowly up to her soft, full lips. Her playful smile radiated throughout the room, capturing the eyes of the men, who dared not smile back for fear of a sharp kick under the table from their wives.

After dinner, the guests met in the lounge for another round of talk and schnapps. A small string quartet played in the background. Alexandrine looked for Chlodwig but was not able to catch his eye. The princess stayed close to him, taking his arm while he mingled with the other guests. Later, the men adjourned into one of the drawing rooms for brandy and cigars. It seemed as though they sought respite from the ladies chattering on about the latest fashion or hats. Once the men left, the women adjourned into another salon, where they quickly found seats in groups with their friends. Alexandrine, still feeling the numbness of her discovery, arrived last, looking for a comfortable seat away from the gossiping women. She found a seat behind a pillar. Her good friend and hostess, Baroness Elisabeth, joined her. From this vantage point, they were out of sight of the other women and could talk privately.

Elisabeth asked Alexandrine about her trip to the Holy Land with the Countess von Hahn. "It was a memorable trip, and I should like to go again sometime," she answered.

"And how are your circumstances now? Are you in a better financial situation?"

"I am happy to say I am. Mr. Erzberger has reinstated my allowance, which is quite adequate."

"You seem much happier than when I last saw you."

"Oh, yes, I am," Alexandrine said somewhat reluctantly, as she was not wanting to say anything about her new friend, Count L, or give away the astonishment of seeing him here. In the next moment, the thought of him in the adjoining room caused her to go pale. The shock of seeing him came back into her memory like an assault on her senses.

Seeing the change come over Alexandrine, the baroness asked, "What is wrong, my dear friend? Are you ill?"

"Not at all, Elisabeth. The heat in the room affected me momentarily. Do not worry."

Somewhere from behind her, Alexandrine heard low voices in an intimate conversation whispering like two lovers. She soon discovered these were two ladies whom she met earlier, thinking themselves private, talking of scandal. Alexandrine strained to hear what was so secretive that they had to whisper. She could only hear a few words: *affair, scandal,* and *divorce.* She knew at once they were gossiping about her.

"Never mind them; they have nothing better to talk about, and they surely won't talk about their own indiscretions," her friend reassured her.

"I'm sorry, Elisabeth, I am feeling quite not myself tonight. The heat is too much to bear. Please excuse me as I wish to go outside for some fresh air."

"Of course, my dear friend," Elisabeth said, taking Alexandrine's hand. "You will surely feel better once you've enjoyed the cool mountain air on the balcony."

It wasn't only the heat that Alexandrine wanted to get away from. The gossiping women and the thought of Chlodwig in the next room were on her mind. She would have left altogether, but her leaving would have given rise to more gossip. *The fresh air will surely clear away the fog in my mind, and I'll find clarity again,* she thought.

She was looking out over the garden, revisiting the past in her mind: her indiscretion and how it had followed her even so far as Austria. She felt the pain of this and wondered if it would ever truly go away. She would not have been so shocked when Chlodwig was announced earlier in the evening had he revealed himself in a gentler manner. The sudden revelation rocked the very foundation out from under her.

It was at that moment when she felt a hand on her shoulder and a wisp of warm breath on her neck. She turned around and found herself looking into Chlodwig's eyes. He had the look of a guilty child. A sudden restriction paralyzed her throat. He handed her a glass of sherry.

When she found her voice, she could only blurt out, "Is it you, my Count L? Why have you deceived me so?"

Even while her mind and heart were in confusion, there was not the slightest lessening of her feelings for him when she saw him standing there next to her.

"My dearest Alex, I regret not having told you sooner of my position, and it is unfortunate how this was revealed to you. We will talk later. I must leave you now, but we shall see each other soon." He turned and hastily returned to the party.

After he left her standing there, she wasn't sure which was worse: seeing him with his wife or his sudden departure without so much as a cursory explanation. She wondered how he would explain this sudden revelation to her.

In her room that night, she had reasoned that she could no longer stay his friend. The pleasant days of joy, which grew stronger with each of his visits, could no longer be. The pain so deep and unrelenting did not let her sleep that night. In the long night, she could only think of the loss of her friend and contemplate the years ahead, stretching endlessly, in which she would have to go on living without him. She had youth, beauty, and high birth, which destined her to take a leading part in the world, to accept admiration as her due, but it was never realized. Now, she thought, *what fate loomed before her? A dreary, monotonous life?*

The air was still. Salzburg was quiet now, and in the silence of the night, in the stifling heat, her face wet with tears, she bade him goodbye.

When Alexandrine returned to Munich, she sent a note to Friedrich. In her precise handwriting, it said, "I need to see you." He, of course, came quickly to her.

"Why did he deceive me so? And you? You knew all along and said nothing!" She was angry, and the words stung.

Bodenstedt, who still secretly loved her, understood why she felt deceived. He said in the gentlest way, "My dear Alex, he did not intentionally do you harm. He only wanted to be your friend without the encumbrances of his title or marriage. He is loyal to his wife but has found in you a friend who shares his passion and interests. After hearing from me how deeply you suffered at the hands of your in-laws, he wanted to offer you his aid and stand by you. Nothing shall change as I know he loves you but dares not say it."

"But I know so little about him. In the months we were together, I never asked, and he said nothing. Tell me, Friedrich, what was his intention?"

"I may know Chlodwig better than most as he has been my friend for many years. From the time of his youth to his last years, he will be a statesman. Together with his diplomatic and political abilities, he possesses a sensitive soul. He is made of a different cloth. On one side, he is all reason and calculation when it comes to his political views. On the other, he has a deep and profound need to have a close union with a sympathetic person. The desire to share his emotions and sensations with another soul like his is deep within his nature. He would have only a woman as his confidant. At first it was his sister Amalie. She is a dreamy and beautiful creature. To her, he confided his budding romance with Princess Marie. Before and during their first years of marriage, he depended on Amalie as a confidant. She was a safe harbor and refuge in all the fatalities of life."

"Does he no longer love his wife?" Alexandrine asked.

"He loves her most dearly. In the early years, they shared a deep love. His greatest joy is to have a woman by his side. Together they shared much: reading, poetry, the arts, and music. Their life together is preserved by the friendly character of their nature, which was assumed in the first days of their union. That is not to say he cannot find another confidant with whom he can share a radiant joy of reason, mystical dreaming, and poetry. That person is you. Somehow, he knew it from the first day he saw you at the theater."

Alexandrine understood what her friend was trying to say, but nevertheless, she was still feeling the suffocating betrayal of that evening in Salzburg.

Several days later, a letter arrived:

> *When you receive this letter, I will already be in the Berlin train station, whence I soon depart for Munich. I implore you, do let me have a word saying when I may come to see you.*

It was signed, *"Your unchanging friend, C H."*

When the room fell quiet that night after receiving his note, Alexandrine drifted into a restless slumber. In her dreams, she heard whispers: "Take his hand, this noble friend who offers you love and friendship, one who will lift up your pride once again. This is not as with the handsome Scheffer, who awakened a young girl's passion. No, this is different. You are entering into the world of love with a man who is equal to you in mind, soul, and thought."

It was in the morning that she knew, deep within her heart, she could not prevent his coming. She wrote back, giving him a time that he may come. The prospect of a new and different life with him was growing within her heart. Her earlier attraction to him as a fascinating companion was turning into a new passion. Her newfound relationship with the prince would surely come dangerously close to a precipice.

Would she fall into the void? Would she lay there broken, never to be her former self? Another fear sprouted its ugly wings: Would he, too, have doubts about shattering their former tranquility together for something that, once started, could never be reversed to what it was before? Would he also long for the quiet evenings in conversation and the trust they shared, knowing it could never be the same? The real question in her mind was the most important one: Would or could he not ever again be to her what "Count L" had been?

When a carriage drew up to the front of her house, Chlodwig stepped out. She knew her whole future would be decided today. She peered through the window and could see the strain on his face. Upon hearing his footsteps when he arrived, a flood of happiness beyond anything she had known in a long while overwhelmed her. She could not restrain herself and welcomed him warmly. All her struggles vanished as he looked upon her face so charmingly. His radiant blue eyes, full of trust, worked their spell on her. She knew at once that her future lay before her with him at her side.

When he took her hand in his, he looked into her eyes and softy said, "My dearest friend, do not take your hand away; do not be angry with me any longer."

It was her anger at his deception, and her instinct for the truth, that only enhanced his admiration for her.

As Alexandrine listened quietly, she opened her heart as he said, "It was when you confessed to me the troubles that caused your suffering that within my heart sprang the strongest desire to stand by you and to abate the persecutors who caused you the loneliness you have felt. The thought of offering you my aid under my own name was painful to me. It was a diplomatic deception. Perhaps I should have been content with our first meeting, but I could not. After that day, I could no longer leave you because I was carried away by the sincerity of your soul and your beauty. You possess all the qualities that I so highly prize in a woman but have seldom found."

Alexandrine was close to tears when he spoke those words. He reached up to stroke her cheek and gently said, "I offer you no promises, only that you can depend on me for an arm to lean on and my protection throughout your life. Do not turn me away. Without you, my life would be a desert, empty and desolate."

He knew what lay in his own heart but now hoped for only one thing: that she would love him as he loved her. Deep emotions overcame him as he declared his love for her.

"Let me be by your side; break free of all others. I will be your true friend and cherish you forever."

With his words, Alexandrine's mind and heart abandoned all the discord she had felt for the past days. He, in one short stroke with those words, became her refuge, her protector, her lover. His profession of love brought her the joy she had sought for so long. Since her divorce from Erzberger, she had been a pariah. But now, in the mantle of protection from the prince, she would enter a new world. The flood of disappointment, anger, and despair was loosened at long last. In this short hour, she felt her whole life had changed.

Sitting next to her, he caught her hands in his, brought them to his lips, and kissed them tenderly. She gazed at him, and all at once, he became so dear to her. Her heart swelled, and she could not imagine a life without him. He enveloped her in his arms and kissed her tenderly on her warm, inviting lips. Nothing more was said, and their friendship was now a ship perfectly set upon golden, still waters, ready to sail forth.

Chlodwig did not return to his club, or to Bodenstedt's house, that evening as he had always done. Instead, Alexandrine took his hand and led him upstairs to her bedchamber. He stood gazing into her lovely face while he unbuttoned her blouse and the laces to her bodice. She let her skirt fall to the floor. He removed his jacket and placed it carefully on a velvet chair waiting for it in the corner of the room. She untied his tie, and as she unbuttoned his shirt, her hand searched under his undershirt to feel the warmth of his skin. He wasn't muscular, but his body felt strong as she caressed it.

As Alexandrine sat on the bed to remove her undergarments and stockings, he turned down the gas light. As the room bathed itself in velvet darkness, they slid under the silk coverings of the bed. They delighted in the pleasure of their bodies touching in an embrace; their lips searching, getting to know each other; and, at last, the release of their passion. It was then that their life together was forged.

⁓

After it was known that Prince Chlodwig had taken Mrs. Erzberger as his mistress, she attained a new status in that particular circle of Munich society. The new world in which she was so suddenly thrust would now prove to take her in its arms. After all, other men had mistresses, and as long as there was no scandal and the wife's position was not threatened, society would look the other way. Even the gossipers who maligned her not so long ago suddenly found her "respectable." It was, however, motivated by a different standard. She might be helpful, having the prince's ear, to attain whatever end they desired. Alexandrine knew this and was not influenced by their sudden invitations.

To no one's surprise, her former in-laws also approached her. Each one sought some favor from the prince. They could not prevail. Alexandrine's in-laws likely would not have pursued her with their vile pamphlet had they known that one day in the future, his Royal Highness, Prince Chlodwig von Hohenlohe-Schillingsfürst, who was already long ago cast into the political arena, would soon be appointed nineteenth minister-president of Bavaria and then vice president of the German government, German ambassador to Paris, the German Secretary of State of Foreign Affairs, governor of Alsace-Lorraine, prime minister of Prussia, and finally, toward the end of his life, chancellor of Germany. All this by never taking a single political step or delivering a speech without discussing it with her. The irony of this was beyond words. And Alexandrine delighted in the thought.

Chlodwig, with his newly extended duties and his more recent work on the unification of Germany, was frequently away from Munich for long periods of time. During those days and weeks, Alexandrine's evenings were again dark and melancholy. Even in his longest absences from her, she could sense his essence hanging in the rooms. It gave her only small comfort.

Before he left on one of his long trips, she asked him to write to her. "Please write, dear friend, so that I may know you are well."

"Perhaps you will also write me a line or two in return. It would brighten me and assuage my lonely hours," he said.

Within a day, she wrote to him of her loneliness for his company and how she missed the evenings of lively conversations and his frequent requests for her assistance in preparing one of his speeches. Not long after, she received his letter:

> *As you already know that I dislike writing, and write rarely and briefly you will, my indulgent and kind-hearted friend, forgive this belated answer to your last letter. That you should have put faith in my vague words is worthy of you and the proof of a noble disposition. Only those who are themselves deceptive see deception where none exists. Nothing is more attractive, more enchanting in a woman than truthfulness, and nothing is more unusual. I believe that you are one of the exceptions. And through that you become for me a magnet from whom I cannot escape, do as I will. I await the moment of my return to Munich with great impatience, but unfortunately several weeks must elapse before I can come. In the meantime, keep me in kindly remembrance.*

It was signed "C. H."

It was their mutual respect and boundless trust in each other that made their lasting love possible. It was that which drew them ever closer together for the next thirty years.

Prince Chlodwig at his desk in Schillingsfürst

Prince Chlodwig at age eighty

Princess Marie von Sayn-Wittgenstein, wife of Prince Chlodwig

Prince Chlodwig at age twenty-seven

Alexandrine at age seventy

Author's grandmother, and Alexandrine's granddaughter, Gisela
Karolina Baroness von Hornstein

Castle Schillingsfürst

Altaussee

18

A Surprise Visitor

*I*t was not long after Chlodwig's return from one of his long trips away that he sent for Alexandrine to come to Schillingsfürst. He wrote:

> My ladies depart this evening and I accompany them
> for some leagues, but then return immediately, so that I
> shall be here again tomorrow. I hope to find a letter from
> you when I get back. Do not make me wait too long, dear
> Alex—I am so depressed that I really need a word from
> you. I shall now be quite alone, and shall miss you more
> than ever. If you are well, and if your heart whispers such
> a wish to you as one to see me, and if you do not dread the
> fatigue, do come. A thousand kisses.

She came by train and was met by his fine royal carriage, with its crest on the door, pulled by two marvelous black horses and three groomsmen. They were sent to bring her from the station to the castle. She was confident that his wife and family were presently away and would not return for some days. As the horses sped on, passing rolling hills with sheep and cows lazily grazing in verdant pastures, the meadow turned into thick and dark foreboding forests. It was evening before she arrived, but there was still enough light to see the castle high above the village, rising up majestically with lights gleaming from the many windows lighting the way. Driving over the large outer-moat bridge and then the inner-moat bridge toward the inner courtyard, she could finally see Castle Schillingsfürst. Approaching closer, she could see the main house and, on either side, equally large buildings.

She was surprised to see Chlodwig waiting for her on the main steps to the castle. The footman lowered the steps of the carriage, and she stepped out. A slight breeze blowing through the courtyard caught her skirt, and it billowed up. That slight movement of her gown made her seem to float from the carriage. The footman led her up the steps to the waiting prince.

"My dearest," he said as he lightly kissed her gloved, outstretched hand.

"Count L," she responded, smiling mischievously. Her eyes caught the lamplight and sparkled in the dark night. They both broke out in laughter at the reference to Count L.

Inside the great hall, pointing up the grand staircase, he said, "A room has been prepared for you, and after you have refreshed yourself and changed, we shall dine together in the small salon." Another footman led her up the stairs.

Alexandrine was happy for the few moments of rest after her long journey. She looked forward to an evening with him, hopefully away from the servants. It seemed to her there was a multitude of them. One or two at every door, dressed in the finest uniforms, ready to spring forward when she approached to open any door for her. She was used to servants as she spent many years in her youth in houses not as grand as this but grand nevertheless.

The maid assigned to her already had a warm bath waiting for her and proceeded to remove Alexandrine's clothing. The maid sponged her with warm bathwater and scented soap, soothing her after the long and dusty ride up to the castle from the station. After searching for a suitable gown for the evening, the maid proceeded to brush Alexandrine's hair. She had never seen hair extending down a lady's back almost to her ankles before and did not know what to do. Most of the ladies she cared for would keep their hair cut to a shorter length. Seeing the maid's distress, Alexandrine quickly plaited it and showed her how to fasten it around her head with ribbons to keep it in place.

When Alexandrine was ready, the maid called for a footman, who guided her to a small dining room, where Chlodwig was waiting. The table was beautifully set, and a small dinner was served by more footmen, who stood by to offer any assistance as required. After dinner, he took her arm and led her into his study. This room was quite large, filled with heavy, elaborately carved dark-walnut furniture; fine leather chairs; and wooden bookcases containing his vast library of books, all of which were beautifully leather-bound. The bookcases covered one wall from floor to ceiling. The room had a masculine feel but was truly elegant in its furnishings and decor. Life-size paintings of men in uniform and ladies in great gowns hung on the other wood-paneled walls. Soon, the grand door to the room opened, and the butler arrived with a silver tray and brandy.

Alexandrine took a particular interest in the ancestral life-size paintings in their elaborate gilded frames. "Tell me, Chlodwig, who are these men in their magnificent uniforms?"

He was pleased that she had an interest and started with the one closest to the door. "This one is my eldest brother, Viktor Moritz Karl, the first prince of Corvey. As first born, he was the heir to the principality of Hohenlohe-Schillingsfürst but renounced his rights and was made duke of Ratibor and prince of Corvey by King Frederick William IV of Prussia. The next painting is of my father, Prince Franz Joseph von Hohenlohe-Waldenburg-Schillingsfürst, who died in 1841."

"I would like to know more about your father. What was he like?" Alexandrine asked.

He answered, "My father wanted a military career but was disappointed when he could not have one. I knew him to have a melancholy strain in his character, although he was a great wit and could be very merry on occasion. His greatest characters were his kindness, courtesy, and amiability. He was universally popular. My love of history and politics probably came from him as he was keenly interested in both. When I was a child, he appeared immensely tall with a will of iron and a sour disposition. There were two ways to deal with him: you could go under, or you could go away."

That amused Alexandrine as this seemed to be the general character of her father.

Continuing to walk around the room, the next painting Alexandrine saw was the solemn face of Prince Philipp Ernst. "Philipp was my younger brother," he added. At this, Chlodwig became melancholy and said, "Phillip was my favorite brother who was closest to my heart and with whom I thought and felt in such perfect harmony. I told him once I have never entrusted to anyone else as he understood everything. He was indulgent to the feelings of others, gentle and lovable."

Seeing the sadness in his eyes, Alexandrine asked, "You speak of him in the past tense. Do you mean he no longer lives?"

"Sadly, Philipp died after a long illness in 1845. This event was the beginning of a time when my natural cheerfulness and optimism were shattered with his death. It was because of Philipp that I became master of Schillingsfürst. After my father died, I renounced my own birthright to Philipp on the stipulation that if he should die, all rights, properties, and principalities would revert to me. As it happened, sadly, Philipp died only four years later."

"My dearest, I cannot express to you how sad I feel over what you have just told me. It seems you were true kinsmen in your natural kindnesses. I had no such rapport with my brother. In fact, I hardly knew him as we were separated much of our lives."

Alexandrine was interested in one particular painting. It was a beautiful woman dressed in a delicate pink gown embroidered with pink and white roses; a small piece of lace framed her delicate face. He said, "This is a portrait of my mother, Princess Konstanze of Hohenlohe-Langenburg. She was an exceptional woman."

"Ah, Langenburg! That sounds familiar as I believe I know this family. Of course, by name only. She is quite beautiful," Alexandrine said, admiring the painting.

"Yes, of course, the name Langenburg is well known. My mother's sister-in-law is Princess Anna Feodora Auguste of

Hohenlohe-Langenburg, who married my mother's brother, Ernst I, prince of Hohenlohe-Langenburg. She is also the half-sister of Queen Victoria of the United Kingdom."

"I believe that I was told this. Princess Feodora and Queen Victoria of England share the same mother, Princess Victoria of Saxe-Coburg-Saalfeld," Alexandrine added.

"You are quite right about that," he answered. "Princess Victoria's first husband was Emich Carl, prince of Leiningen. He was Feodora's father, who died in 1814. Victoria then married the duke of Kent, who was the father of Queen Victoria. By all rights, Victoria and Feodora are sisters. She spent much time in England with her half-sister as a companion. Queen Victoria was devoted to her elder sister."

"Yes, of course, I have heard of the relationship of the Langenburg family to the Queen of England, but I did not know of your connection to them. You sound very affectionate when speaking of the Princess Feodora."

"Yes, I am very fond of my aunt. She has helped me in my career more than once. I had the honor of escorting her to England a few years ago to see her sister."

There were more paintings she would have liked to see, but the long day was nearing the end, along with her endurance.

Sensing her tiredness, he said, "We shall retire early tonight, my dearest, as we have much to do tomorrow."

She smiled at him most lovingly. He thought to himself that when she smiled, her beauty took on an enchanting quality. He took her hand in his, kissed it softly, and led her to the stairs, where her maid was waiting to take her to her bedchamber.

Her journey had taken a toll. She was eager to go to bed. She did not dream that night and awoke in the morning refreshed.

Chlodwig had prepared for their day together. A ride in the morning would invigorate them both. Two spirited horses were brought forth by the grooms, one with a side saddle and the other with a regular riding saddle. She would have preferred to ride astride as she had done in her youth, but this was not the time. They rode off toward the meadows, which later turned into forests. Their ride was gentle enough, but she longed for the wind in her hair, so with a swift kick to her mount, she burst away from Chlodwig.

He spurred his horse on, sparing nothing to catch her. Her skirt was billowing in the wind; her hair, now loosened, flowing behind her as she raced through the forest. She kept on daring him to catch her, but she was still much too far ahead. As she approached an embankment covered with leaves and branches, her horse took the leap with ease. She thought herself an expert rider and was sure he was too. She looked back and saw his horse balk at the same hidden barrier and did not jump. She turned her horse around to meet up with him. He was clearly angry and scolded her for her mischievous adventure. He could see she was fearless and afraid of nothing. She only smiled at him with that seductive smile that had always stirred his passion.

With that smile, the anger left him. He said, "You lovely thing! Now with your loosened hair, your blazing eyes, you seem like some wild Amazon at the head of a warlike troop. I feel as if you belong to another world and not this commonplace one of ours."

They both dismounted, placing themselves in the shade of a tree. A warm breeze blew, and the limbs of the tree overhead stirred. His eyes were now soft with forgiveness. He folded his arms around her. They were content to savor their intimacy in each other's arms. At that moment, she loved him honestly for his loving nature, his brilliant mind, his strength of person, the breadth of his compassion and patience. She loved him as a woman and was content to stay a while in the warmth of his love with his arms around her.

They spent the rest of the day exploring the grounds on foot and in a pair of pony chaises. The weather was of no concern; it was fine with only a slight breeze now and then. In the evening, after dinner, sitting in the radius of charmed candlelight, they reveled in tender feeling for each other. She played the piano, while he sat with a glass of brandy, watching her move her hands ever so elegantly over the keys.

The next afternoon, after another day of joyful riding and enjoying the natural beauty around Schillingsfürst, they were sitting together in one of the salons reading poetry to each other when they heard a carriage rumbling over the inner drawbridge. It was clear from the flurry of servants bustling about that it was Princess Marie's carriage, which was already in the courtyard. Alexandrine's face went pale. "I have to go immediately," she blurted out with panic in her voice. He caught her hand as she started to leap up from her chair.

"There is no need to go," he said as he stood up waiting for Marie to enter the room.

Princess Marie strode into the sunlit room with dignity and grace. Alexandrine's mind ceased to function, and she could not speak. She could only stare at her. She was a stately, mature woman with the look of royalty, which suited her. She looked very much a princess in her heavy satin gown, even though the weather was warm. Alexandrine was nervous, the princess dignified and composed.

He introduced her to his wife as Alexandrine, Baroness von Hedemann of Hedemann-Heespen. Alexandrine bowed to her.

"How do you do, Baroness?" she said as she took off her gloves, handing them to the footman, who was always nearby, before sitting down on the settee. "Please sit down, Baroness. I would like to know more about you."

The butler arrived with coffee and cakes. It was a pleasant enough afternoon, with the princess telling them of her travels and the reason for her sudden return to Schillingsfürst. Afterward, the princess excused herself. Before she left the room, she asked Alexandrine if she cared to stay for supper.

Uncomfortable as she was, she agreed to stay. The dinner was elegantly served, and conversation was light. Alexandrine no longer felt out of place as the princess treated her with gracious attention. The princess was an intelligent and well-educated woman whose heritage Alexandrine thought to be quite remarkable. After dinner, Alexandrine gathered her belongings and left the castle. A carriage took her to an inn in the village. The next day, she returned to Munich by train without seeing Chlodwig.

Following the incident at Schillingsfürst and meeting the princess, Alexandrine was determined never to go to the castle again. A few days later, she was surprised to be called on by the princess's solicitor. She invited him in, offering him tea.

She could see he was uncomfortable as he said, "I have

been charged with the duty to come to you with a declaration from her Royal Highness, Princess Marie."

"And what might that be?" Alexandrine asked, already knowing that she would not like the answer.

The solicitor stuttered as he read the document: "This document, signed by me, Princess Marie von Hohenlohe-Schillingsfürst, does hereby request you sever all contact and relationships with my husband, Chlodwig, now and forever. My health and well-being will suffer greatly if you do not do so immediately. Should you resist, the consequences to you will be great." The solicitor added, "Her Royal Highness, the princess, would suffer greatly if you do not comply with her wishes. She has charged me with the duty to impress upon you the seriousness of her request." With that, the solicitor bid her farewell and left.

Alexandrine did not know what prompted this visit from the solicitor as she was sure there could not possibly have been any indication of anything to her visit to Schillingsfürst but a social call. Or perhaps the princess was more perceptive than she thought her to be.

When Chlodwig returned to Munich, Alexandrine reported to him this meeting with the solicitor and his reason for the visit. He took it lightly. "Do not concern yourself, my dear Alex. It will be righted." After a few days, Alexandrine learned that the solicitor was summarily dismissed.

Chlodwig's growing relationship with Alexandrine did not in any way diminish his love for his wife. The diplomat used those skills to convince Marie that she was a constant force in his life, and he depended on her strength and steadfastness. She knew this and said no more.

Not to be denied the pleasure of Alexandrine's company, or the comfort of his palatial home whenever he desired, Chlodwig continued to invite Alexandrine there while the princess was well away and not likely to interrupt them again.

19

Gossip and Politics

Neither Alexandrine nor Chlodwig was blind to the fact that their relationship could not remain a secret within the prince's political circle. Public opinion was busying itself against him with whispers and undertones by his political adversaries that threatened to become openly public. His liberal leanings would soon become fodder for the antiliberal factions, which, in due course, would use any kind of scandal against him.

In 1864, Ludwig was crowned king of Bavaria after the sudden death of his father, King Maximilian II. Sentiments against Chlodwig soon reached Ludwig's ears. Because of his true affection for both Chlodwig and Alexandrine, he intervened. He begged the prince to separate himself from Alexandrine, at least for a short while, to silence any future scandal and those who opposed him.

Chlodwig agreed with Ludwig that it was in both their best interests that Alexandrine should leave Munich to stay with her friend Baroness Elisabeth in Salzburg. She took Hermann; his nurse; and Maria, her maid, and remained with her friend for six months in the hope that the gossip would evaporate once there was no more to talk about. Chlodwig, however, did not want to be separated from her. He visited her in Salzburg as often as he had the opportunity to do so or invited her to stay with him at Schillingfürst. After six months, Alexandrine returned to Karlstrasse.

During the next few years, their time together was spent more discretely while in Munich. Even on her visits to Castle Schillingfürst, they became more reclusive. Those days were spent reading, writing poetry together, discussing his next political objectives, riding, or walking through the forests that surrounded the vast estate. One evening while playing the piano, with candlelight casting a soft glow onto her face, Chlodwig watched Alexandrine intently, remembering the first time he brought her to the castle. He sat next to her and kissed her tenderly on her neck as he said, "Do you remember the first time you were here with me at Schillingfürst?" They both laughed, recalling the awkward moment when his wife, Princess Marie, arrived unexpectedly.

Chlodwig's meetings with Bismarck were now about the November Constitution being written for the joint affairs of Denmark and Schleswig. It was still in draft form when the Danish king, Frederick VI, died at this critical time. The new king, Christian IX, felt compelled to sign the draft, violating the London Protocol of 1852, which affirmed the integrity of the Danish federation. Bismarck issued an ultimatum to Denmark demanding the draft constitution be abolished within forty-eight hours. The demand was rejected by the Danish government. In doing so, Austria and Prussia declared war on Denmark on January 14, 1864. The war was short-lived, ending on October 30, 1864. At a peace treaty, the Danish king renounced his rights to the duchies in return for the emperor of Austria and the king of Prussia ceding Schleswig, Holstein, and Lauenburg.

It was in 1864 that Chlodwig heard of the sudden death of Prince Albert. He was truly saddened by the news as Albert had been his friend during his school days. Even after his marriage to Queen Victoria in England, Albert kept their lines of communication open, often seeking Chlodwig's advice. Soon after Prince Albert's death, he received a communication from Queen Victoria. She wrote that with Albert's death, she no longer had a reliable connection with Germany and wanted to express her confidence in him to keep her informed of German social and political conditions from time to time. Of course, he graciously accepted her request.

After the Austro-Prussian War of 1866 was fought between the Austrian Empire and the Kingdom of Prussia, each aided by various allies within the German Confederation, Chlodwig argued for a closer union between Bavaria and Prussia. King Ludwig II of Bavaria was against any dilution of his power. However, Otto von Bismarck, who was, at the time, minister-president of Prussia, had access to a large sum of money as part of the fortune the royal House of Hannover received from Prussia after the annexation of Hannover by Prussia. It was intended to fight Hannovian loyalists. Bismarck secretly gave a large sum of this money to King Ludwig II to pay off his large debts. Ludwig came around.

In 1866, Chlodwig succeeded Baron Karl Ludwig von der Pfordten as minister-president of Bavaria. This appointment by King Ludwig II was believed to be at the instigation of the composer Richard Wagner. Wagner was a court favorite of

King Ludwig II. Much was said about Ludwig and Wagner's relationship—not always favorable. Chlodwig regarded Ludwig as the most amiable and engaging sovereign, noble and poetic in nature, and his courtesy was a natural expression of a truly kind heart. Wagner, of course, admired his defense of Ludwig. It was when Ludwig consulted with his friend Wagner that the latter expounded on Chlodwig's intelligence and political acuity, which ultimately led to the confirmation not only as minister-president of Bavaria but also as minister of the Royal House and of Foreign Affairs and president of the Council of Ministers.

Alexandrine received a letter from Chlodwig with only these words: "I am it!" She knew immediately what those few words meant. He was, at last, recognized for his contributions and involvement with the Prussian and Bavarian governments in achieving alliances and unification of all the northern German states.

Happiness can only last so long before sadness pays its grim visit. In July of that year, Chlodwig and Marie's nine-year-old son, Albert, fell ill with diphtheria. Chlodwig rushed home to be with Marie and his son. The doctor tending the boy saw little improvement. Within a few days, young Albert died. Marie and Chlodwig tried desperately to console each other in a grief without measure over the loss of their son.

With a heavy heart, still grieving for his son, he returned to Berlin. As head of the Bavarian government, he took on the challenge of finding some basis for an effective union of the South German states with the North German Confederation. During the three years in the office of minister-president of Bavaria, he was possibly the most important statesman in Germany next to Bismarck. In his capacity as minister-president, he carried out a long-needed reorganization of the Bavarian Army using the Prussian model. He brought about the military union of the southern states and the creation of the customs parliament, to which he was later elected vice president.

20

Altaussee

After another long absence from Alexandrine, Chlodwig could no longer stay away and returned to Munich. He told her, with marked sadness, of his son's death. He laid his head on her shoulder and cried bitterly. Alexandrine stroked his face and ran her fingers through his hair with care and understanding. She, too, started to cry as she could not bear to see him in such anguish.

Tired from his lengthy negotiations, speeches, and meetings, Chlodwig proposed a time of relaxation at one of his residences in the Austrian Alps. "I have not been to Altausee in several years and would very much like to spend the summer there with you," he said. Alexandrine, hearing the tiredness in his voice, was delighted that he would seek rest. But, more than that, it gladdened her heart that they would, at long last, have more time together.

The village of Altaussee was spread around the crystal-clear mountain lake Bad Aussee and was under the watchful eye of the Loser Plateau. It was a typical Austrian mountain village with small brick houses, flower boxes outside the windows, and gardens overflowing with more flowers. Altaussee was best known for one of Austria's most interesting attractions, known throughout Europe as the largest salt mines in the country.[6]

As Alexandrine was still on good terms with the Scheffers, she placed Hermann with them for the month she would be gone. They were happy to have the boy to themselves for such a long time. Hermann was beginning to take on the image of his father, to the delight of his grandparents.

As this mountain village was a favorite refuge for Austrians and Germans alike seeking a safe haven from the heat of the cities in the summer months, many of Chlodwig's friends and colleagues also sought Altaussee for quiet relaxation and respite from the burdens of everyday stresses. Before leaving, he arranged for Alexandrine to stay at an inn not far from his house to avoid any more vicious gossip, which her visit would surely evidence. Leaving the city behind, the train took them through the Austrian Alps and then by carriage to their destination. The house, once a small hunting lodge, was purchased many years earlier by Chlodwig, and he and Marie spent many days there with their growing family. He enjoyed the area for its hunting and Marie and the children for its clean, pure mountain air. Over time, the once-rustic hunting lodge became a charming and comfortable villa. He continued to spend his summers there whenever he could. Princess Marie, now well into middle age, was not inclined to spend her days in

---

6   Between 1943 and 1945, the extensive complex of salt mines in Altaussee served as a huge repository for art stolen by the Nazis. It also contained holdings from Austrian collections. Initially, in August 1943, art treasures from Austrian churches, monasteries, and museums were transferred into the mines for safekeeping, followed by, starting in February 1944, a stock of about 4,700 works of stolen art from all over Europe.

the countryside any longer, preferring instead to stay in one of the European spas. In recent summers, her husband would establish her in a lavish spa in Baden-Baden or somewhere in the south of Italy, and he would retreat to Altaussee for rest and an occasional hunt. When Alexandrine agreed to go with him, he was overjoyed to be able to share his love of nature with her, which in these beautiful surroundings was in abundance. Here they would find long, quiet days, the natural beauty of the forests, majestic perpetually snow-covered mountains, and the lake catching streams of sunlight on its crystal-blue surface.

Over the next weeks, they shared many blissful days together, taking walks in the woods over paths lined with tree roots or riding through the flowering meadows that surrounded the village. On warm, sunlit days, they basked peacefully in the shadow of the Alps, sitting quietly in the meadow with a picnic lunch. The moonlit, silent evenings they spent reading or taking turns writing poetry to each other.

On other days, they walked together into the village. On one particular day, the weekly street market in the center of town was underway. A mixture of bustling local peasants, tradesmen, and farmers set up their stalls, filling them with their wares every morning in the hopes of selling to the many tourists who flocked to this quaint little town. All heads in the market bowed when the prince appeared. He tipped his hat to everyone he met. When, by coincidence, they met one of his friends, he politely greeted them and continued on to let them speculate whatever they wanted. He was in too happy a mood to care.

They continued down the street, visiting each stall and lightheartedly chatting with the farmers while buying ripe plums, apples, and berries. After they could carry no more, they took their overfilled baskets of fresh fruits and vegetables, climbed up the hill back to the villa, and brought them to the cook. The cook, a local woman who came every day to prepare Chlodwig's meals, was happy to see the bounty they brought her. She did not prepare elaborate meals as the cooks at Schillingfürst would have, but neither he nor Alexandrine minded. They were simple meals that any farmer's wife in the region would prepare for her own family. Most evenings, they were served a little pork or sausages with sauerkraut and potatoes. For dessert, she made plum cake with streusel topping. It suited them as part of the country life in the Alps.

While there, they had occasion to make the acquaintances of the Hungarian Count Hunyadi, Baron Sala, and an opera singer. They all courted Alexandrine with special favors. There were flowers, notes, and unabashed flirting. Chlodwig only found it amusing. One day, during a walk through a meadow with Count Hunyadi, a large horned bull suddenly appeared on the path. Alexandrine's courtier, the count, bolted, leaving her to face the bull. To the rescue came Chlodwig on horseback, who, like St. George with a sword, saw Alexandrine in danger and attacked the bull. The farmer who owned the bull and who had followed it up the path rescued the animal from the prince just in time to save it from a piercing. Alexandrine, however, was saved. That evening, they both laughed over the not-so-chivalrous behavior of the count. Afterward, Chlodwig would often remark about the event and caution Alexandrine to leave her three adorers to their own devices.

Chlodwig himself was not entirely free from the guile of a certain Frau von Binzer, who lived in a house nearby during the summer months. She was curious about Alexandrine and wanted him to take her into his confidence. But he turned a deaf ear and delighted in giving her no information. Nevertheless, Alexandrine was glad when the curious frau was gone from Altaussee and back in her home in Augsburg.

On an evening when a light rain made its appearance on the panes, a feeling of melancholy overtook Alexandrine. She longed for the touch of her children, to hold them to her breast, to sing them lullabies while tucking the featherbed around their sweet little bodies. Her loneliness for them never abated. She stared moodily out the window, watching the rain droplets land one by one on the window and on the tree leaves outside as they slowly dripped to nourish the ground.

"My dearest, what sadness are you feeling today?" Chlodwig asked. She looked at him with eyes filled with pain and a lone tear clinging to her cheek.

"I long to see my children. I have not seen them for several years or heard if they are well. I do not know if they are happy," she said with sadness clinging to each word. She leaned against him as he put his arms around her in a gesture that meant more than any words. In the gentlest way, he asked her to tell him her thoughts.

She poured out her unhappiness. "I have often wondered how my mother could have abandoned me, and I, as a mother, live in agony every day without my children. I fear that one day even Hermann will desert me. He loves the Scheffers and may one day want to leave me to live with them. He will grow up in a bourgeois, humdrum, unimaginative world and know nothing of me or the love I have for him."

"Alex, do not worry so much about Hermann. He loves you, and I am sure he will not leave you," he said to her, wiping the little tear from her cheek. "I know nothing of your mother and why she abandoned you. Won't you tell me what you have buried in your heart all these years?"

She had never spoken of her mother to him or anyone else. She was ashamed and hid it from everyone. She began by telling him, "My father never spoke of my mother. In Nysa, I can remember sitting under a life-size portrait of a beautiful red-haired woman wondering if it was my mother. In the painting, she wore a magnificent gown with a jewel-encrusted bodice and roses strewn around her feet. I thought how exquisitely lovely she was except for her eyes, which seemed to look down upon me with a cold countenance."

Seeing the sadness in Alexandrine, he asked, "Did your father not think it important for you to know about your mother? It appears, if the portrait is your mother, then you must surely be told."

"When I was sixteen, I implored my father to tell me where she was. He said that my stepmother forbade him from mentioning anything about her. He would not risk her ire. After much pleading, he finally relented. He made me promise that I would tell my stepmother none of what he was about to say to me. My father went on, in stinging truthfulness, of the circumstances to which I was born, how my mother became insane and was placed into an asylum while she was pregnant.

"I was born in that institution. The doctors would not allow my mother to keep me, so my father took me away and raised me, my two sisters, and my brother alone with only a nurse to care for us. After some time, he decided he could no longer manage four children who needed a mother. I was six years old when he remarried. I have no fond memories of my stepmother.

"No amount of pleading on my behalf would open his heart to tell me anything more about my mother. I wanted to know where she was or what happened to her for all these years. Finally, in a moment of weakness, he relented. He told me the name of the asylum where I was born. He also said she was released many years after my birth and was now living in Breslau in the region of Silesia."

"Did you go to Breslau?" he asked.

"I did nothing until an opportunity presented itself the following summer. My father and stepmother decided to go to the cool and quiet mountains in Switzerland. I wrote a letter to my mother in Breslau telling her that I wished to see her. To my surprise, I received an answer from her a few weeks later, and a meeting was arranged. I was overjoyed to at last meet this woman who was a mystery to me. On the train to Breslau, I gave much thought to what I would say to her. What could I say to a woman whom I had never known? All at once, I wanted to pour out all my love to her, which for so long I had yearned to do.

"The meeting was to take place in Café Liszt, a small coffeehouse in downtown Breslau. I arrived early to pick out a table by a window so I could see her arrive. When she appeared, she was still the exquisite-looking woman I remembered from the painting. She was tall and slim, holding herself regally as she walked into the café and seating herself at the table across form me. At first, neither one of us spoke as I'm sure she did not know what to say, and neither did I.

"What I had hoped for was a warm embrace from her, but I only received those cold eyes, which appeared to critically assess me. Her first words were an apology for choosing the plain and simple café for our meeting. She said, 'Of course, there are white linen tablecloths and napkins,' as if to offer a little warmth to relieve the icy chill that hung over us.

"I ordered a light luncheon, but she only asked for coffee. At last, she showed some interest and asked me about my life. I did not get the impression that she cared but was only making conversation to pass the time. After lunch and her third cup of coffee, she stood up, went over to me, placed a cold kiss on my forehead, and was gone. I never saw my mother again."

Silent tears ran down Alexandrine's cheek when she finished her story. Chlodwig wrapped his arms around her and said, "My dearest Alex, let the past slumber. Those days are gone and serve no purpose in remembering. It will only cause you great unhappiness."

They shared many more days in Altausee before a cold burst of mountain air blew down from the peaks as a reminder that summer was at its end. Their days of love and laughter were drawing to a close. Alexandrine desired one more trip to the market before they left this idyllic place. He did not go with her, explaining he had to attend to some urgent business. Alexandrine did not mind going alone as she often did. She enjoyed walking in the clear mountain air; smelling the fragrant scents of the flowers, leaves, and grasses; hearing the birds' joyful songs; seeing the forest creatures running away from her as she walked along the winding path down to the village.

Chlodwig engaged himself at his desk while she was gone, going over his accounts and writing a letter to his wife, Marie. He intended to return to Schillingsfürst soon and wanted her to know he would be staying a few days to look after the tenant properties and go over the annual accounts with his steward.

He was looking forward to seeing his children and spending some time at the castle. He sent for a messenger to deliver the note to his wife at Schillingsfürst.

Having finished with his correspondence, he sat outside to enjoy the sunshine. In that drowsy afternoon, he was flooded with happiness and the peacefulness of the moment when suddenly he saw Alexandrine coming through the trees with the sunlight flitting through the leaves, splattering shapes across her face and onto her cream-colored cotton dress. Her little straw hat did not hide her face, and he could see her eyes in all their radiant beauty. She smiled at him. He walked out to meet her and took the basket filled with fruit in his hand. She wrapped herself around his free arm as if it were the natural thing to do. Thus, they walked with such comfort with each other back to the house. That evening, their last one at Altausee, they sat together in the glow of a soothing fire. She leaned against him. In the warmth of each other's love, and in their own quiet way, they thought of their days together in the idyll of this place.

Wherever he was, whether on his travels or in Schillingsfürst, Alexandrine was always as close to him as his own heart. He felt tied to her by a bond so strong it could not easily break. If it would, he would find it impossible to bear. For now, he would not think of such things; he would just enjoy the memories of the past summer with her at Altaussee.

As they parted, he said, "Farewell, farewell, my dear friend, my good comrade. All others are so alien to me, so uninteresting. No one knows where my longing lies. It is you who are my joy, my sunshine. I must leave my dear oasis as the desert swallows me up."

She, too, felt the same as she left this peaceful place in the mountains. Their daily companionship had become a habit to them. No, it was more than that. It was an absolute necessity binding them together.

21

Letters

After the summer in Altaussee with Alexandrine, Chlodwig returned to Schillingsfürst. No matter where he was, his mind could never completely find rest. Mostly, he busied himself constructing plans for the future of Germany and his career. But when he had leisure time, he found it comforting to compose poetry or find solace in nature. The natural beauty and sereneness of his properties there gave him that opportunity. As an avid sportsman, he often went on hunts but then could be distracted by a butterfly flittering around on tall grasses. Sometimes, a bird singing him a song would distract him. A story often told by his companions was on the day of a hunt in Austria for chamois. While his guests were pursuing their prey, he was sitting in the grass reciting a poem to his sister Amalie when the chamois appeared before him in plain sight. He did not reach for his gun, and in an instant the chamois was gone. This created much amusement that evening at dinner.

"Are you a hunter or a poet?" they asked.

"It would seem that I am a poet," he answered.

After he concluded his duties at his estate, he was once again on his travels to attend to his obligation as president-minister. In spite of his many travels, which consumed his busy life, he continued to find time to write to Alexandrine. And she, in turn, would write to him as he was becoming more and more the focus of all her thoughts. Alexandrine, although lonely for his companionship, nevertheless would not burden him with her feelings as she was proud of his dedication and zeal as a statesman.

On September 30, he wrote:

The subscript of my paper shows you that I am on the road. It is too early to go to bed, so I have got some paper from the postmaster to write to you on. How sad it is to be writing to you again, after having such a good long time together without needing that pis aller for exchanging our ideas. Our departure from Altaussee made me feel unusually melancholy and "lost". I don't know what I shall do now that I can no longer go to "The Market". That hour was the axis of the whole twenty-four. You don't know what you are to me. I am spellbound in your magic circle, and could not get free even if I would. How often today I wish that you were with me, on my lonely journey. It is a fine road through the Emstal, and wonderful sun and moon effects made it still more charming, as Frau Binzer would say. I took a stroll in the village where I lunched. A man came up as if to greet me, and as I looked at him in surprise and rather coldly, he excused himself: "I thought you were Herr Limberger." So known herewith that I have a double called Limberger. I should like to make his acquaintance.

Alex replied, thanking him for his letter. "I am counting the days until your return. In your absence, your letters provide me with much comfort and I look forward to your next correspondence which I hope will be soon. In the next few days, I will travel to Augsburg in the hopes of visiting with my children should their father permit it."

A letter from Chlodwig arrived almost a month later in October.

Forgive me, dear Alex, for breaking my promise. I got through my journey so quickly, and was so busy when I reached the end that I could not find a quiet moment in which to write to you. I have been back here some days, and I have had no letter from you in some time. I gather that you are in doubt as to my whereabouts. I passed through Munich on the very evening that you must have left it. I stayed only half-an-hour, and did not go beyond the hall of the railway station when one can see into the town. It was night and there was a thick fog in the streets. I looked at it very indifferently for I knew you were not there.

I can't say that I feel exactly in a rosy temper right now. I never am when long parted from you. I miss you as one misses the flowers in autumn, and now the sun and the warm promising airs of spring. I droop and grow bitter and sullen. But sometimes your face comes to me in a dream.

> *Even when comes the morning,*
> *It does not go away,*
> *So, in my heart I bear it,*
> *Through all the live-long day.*

That is just what has happened to me today and the dream has reminded me that it is my turn to write.

It was signed, *"Your faithful friend."*

He returned to Munich soon after his last letter. Once again, evenings were spent in conversation over politics as he happily shared his days in Parliament with her. He was a most capable public servant and happy to share his political views with Alexandrine as it was her opinion he greatly valued. And she admired him for his intellect and diplomacy in handling the most critical of matters.

On many of those evenings, his old friend Friedrich von Bodenstedt joined them for more lighthearted conversation and a game of cards. Friedrich, always happy to spend an evening with Alexandrine, could not refuse. When she entered the room during one of his visits, he thought it was as if the sun was rising over this lovely creature. Worshiping her was enough for him without the encumbrances of a love affair. Now having been the instrument of Chlodwig's attraction to her, he rued over his reluctance to make her his as he had obviously wanted to do. Being invited to spend evenings with her, even with his friend by her side, gave him some reward for years of his devotion to her.

Bodenstedt thought of himself as a lover of all women. Although his love interests before were somewhat lighthearted affairs with actresses and sometimes aristocratic ladies who were oftentimes married, he did not commit himself to any. He was more interested in showering them with his charm rather than hoping for any domestic happiness by tying himself to any one woman. To him, Alexandrine was quite different. She could steal his heart without any measure on his part.

More days at Schillingsfürst followed. Whenever she arrived, she asked if the princess would arrive again, teasing Chlodwig about the first time she visited his castle. She would then break out in laughter. He thought her laughter was the happiest of all sounds and did not mind her teasing. He would assure her there was no chance of an early arrival by the princess, who was well entrenched at her estate in Mir.

The elegant charm of the princely castle suited Alexandrine. The open windows in spring brought in the lovely scents of the garden. There were walks in the forest and rides in the pony cart or on horseback. They would often ride early in the morning. Alexandrine's penchant for riding dangerously continued to anger him. She would spur the horse to a gallop, her hair ribbons flying in the wind. He, finally catching up with her, did not slow her horse. She sped through the forest until, in one quick moment, a deer leaped from behind the trees in front of Alexandrine's horse. The horse shied and reared. As an experienced rider, she maintained her control and steadied the horse. When he caught up with her again, he was red with fury. They both alighted from their mounts. He was still shaking from the chase when he led her to a small clearing under a large black walnut tree, where they sank into the grass.

Chlodwig clung to her. In a quivering voice, he said, "What would I do without you? I would turn to dust. I could not live without you for even a moment in time."

Her face was shadowed by the overhanging branches, and yet he could still see her eyes sparkling from the excitement of her wild ride. Slowly her eyes took on a softer gaze, speaking silently of her love for him. As their lips touched, a tide of joy enveloped them both. At that moment, they knew that their deepening love for each other could not be doubted. Alexandrine felt as though she was in an enchanted dream in the arms of this most dear man. Her mind ceased to function as all her sensations floated on a buoyant cloud of happiness with his every touch. The intensity of their passion at that moment surprised them both.

22

A Prince Is Born

It was not long afterward that Alexandrine discovered she was to become a mother. Her delight at having Chlodwig's child binding them together even more was her most secret dream. She would at last have a child no one could take from her. Even Hermann was no longer hers as he spent most of the time with the Scheffers. After consulting her physician, she was assured she was healthy and would have no problems with her pregnancy. However, a greater problem presented itself. She was no longer able to hide the signs of pregnancy. Her face became rounder; her skin was no longer pure as porcelain. She was needing to have fuller dresses made to hide her ever-increasing roundness.

During her time in Munich, Alexandrine became known to a Frau Eckl, who had a haughty, proud face with high cheekbones and a straight, sharp nose. Alexandrine found her plain but, in some strange way, fascinating. They became friends. One day while visiting her friend, she advised Alexandrine to leave Munich as the gossip her pregnancy would invoke among the Munich elite would be disastrous to her and to the reputation of the well-known president-minister. Chlodwig agreed and soon thereafter took her to Thüringen, where Frau Eckl had secured a place for Alexandrine to stay until the baby was born. Her friend offered to stay there with Alexandrine until the birth. Not wanting to offend her friend, Alexandrine agreed.

Seeing the little house that her friend had secured shocked Alexandrine. To her, it was a horrid little place. Almost primitive. The furnishings were crude and not well made, the floors barren; little ornamentation existed, if any. Pulling aside the shabby coverings of the dull and dirty windows, she could see only more squalid houses like the one she was living in. Alexandrine thought she could not endure staying in this place, but there was nothing else to be done.

Alexandrine wrote to Chlodwig frequently over the next weeks lamenting over the place she was destined to live until their precious child was born. He wrote, "I cannot tell you how painful it is to me to know that my dear sweet Alex is in that uncomfortable place or how I count the days until you are emancipated therefrom and there was nothing to be done and nothing better to be found. But it is a great defect in our social system that better arrangements are not made for such eventualities."

Alexandrine had by then convinced herself that Frau Eckl had acted with good sense as remaining in Munich would have brought about unpleasant gossip. She accepted her situation because any gossip against her morality that found its way to her children would ultimately harm them. But could her friend not have found better lodgings?

An event took place during her confinement that caused both Alexandrine and Chlodwig to enter into illogical arguments. One day, Frau Eckl visited Chlodwig in Munich. He was staying with Bodenstedt at the time. How she found him he did not know, but he found it interesting that she could. She and Chlodwig spoke only briefly, the subject of which was how much she cared for Alexandrine's welfare. He thanked her most sincerely for her good friendship, whereupon she left.

When Alexandrine found out about the visit, it angered her greatly. It conjured up evil thoughts in her. Although she had already accepted her situation, she still had not forgiven her friend for bringing her to this wretched place. She thought of it as nothing short of treachery. And then the total affront of visiting the prince during her absence and being told it was just to "talk with him." In her anger toward Eckl, she conjured up all the hatred and sinister reasons she could as to why the woman visited him. She heaped them on Chlodwig in all her fury.

After her hysterical outburst over the "beastly Eckl," she received his letter, which he wrote in haste to explain that it is reasonable for the "hot tempered creature" she is to act this way. But applying a little reason would be desirable.

"Are you jealous?" he asked when he saw her soon afterward. He went on. "You need not be. There is no one on this earth that would take me from you. It is you I love most sincerely, and if you are so inclined to worry, then do not. It is not in me to betray you."

He, in his infinite goodness and understanding, forgave her for her jealousy. He knew well her passionate nature and that all this vehemence against Frau Eckl would soon disappear. She had once been a friend with whom she spent many days talking over coffee and cake. She knew Alexandrine's innermost secrets as well as her fears. But after what Alexandrine thought was a betrayal, she would no longer call her a friend. As a result, she proceeded to call her Frau *Ekelhaft* as the word in German means "Mrs. Loathsome."

The child, loved so much while in her womb, was born in that miserable house. A secret pleasure welled up in Alexandrine, not in her mind but from some deeper place. When this golden child, a son, arrived, it was as if the sun finally shone again upon her heart. This child, his child and hers, would compensate for all the misery she endured of late at the hands of Frau Eckl. At the time, Chlodwig was in between journeys to Berlin but hurried to Thüringen to hold his little son in his arms. He welcomed him with utter delight.

She was not yet fit to travel so stayed on in that squalid little house that she had to call home these past months. But she was happier now than she had been in months. She had their son in her arms and at her breast.

This was a particularly busy time for Chlodwig. As minister-president of Bavaria, long sessions of endless meetings awaited him when he returned from his short visits with Alexandrine and his son. He was taxed to the limits of his strength and endurance in endless days in Parliament and travels to Berlin. He managed to tear himself away to visit them, each time more tired than the last. After every short visit, he tore himself away with a heavy heart and tears in his eyes as he bent over the sleeping child to kiss him goodbye.

The day finally arrived when the doctor released Alexandrine from her "prison." Her heart overflowed with happiness as all her wishes had come true. The noblest of all men loved her, and she had a child of his. There could be no greater gift. Before the birth of their son, they both agreed that the child should remain in the country away from the smog and noise of the city. He pleaded with her to take him to a place where there were people to lovingly care for him and whom she absolutely trusted with his child. He also asked the doctor to give her absolute precautionary instructions to care for herself during the journey. The doctor also expressed his concern as he knew well Alexandrine's impetuous nature, which, even in her confinement, could not find rest.

Fate once more laid an ugly hand upon Alexandrine. The child did not live long. This baby so longed for, so loved and cherished as the unbreakable bond between her and the man she loved, lay before her white and limp. When their son, her joy, was buried, her grief plunged her into such depth of misery, from which she thought she would never return. Even Chlodwig was not there with his sweetness and love to comfort her. He was at Schillingfürst and had not received the news before Alexandrine returned to Munich. As soon as he heard, he rushed to her side. It was at great sacrifice of time and energy that he could manage to see her even for a short time. Nevertheless, she was happy to hear his dear voice and feel his arms around her until his duty called him away again.

While away, he wrote endearing letters to her, but they did not give her solace. Her state of mind did not improve. Being kindred spirits, they often knew each other's thoughts and feelings, no more so than they did now. The more she withdrew into herself, the more he wrote to show his devotion to her. He knew well the pain of losing a child. The loss of his son Albert had cast a shadow over him that lived on in his fragile heart. And now another son was lost.

In June, a short time after their little son died, he wrote:

Although you have only just received a letter from me,

I cannot help writing to you again. I know that you are doubly alone now and have no-one to tell your grief to. So, I want at least to show you that I am with you in spirit. That I am always thinking of you and caring for you. I am afraid you are not well for you do not write to me and in your last letter you said "more tomorrow". I think it is very natural that you should not have the energy to want to write and I do not ask you to weary yourself by doing so. If I could have you here in this solitary tranquility, cherish you and amuse you, you would soon be comforted and restored.

I understand so thoroughly what you must be feeling. For months you have lived on the thought of our child and you have suffered for it and cherished it. Now all the world of dreams and hopes are gone. Such a thing is hard to bear. The thought of you in pain follows me all day and I count the hours impatiently until I can be with you again. In the meanwhile, I kiss you in my imagination more lovingly ever more than usual.

It was signed, *"Your truest friend."*

23

Princess Elisabeth Clothilde Gisela

During the summer months, when Munich smelled of sweaty horses and rancid garbage, Alexandrine and Chlodwig again spent a few short days, as his duties allowed, in the cool mountains of Altaussee.

Not long after another summer there, Alexandrine told Chlodwig the joyful news. She was pregnant again with another child. This time, she stayed in Munich but away from the eyes of gossipers. Their daughter, whom they named Elisabeth Clothilde Gisela, was born on February 28,1870, in Munich. When they spoke of her, they preferred to call her Gisela or Gisa. She would be their last child as Alexandrine was now thirty-seven years of age. Gisela was frail and unhealthy at birth, which gave Alexandrine much cause to worry after losing her dear son not long before. Because of the child's frailty, Chlodwig decided to take Gisela and Alexandrine away from the unhealthy, smoke-filled air of the city to Pasing, where his precious daughter would surely thrive in the fields and meadows of the countryside. Once Gisela's health improved, they both decided that she would remain there until she reached school age. Gisela did indeed thrive under the constant attention of her mother, who found maternal devotion to this child her most fervent desire.

Gisela was full of sweetness, unlike her family ancestors the Heespen Cossacks but more like her father's more restrained and refined nature. She blossomed into an exquisitely beautiful child with a radiant, loving nature. Chlodwig worshiped his daughter with ever-renewing fascination when this dear golden-haired child looked up at him with her brilliant blue eyes. When he came to visit, she would rush to him, and his heart filled with love for her.

He would say, "When this sweet child rushes to me, with all joy and welcome, I feel the freshness of my youth return." Gisela learned quickly the power she had over her father and how irresistible she was with her sweet words and laughter.

His additional duties as the minister of the Royal House and of Foreign Affairs took him farther and farther away. He had spent the past two years back and forth between Berlin and Munich advising on the North German Confederation. In the next four years, measures needed to be consolidated such as the free movement of citizens within the territory of the confederation, a common postal system, common passports, equal rights for the different religious denominations, a unified measures and weights system, and a penal code. Throughout that period, Chlodwig relied on Alexandrine as an observer, private "diplomat," and counselor in his political sphere. She was proud of his political ambitions and his feel for politics and was happy to become a part of it.

During those years, he was seldom in Munich as his travels to other countries became more frequent. When he finally was able to come to Munich, he was totally exhausted. Alexandrine sat with him, stroking his forehead to relieve his worry lines. He soon fell asleep. Not wanting to wake him from that restful slumber, Alexandrine slid out from under his arms, covered him with a light blanket, and then went upstairs to her own bed.

With his frequent trips away, Alexandrine's feminine heart was forming illogical jealousies. He was universally admired by women and sometimes aggressively pursued. While he was away, he often wrote about meetings with women of his acquaintance. In one letter, he wrote, "There are no women here with red hair so you can be at peace about that!" She knew he admired women with red hair. Had he not been drawn to her for her auburn hair?

One night, she had a dream that he was in a room full of beautiful women whose hair was dyed red with her blood. She wrote a poem about her dream and sent it to him, which caused him to fall over with laughter. He told her later that his amusement was one of the most beautiful moments in an otherwise dreary time as he was on endless journeys back and forth to Germany and France. She titled the poem "The Dream":

> *I saw you today*
> *In a golden hall,*
> *With your cheerful laughter*
> *At a festive ball.*

Alexandrine

And saw standing around you
I don't know what I said,
All too many women all,
With hair so long and red.

You looked at her, a look that
Plunged into my heart.
I heard you say something
And in my dream cried out.

Oh, talk no more of that,
Look now at her hair,
It becomes even redder
As my heart's blood adheres there.

But even as he scolded Alexandrine for her untoward jealousy, he himself was not entirely exempt from this weakness.

That same blind confidence in each other was tested and proven safe much later when she had a long acquaintance with the Swiss poet Heinrich Leuthold.

24

An Ardent Poet

*H*einrich Leuthold was a renowned poet from Switzerland who studied law in Zurich and Basel before moving to Munich in 1857. There, he joined the poets' society *Die Krokodile* (The Crocodile). Although considered critical in his manner by other poets whom he alienated, he nevertheless was considered an endowed genius in Munich's literary circles. He published a number of poems throughout his short fifty-two years.

During the time Alexandrine lived at Karlstrasse, Leuthold lived in the vicinity and, having seen her many times, tried desperately to meet her. The elusive Alexandrine successfully evaded him until one eventful evening when they found themselves together with other writers and poets at a mutual friend's house. During the evening, there were lively conversations until Alexandrine's name was mentioned by a group of guests, which included Leuthold. Baroness von Gratz, a friend of Alexandrine who happened to pass by, overheard an unfavorable remark made about Alexandrine by Leuthold. The baroness quickly reported the insulting remark to her.

Alexandrine, outraged by this, called on Baroness von Gratz to invite Leuthold to come to her house on the pretense of another evening of poetry. Unbeknown to Leuthold, Alexandrine would be there waiting for him. Upon seeing Leuthold, she asked him with vehemence, "What right gives you permission to assault me in this way?"

He could see the blood boiling in her eyes. With a devilish smile on his face, he said, "Baroness, that was the only way I could meet you."

Still seething, Alexandrine answered, "You poets have a peculiar way to attain someone's friendship."

When he looked at her with the most mournful eyes after her retort, she lost her anger toward him. He stayed until late in the evening, reading more of his poetry and then parts from his newest epic poem, *Penthesilea*. Alexandrine could not help herself as she became increasingly enchanted with this poet. His pale face took on a new life when Alexandrine looked at him. And she suddenly fell into his poet's world. It was from that day forward he knew they would become friends.

That night was, for him, the start of pain and loss for loving Alexandrine while she kept her distance. She could not quite find in herself any love for this broken poet, while he adored her youthfulness and spark for life. His poem *Lenzlied* (*Spring Song*) brings to light a gaiety in his heart and the love he felt for her:

> *Timid hopes and sweet illusions,*
> *Gently stir within my soul*
> *Wild, long-hidden dear delusions,*
> *Seem to break from my control;*
> *Is it a tear so softly flowing?*

Or a song that strives to say . . .
It is your lot in radiance and perfume
Your happiness to have.[7]

Alexandrine, ever cautious to preserve her relationship with Chlodwig, would not commit to Leuthold anything but a friendship. Over the next weeks, Leuthold would often come uninvited for dinner at her house and then spend the evening with her. The evenings became later and later as he would not easily leave until he made his feelings clear to her. He often overwhelmed her with his devotion, which he could not hold back.

On one particular evening, she talked about Catholicism, which to her was of burgeoning interest. When she spoke of the Catholic Church, he became so agitated that his face reddened and his eyes rolled to the back of his head. It was believed he had a brain hemorrhage. Seeing the pain he was suffering and believing it was her fault, Alexandrine took him into one of the guest rooms and put him to bed to nurse the sick Leuthold well again. From that day on, he remained in her house as he refused to leave even when he felt well again.

The gossip in Munich flourished again with great vigor over this new development in the house on Karlstrasse. The Munich historian Karl Alexander von Müller wrote about her fanning the flames of gossip, calling her "Leuthold's Penthesilia." When Alexandrine took him out in a carriage for fresh air around the streets of Munich, looking quite well and obviously happy to be in her company, the gossip exploded. Chlodwig, too, showed his disagreement concerning Leuthold living in her house. In the letters he wrote to her, he expressed his

---

7   Transcribed by the author from a poem by Heinrich Leuthold.

feelings of jealousy. She reassured him that there was nothing to it. "Leuthold is sickly and wretched. I only mean to make him better. You have no reason to concern yourself with him as he is only a friend and no more," she wrote him. She was so convincing that he believed the jealous feelings he had were foolish and wrong. With that, Chlodwig, in his goodness and trust, understood there was nothing more to it than a friendship. He would say no more.

However, Leuthold was not inclined to think of only friendship where Alexandrine was concerned. He continued to overwhelm her with his pronouncements of love in person and in his poems. Somewhat healthier, he still refused to move out of her house. When she was not there, he wandered around the home like a lost soul, uttering, "But in vain is all my calling, and listen too in vain echoes only to give me answers."

After what seemed to Chlodwig long enough for Leuthold to recover from whatever malady caused him his pain, he urged Alexandrine to look for another home for the poet. He had reached his limit of patience with Leuthold living in her house. After much convincing and cajoling, she finally persuaded the pitiful, love-stricken Leuthold to move out of her home. It was there, alone in his new dwelling, that he fell into total disintegration. He wrote constant letters to Alexandrine lamenting his life. In one of these, he ended with, "I carry in me a song that was begun—but just as it was most sweetly sounding, it broke off in a shrill dissonance. Now it is too late—I shall not find its close—I have missed the song of my life."

In spite of Chlodwig's indifference to him, Leuthold had an admiration for him as a statesman. On the prince's birthday, March 31, 1876, he wrote a poem in his honor entitled "To

Prince Chlodwig von Hohenlohe." With the poem, he sent a
laurel wreath.

> *I feel right well, the while the crown I twine*
> *Of laurel round the brow so garlanded,*
> *How deep the country's gratitude, and mine,*
> *How poor, how vain this offering, how dead,*
> *How all unworthy of the man who checks,*
> *Gazing into the face of times to be,*
> *The pages of their history, and decks*
> *The times that are with leaves from this same tree.*

In June of 1877, he wrote another letter to Alexandrine in
Paris, where she was with Chlodwig at the time. It filled her
heart with compassion:

> *Dear Alex, every day I have intended to answer your*
> *letter, but I could not through inward agitation. All my*
> *friends think that you have given up on me, but I believe*
> *inviolably in your affection for me, and in your fidelity. To*
> *myself I am a martyr, and live like an anchorite—lonely*
> *and forsaken, while you are yielding yourself to another*
> *in love.*
>
> *I had no idea how terribly this involuntary abnega-*
> *tion on my part would affect my state of mind. You talk*
> *of material sacrifices made by you; I count them as small*
> *compared with the agony of soul which I feel at your giv-*
> *ing your incomparable charms exclusive to another. But*
> *still I trust in your word, and hope that I shall again caress*
> *and kiss your fair and generous hand.*
>
> *What made you speak of the ideas of your son Her-*

mann, as if I had quite forgotten you and how can you doubt my silence? Since your departure, I have never spoken your name to a stranger; only once did one of my friends put a question concerning you. I was silent, but the tears came into my eyes. He apologized and did not press for an answer.

Day and night I think of you alone, and never, never has a man loved you as I have loved you. I only fear that I may go crazy before I see you again. The silly verse is always surging in my ears:

> *You dear, sweet, loving heart*
> *Forgive me my deep smart.*

I am unhappy and feel quite ill. I eat only once a day and then very little. Everything is costly and I seem to need more money than I thought I did. Life without you is nothing but misery. I must see you soon again or I die.

Your unhappy, Heinrich

After reading the letter from Leuthold, Alexandrine wanted to go immediately to his side and comfort him in his pain. "My dearest, men don't go mad or die for love," Chlodwig said. Alexandrine stayed in Paris a few more weeks when a letter arrived from her son, Hermann, telling her the frightful news that Leuthold actually had become insane. She left immediately for Munich. She was too late. In July 1877, Leuthold was already in an asylum.

She found him in a straitjacket. Out of her goodness of heart, she sat with him every day for hours at a time. He, like a child, listened to her consoling words, saying nothing. Only a few times during her visits was his brain clear enough to say a few words. Alexandrine, unable to see him in this place and in such a condition, took her friend out of the asylum and back to her house with the thought of restoring him to good health. There seemed to be no improvement as his periods of lucidity were few and far between, and to compound it, his deliriums were more frequent.

Distraught over the eventuality of not being able to restore him to good health, Alexandrine took him to Zurich, his home city, and placed him in the care of doctors at Burghölzli Asylum. It was a sorrowful journey to Switzerland, dark and melancholy. After leaving him in the care of the doctors, she took the train back to Munich. During the trip, she had nothing cheerful to sustain her. She found everything unbearable. Over the following year, the doctors at the asylum kept her informed of his condition, which sadly was not improving and was becoming worse.

Sensing Alexandrine's suffering after hearing the condition of her friend Leuthold worsen, Chlodwig bade her to go see her sick "Achilles." In June of 1879, she arrived in Zurich. She was surprised to see that he recognized her but had no remembrance of her name. He cried as a child when he saw her and said, "Now that I have seen you again, I am glad to die."

She returned to Munich saddened but happy to know her visit had gladdened him. A telegram was waiting for her. Leuthold had died. In the years following his wretched demise, she often wondered if his love for her, which she did not return, led to his suffering and eventual death.

In all the years caring for her friend, she never held anything back from Chlodwig. He knew of Leuthold's love for her. She shared his letters and poems with him. He knew of her devotion to him both spiritually and financially. Because of Chlodwig's absolute trust in her, he did not have the least suspicion that her feelings for her friend were anything other than a true friendship.

Their relationship only strengthened as he admired her for her truthfulness. His was a generous soul, and she could do nothing to damage it even when another came into her circle with a burning passion for her. Against her will and without any response from her, this suitor pursued her with all the means he could devise. She closed her door to him, but he turned up unexpectedly in other places. Not finding her available to him, he wrote letters of his undying love for her. His letters were full of insanity:

> *I must write to you once more, and I will force you to hear me. I ask you this: If you do not love me, why do you come to me in dreams every night and whisper such strangely maddening things in my ear? Your image is gradually draining my life blood, and usurping every motion of my brain. Aye, defend yourself, struggle and fight with me—but then let your weary head rest on my shoulder.*

And so forth.

Chlodwig could not save her from his insanity, so she took matters into her own hands to end her persecution. She handed all the letters from him to Father Obercamp, even though it grieved her to do so. She did not want to ruin this man's life, for he had committed no crime but to burden her with his love.

When she saw Chlodwig again, she confessed to him all that had happened. In him, she found a generous soul with indulgence and understanding. Alexandrine felt that he clothed her with qualities that were only a reflection of his own. She was not so inclined as he was to turn away from her jealous nature.

Despite their limitless love for each other, despite the warm friendship, doubt and unreasonable jealousy were things Alexandrine could not control within herself. When, on one of his journeys, he encountered a certain countess whose objective was to be courted by Chlodwig for the sole purpose of linking her name with his, he in his truthfulness told Alexandrine. He explained to her there were no grounds for jealousy as he was the object of gossip by the unnamed countess, who conspired against him. He was only the scapegoat. Alexandrine, with a true woman's heart, could not be solaced by his consoling words mingled with kisses. She was sure that the sun would only shine a short while until the next time.

25

War

$\mathcal{F}$inding his days beyond his endurance to continue at such a pace, Chlodwig made the decision to petition King Ludwig to release him from his additional duty as foreign minister. He sent a resignation to the king. Not receiving an answer, he went to the palace, where the king received him cordially. The king told him that he regretted the current state of affairs and that it had come to this. Ludwig protested that he wished to act constitutionally but stopped at the point that his resignation was a weak surrender. After more discussion about constitutionalism, absolute monarchy, and such, he asked if Chlodwig would temporarily continue to conduct the business of his office. Chlodwig agreed as he admired King Ludwig and was sure he would still, at some later date, grant the petition. He often told his friends that his opinion of Ludwig was that he was the most amiable and engaging sovereign. He was not only courteous but also kindhearted.

Chlodwig continued to request his release from his duties, trusting Ludwig explicitly. But when several months went by and more petitions were sent to the king and denied, he felt strongly that he would never be released from his position as foreign minister. Finally, his long sought-after letter arrived on March 7, 1870.

> *My dear Prince—You have repeatedly petitioned me to relieve you of your duties as Minister of the Royal House and of Foreign Affairs. After careful investigation of the circumstances, I have assented to your request today in consequence of the personal motives you have adduced. In making this explanation to you I feel myself bound to express to you from the bottom of my heart my appreciation of the self-sacrificing devotion and unfailing loyalty which have marked your tenure of office. To give tangible expression to this appreciation I have included you, my dear Prince, in the roll of Capitularies of my knightly order of St. Hubertus.*
>
> *In the renewed assurance of my good wishes, I remain, ever*
>
> *Your affectionate King Ludwig.*[8]

When the letter arrived, Chlodwig read it to Alexandrine, who was delighted as she knew how much he wanted to be released from his position as minister of fowreign affairs. She smiled happily at him and said, "This is good news, my friend, as this has bankrupted your good nature and sensibilities for so many years. At last, the king has bestowed upon you his appreciation for all you have done for Germany and the sacrifices you've made." She could see the stress and strain leave

---

8   William Heinemann, *Memoirs of Prince Chlodwig of Hohenlohe-Schillingsfürst*, Vol. 2 (Friedrich Curtius: London, 1906).

his body. That evening, they sat quietly, each in their own thoughts.

It did not last. The Bavarian Upper Chamber of the House was in deliberation as the outbreak of war with France was imminent. A bill was introduced in case war should prove unavoidable. An immediate and extraordinary vote of credit of 5,600,000 gulden was provided for the fitting out of the army. An increased budget needed to be approved for the upkeep of the war. The bill was passed unanimously but not without criticism of its legitimacy.

Chlodwig confided in Alexandrine that afternoon. "The bill passed one hundred and one to forty-seven. The day after, the House met in a secret session. It was decided at that session to pass the bill in the public sitting but without discussion. The bill was then passed unanimously. I asked if I could speak as I had been silent too long."

"Did you speak?" she asked.

"No, I only asked if I *could*. The problem is that I need only to raise my finger, and I would be made foreign minister again. I let that go. I should not like to be the one to bear the responsibility for what will happen to Bavaria in the next few months."

"Of course, Chlodwig, you are right," she said. "You need no more burdens."

"As it turned out, I thank God that the bill was accepted. Had neutrality been decided on instead of a war vote, the entire Cabinet would have resigned. I would have most certainly been called upon to form a new Ministry. This would have been a dangerous time because, if the French were victorious, I would have been in the company of all those who wanted war, and I would be driven out in disgrace. I will go to Schillingsfürst for a few days before I return to the House. It seems rumors are increasing of the threatening attitude of Austria, which will have to be dealt with when I return."

Alexandrine listened to him with full attention and was somewhat fearful, not so much of a war with France but with worry over Chlodwig's state of mind.

He returned within a week. Alexandrine asked, "How was your visit to Schillingfürst?"

He answered, "On my way, I saw many soldiers on the road. The peasants are very vocal, saying that the only way to have rest is to have war. Their hatred for Napoleon is great. A parson is said to have had his ears boxed by a noncommissioned officer and then to have been arrested. A notice has been posted that such incitement will be treated by military law and punished with death."

Alexandrine's face took on the look of horror as she said, "Are things so bad in the country that people have to fear being sentenced to death for their beliefs?"

"It appears so, but the threat has restrained some of those who would incite."

"What is Prussia's position on the war?" Alexandrine asked.

"I had occasion to meet with the crown prince, whose first words to me were 'you were right,' though I did not know to what he was referring. It appears it was with regard to a conversation I had with him, at which time I had expressed fears of the warlike intentions of France."

"And what did the crown prince say to that?" she asked.

"Only that the French emperor is blind to think he can

win a war. Even if we were victorious, we could gain little since it is not possible to determine in what way affairs in France would have to be shaped to ensure a lasting peace."

"And Austria? How does it fit into the plan?"

"The crown prince is hopeful Austria will remain neutral. The Austrians fear that as a consequence of this war, Germany should unite, and their German providences would gravitate toward Germany. If that happens, Austria's composition might be endangered."

On July 19, 1870, war broke out.

Chlodwig, back in Munich, noticed that inside the waiting rooms of the train station, there was a troop of men in mufti and military caps. At first, he thought they were recruits, but they happened to be ambulance men off to the front. He realized these men were known to him from the city. They were men of all classes who had an irresistible desire to take part in the war.

German forces fought and defeated the French armies in northern France. The war ended on January 28, 1871. The French were no match for the superior trained army and weaponry of the Germans. During the waning days of the war, the German states proclaimed their union as the German Empire under Wilhelm I and Chancellor von Bismarck, with the notable exception of Austria. Wilhelm I was now emperor of the German Empire. For the first time in history, the Germans were united under a nation state. Following unification, Germany became one of the most powerful nations in Europe.

Chlodwig was pleased.

26

Seven Years in Paris

Two years after the end of the war with France, Chlodwig was appointed by Bismarck as German ambassador to Paris. He was to stay in Paris under the direction of Emperor Wilhelm I of Prussia until 1880. A farewell audience was held with the emperor even though Bismarck already gave him his instructions. The emperor expressly emphasized his desire to keep on the best terms possible with France, saying that France should not be too strong but a desirable ally. The meeting ended with the emperor thanking Prince Chlodwig for the sacrifices he would be making by going to Paris.

He reassured the king, saying, "Your Royal Highness, there is no sacrifice on my part that is too great if it serves you."

Later, Chlodwig told Alexandrine of this meeting with the emperor. "It was a very good meeting, and Wilhelm and Bismarck both expressed how important it is to keep France in check without a strong hold on her. He wishes me to ensure that France remains an ally to Prussia."

"I'm sure the emperor has full confidence in you by making you ambassador."

"I believe he does. I am honored that he thinks so," he said.

The next few weeks were taken up by constant meetings with Bismarck and Emperor Wilhelm I in preparation for the best ways for Germany to mend its postwar relations with France. Bismarck's view was that Chlodwig, as German ambassador, would make his objective to reign in Patrice de MacMahon, the elected president of the republic, who, as a staunch Catholic conservative, gained the legitimist sympathies. Chlodwig had one last duty to perform. At a farewell banquet thrown by the Imperial Party, he addressed his resignation from his position in the German Reichstag.

He said, "Gentlemen, I have the opportunity today to express to you how painfully moved I am at the thought that I must now take leave of an assembly in which consideration and respect have been shown me in a measure which is quite disproportionate to my contribution. You give me the opportunity of saying how highly honored I feel to have belonged to an assembly that was summoned to establish the principles of Germany unity."

That evening, he visited Alexandrine and told her of his resignation speech. "I feel flattered by the expressions of their gratitude, but being a modest man, I cannot help that these words lose their luster in my remorseless self-criticism."

Alexandrine saw in him a look of despair and unhappiness and gently said, "You must not think all those who flatter you for all your work for Germany are not sincere. You have done great works and will always be remembered as the builder of a unified Germany. Let those feelings go, Chlodwig. You do not know your own worth."

"I must go immediately to establish myself in Paris. I want you and Gisela to accompany me. However, it would be best if

I go directly. I will send for you and Gisela in a month's time. I will make all the arrangements for your journey to Paris."

"Oh, Chlodwig, I have been longing to go to Paris. I will go to see and learn. But Gisela is still so young. She will miss the countryside and her nurses," Alexandrine lamented.

"Do not concern yourself, my dearest. Gisela will adapt very well, and when she is old enough, she will have a French tutor."

"Oh, you mean for her to become French? Is that what you propose?" Alexandrine said, a little disappointed in him that he would want that.

"Not at all, Alex. Gisela is German and always will be. You must know a French education is a desirable goal. When we return to Germany, she will have benefited from it and will continue her schooling in Pasing as originally planned."

The days went by quickly. By the time they parted, each was looking forward to what experiences would await them in France.

∼

As the train pulled into the Gare de l'Est train station, a brass band welcomed the new ambassador. After arriving in Paris, he went immediately to the German Embassy to meet with his staff. He was informed that his diplomatic attaché, Count von N, would arrive the next day from Berlin. Later, Chlodwig took a tour of the Hotel Beauharnais, a large French townhouse named after the mother of Napoleon III, which would be his official residence.

Since his arrival in Paris came shortly after Napoleon III's defeat in the Franco-Prussian War, he found that everything and everywhere in Paris could be ascribed to Napoleon III.

It did not surprise him as he had known of Napoleon's aspirations to restore Paris's medieval iconic buildings and structures in the aftermath of the French Revolution. After Napoleon III's death in England, the collapse of the Second French Empire was replaced with the Third French Republic, headed by Patrice de MacMahon. It was he with whom Chlodwig would spend much time during his stay in Paris to mend French and Prussian relations.

Alexandrine found the month in Munich useful as she placed Hermann in a school for young boys, paid her housekeeper and cook in advance for the time she would be away in Paris, and saw to her affairs as she knew she would be gone a length of time.

Chlodwig arranged to rent an entire train car for Alexandrine, Gisela, and their entourage. On the day of departure, eleven suitcases and trunks full of Alexandrine's clothing were packed for the seven-year-long stay in Paris. They boarded the train in Munich with a nurse and tutor for Gisela and Alexandrine's lady's maid, Maria. Together with all of their luggage, the entire train compartment was full. The train car glowed with rich oak paneling and seats upholstered in the finest velvet. It was going to be a pleasant journey through Germany and France. Gisela found endless amusements running from one compartment to another, often evading her nurse, to the woman's frustration. Gisela, this child so dear to her mother, was not reined in by her, to the vexation of the nurse.

After two days, the train arrived at the station, belching smoke and screeching, with the steel brakes skidding along the steel track, until it came to a stop near the platform. Chlodwig was waiting there in happy anticipation to see Alexandrine and his beloved daughter. After everything and everyone disembarked from the train, a waiting carriage would deliver Alexandrine, Gisela, the nurse, and the tutor to the chateau where they would live.

"I am so happy to see you, my dearest. And you, too, *mon petite chérie*. You will live here in complete privacy and away from prying eyes. My residence is not far away," he assured Alexandrine as he embraced them both.

When she arrived at the chateau, she was greeted by a staff of four. The cook, kitchen maid, and housemaid all dressed in black dresses, white aprons, and lace caps. The housekeeper welcomed Alexandrine and Gisela along with their little entourage.

"Welcome to Chateau Mirage. *Bienvenue, madame. Je suis Mme Prousey, la gouvernante. Je suis désolé mais je ne parle pas allemande,*" the housekeeper said as she extended her hand to Alexandrine.

In French, Alexandrine said, "Mrs. Prousey, I am happy to speak to you in French as it will give me an opportunity to perfect it while I am here. My daughter Gisela will be taking French lessons as well." With that, Mrs. Prousey smiled and invited them inside.

A few days after her arrival, and having recovered from the long journey to Paris, Alexandrine ventured into the city. There were sounds of workmen hammering and people bustling everywhere. Wide treelined boulevards, fountains, and buildings in blue, white, and pale orange lined the streets, each one more adorned than the next. There were fountains, statues in squares, great buildings with glass domes, shops filled with goods tempting the pocketbook, bakeries with confections that were works of art. Paris was particularly beautiful in the spring. As the carriage turned onto another street, another fantastic row of buildings appeared. At the end of one particularly long and beautiful boulevard, the Arc de Triomphe suddenly showed itself. The carriage passed through its arch driving down the Champ Elyseés to the Place de la Concorde and into the garden of the Louvre. At the end of the garden stood a grand building, which looked as though it was partially destroyed.

"What is this place?" Alexandrine asked.

The carriage driver said, "Here is where the great Tuileries Palace once stood. It was the former residence of all past French kings and emperors. It was burned and looted during the French Revolution. It has been renovated and restored but was burned again in 1871. What remains is only part of the great palace. It will never again be what it was. Today, it is used as the embassy of the Prussian Empire."

This is where Chlodwig will spend his days, she thought to herself.

Everywhere she looked there was splendor: the many gardens, buildings with gilded domes, cathedrals, and the palace. There was a vibrancy there with people strolling down the boulevards, carriages rattling over rough stone streets, and hawkers selling their wares.

Their tour continued to the banks of the Seine, where artists gathered on the bridges with their paints and brushes to paint *plein* air. Lovers strolled along the river, holding hands, kissing under the chestnut trees that lined the walkways. Women with the most enormous hats decorated with ribbons, flowers, and feathers strolled by, holding on to the arms of elegantly dressed men in top hats. The spring air welcomed everyone outdoors. Old people were young again; husbands and wives grew more affectionate with each other—and sometimes not with each other. It seemed as though everyone looked the other way where love was concerned. There were other places in the City of Light to which Alexandrine dared not go where there was a wider scope of relationships not conforming to moral standards.

Paris came to her as a revelation. She did not know much about Napoleon III or the Second Empire, but so far, she could see that among luxury, there was decadence and wickedness. And, in some areas of the city, poverty to the greatest extent.

On another tour through Paris, Alexandrine noticed soldiers everywhere, or, to her, it seemed so. They were dressed in brilliant uniforms—white breeches, gaiters, and tasseled hats—with huge rifles across their chests. Her guide told her, "Those men are not real soldiers as there is no longer a French Army. The Prussians killed them all. They only pretend to be soldiers and are not carrying real guns. We have no bullets." She sensed he was angry over the current situation in France without their beloved monarch. There was a large wound that had not yet healed.

It had only been three years since the surrender of France at their defeat by the Prussians. It was probably the most disastrous war in French history at a huge cost of lives. While France lost 150,000, either killed or wounded in the battles, Germany[9] lost 117,000. The cost to France was also staggering: five billion francs and the provinces of Alsace and Lorraine. The cost to the French people was even greater: starvation.

Only a few months after the defeat of the French government and the imprisonment of Napoleon III, an insurrection by a unit of workers and the French National Guard had seized

---

9   Germany, during this period, was the general term used for all the states of the North German Confederation which consisted of Prussia, and other German states. The southern German states joined in 1870. In 1871, this union of states became the German Empire.

cannons and fortified themselves on Montmartre. A force of army regulators was discharged to recover the cannons and crush the National Guard soldiers. This incident marked the beginning of the Paris Commune, which was now in charge of Paris. In the coming weeks, a siege of the current government took place. The Commune used force shelling the city, impeaching all members of government and confiscating properties. When the archbishop of Paris was arrested and jailed, the people were outraged. There were protests and marches by a group that called itself Friends of Order. They were unarmed and without incident until a group of National Guards stopped them. A volley of gunfire ensued.

The chaos continued with cannon shots growing heavier every day. The Commune looted the churches and denounced all priests. People left the city in droves with whatever they could carry. After tens of thousands fled, the Commune forbade able-bodied men to leave the city. The Paris Commune continued its destruction, ordering the demolition of the Vendôme Column in the Place Vendôme, which honored the victories of the French armies under Napoleon. Another decree was to burn the Louvre because it contained works of art celebrating gods, kings, and priests. This also included demolishing Notre-Dame.

More days of darkness and grief engulfed the city as the Communards continued their atrocities. The archbishop and six other prisoners were shot and dumped in an open ditch. In all, fifty-three other priests were murdered. After two months of terror under the Commune, the regular French Armed Forces under the command of Patrice de MacMahon and the Versailles government marched on Paris and defeated them. After what was called the Bloody Week, the Third Republic was formed. MacMahon was elected president of the republic by popular demand. A staunch Catholic conservative, he, over time, grew increasingly at odds with the French Parliament.

This is what the new German ambassador to Paris came to mend in 1873. It would not be an easy task. Not only did he need to use diplomacy in stabilizing a failing government, but the economic situation in France was in crisis.

27

Life in Paris

After Chlodwig assumed his new position, Paris society fell over each other to be the first to have the venerable Prince von Hohenlohe-Schillingsfürst on their guest list. The first invitation came from Duchesse de G. It was to be a ball in his honor. Of course, he could not decline the invitation from such a prominent Paris socialite. Even though *la noblesse française* was no longer recognized, persons of rank maintained their titles and enjoyed a certain status.

Alexandrine was not so delighted as he was because she did not want to be the subject of scandal so soon. Chlodwig offered his attaché from the embassy to accompany her instead. Her stay in Paris portended a different future for her than she had intended. Even though Chlodwig came frequently to see her and his dear child, he seldom stayed long, as his duties at the embassy repeatedly took him away with each ensuing crisis. He traveled frequently to Berlin to report to the emperor on matters of state. The most recent action by Russia to keep open the outlets from the Black Sea to the Mediterranean could lead to another war. If war did break out, it was the duty of Germany and France by common action, and the united power of their influence, to preserve peace in Europe and to localize the war. On one of those trips to Berlin, Chlodwig met with Bismarck, who had just handed in his resignation as chancellor. To Chlodwig's surprise, the emperor did not accept it. Instead, Bismarck was granted a leave for an indefinite period of time. Bismarck confessed he was not well as his rheumatism was getting worse, to the extent that he stayed in bed for several days at a time. At the same time, the French newspaper *Journal des Débats* confirmed Bismarck's resignation, which, of course, caused many a conversation around Paris.

The night of the first ball arrived. Lately, Alexandrine had the custom of wearing a simple, more form-fitting style of gown, in the latest Paris fashion. She preferred the newer design with its long, slim, body-hugging style that revealed a woman's natural figure. The style of these dresses was heavily decorated with ribbons, ruching, and lace trim. The most accommodating convention was the lack of a restrictive corset. Some women's clothing even took on the appearance of menswear with its emphasis on tailoring. Even men's clothing had changed by 1874, consisting of lounge suits for their slimness of style and narrow silhouette. Men started wearing three-piece suits for more casual attire. Instead of lace or ruffled neckwear, heavily starched collars on shirts, worn high and standing up with turned-down wingtips, were preferred.

Tonight, Alexandrine would wear one of her finest new Parisian dresses. Her maid had already cleaned and pressed it and then laid it out on the bed for her to admire. "Yes, that is perfect," she said to Marie. When Chlodwig saw her in this stunning dress, he was without words. He thought her beautiful beyond any other woman he'd ever seen. He presented her with a diamond necklace, which he fastened around her neck. Her hair, as usual, was braided and twisted around her head and embellished with flowers and ribbons. He whispered in her ear, "You are undoubtfully the greatest beauty in all of Paris."

The young attaché arrived wearing long tails, a white shirt with a high collar, and an ascot; he was holding his gloves, hat, and walking cane in one hand as he took Alexandrine's gloved hand and kissed it in greeting. She thought him to be quite handsome and was much relieved to spend the evening with him rather than some fat, drooling old man whose rheumy eyes looked her up and down with some wayward desire. The three of them left in a hired carriage for the short trip to Maison L' Fleur.

Arriving on a quiet street in Paris, the horses came to a halt at the carriage entrance behind several other carriages arriving at the same time. After a while, their carriage proceeded up to the graceful house built of stone, glass, and ironwork. The house sat between a courtyard and garden so large it seemed better suited for the countryside. They entered on the ground floor and were led up the grand staircase to the reception hall by a handsomely dressed footman.

Chlodwig entered first and was announced to the guests already assembled: "His Royal Highness, the German ambassador, Prince Chlodwig von Hohenlohe-Schillingsfürst." He was immediately set upon by the duchess and a group of men anxious to hear his political agenda for the new governing of France after the disastrous war with Prussia. The next announcement came: "His Highness, Count von N. and Baroness von Hedemann." As they walked in with her gloved hand poised ever so lightly on his arm, all eyes fell on Alexandrine. Floating into the room with the handsome count and in her stunning dress, which fell slightly off the shoulder, she had certainly, at that moment, made her mark on Paris society. Her hostess, clearly in her seventies, tall, slender, poised, and beautiful in a colorless sort of way, greeted her warmly.

She proceeded to introduce Alexandrine to a few of the other women guests, while the men huddled on the other side of the room in deep political talk, sometimes raising their voices in disagreement. Most of the conversations were about war and politics. She heard one of the men say, "The Conservative Party will rally and recover its ground." Another said, "The Conservatives must, in the first place, realize that they are in danger." The count quickly led her away from the group as he thought there was no need to hear their points of view. He brought her to another room, saying, "I have learned that French is the only language for polite conversation. One can talk all evening without saying anything."

Footmen circled the room with silver trays of chilled champagne, replacing every empty glass with a fresh one. By the time the orchestra started playing, Alexandrine felt the effects of the four glasses of champagne she had already drunk. She found an empty chair to take a moment. Looking around the room, she saw it was decorated in the most lavish style she had ever seen. There were Louis XIV gilded chairs covered in colorful velvet and ornately carved and gilded frames with life-size portraits, undoubtedly of bygone relatives. The buffet table was set with crisp white table linens, gold plates, and crystal glasses. All seemed to her beautiful but ostentatious. She compared it to the simpler, more austere Bavarian castles she had lived in with their heavy carved walnut furniture, battle armory displayed on the walls, and bare wooden floors. The table was laden with everything any guest could wish, from the finest Russian caviar to the freshest Atlantic cod, smoked salmon, and roast beef. Port and beer were also served. The French were of a different kind, desirous of a showy and gilded world with gluttonous appetites.

Guests were now gravitating to the ballroom for the first dance. As more people joined in, the orchestra played the *Suite de Danses,* which included the *allemande* and *gigue.* Throughout the evening, Alexandrine saw neither Chlodwig nor her young and handsome escort. But there was no shortage of offers from the other men there, young and old, for the favor of a dance. Her dance card was filled in the first hour. By the end of the evening, she was too tired for even one more dance and wished to go home. She could not find Chlodwig until he suddenly appeared behind her. A footman approached, and when she took the glass, she only pretended to drink it as she knew one more glass would definitely put her embarrassingly on the floor.

"Are you enjoying yourself?" he asked, taking her free hand in his to kiss. "I would gladly stay here with you, but I am missed by the moralizing clods in the next room," he whispered. Alexandrine laughed as he winked at her before he walked back to the smoke-filled salon.

The evening went well into the night, with some of the men off in other rooms for games of chance. There, she found her escort with only a few francs before him yet still betting for one last win. Chlodwig, not wishing to gamble, stood with a group of men discussing the results of the Franco-Prussian war. She heard voices raise whenever the word *Prussia* was spoken. One particular sour-faced man with a receding hairline, bushy side whiskers, and legs that bowed from years of riding was ranting how the French Army still had muzzle-loading guns, which were no match for the superior fire power of Prussian weapons, especially their Krupp's steel breach-loading cannons. "That's how France lost the war," he yelled. An argument then ensued.

"And now we're to unite with Prussia against the Russians. Absurd," another shouted.

"You are the absurd one, Viktor," another man chimed in. "The Russians are only waiting for the fine weather to strike the first blow. By that time, France will be a force to reckon with. *Vive la France*. We will return."

A chorus of voices shouted, *"Vive la France."*

Chlodwig, ever the diplomat, let the men air their views and did not engage. When Alexandrine approached him and whispered in his ear that she wished to leave, he did not try to persuade her to stay any longer at the soirée. He was happy to be rid of the bombastic gentlemen, leaving them to argue among themselves. He then sought out his young attaché, finding him in the game room sorely losing.

"You've had enough tonight, my friend. Your lady wishes to go home," he said a little forcefully over the protestations of the young man. In the end, the three of them left, sharing a carriage, and Alexandrine and Chlodwig were deposited at the chateau. That evening, he stayed the night with Alexandrine.

The next morning, they breakfasted on eggs, two kinds of bread, and a *petit pain*. Two silver pots, one for coffee and one for hot milk, were on the table. Alexandrine picked up the coffee pot and poured it into Chlodwig's cup and then her own. She remarked that the coffee had an exquisite flavor. However, she found German coffee more to her liking.

Alexandrine asked him if he had the opportunity to meet with Princess Pauline Metternich at last night's soirée.

"The Hungarian?" he asked.

"Yes, I believe so if she is the same Princess Pauline who is a patron of Richard Wagner."

"Why do you ask?

"I overheard some of the women talking about her," she replied.

"Well, then, I'm sure you heard more than you wished to hear," he said. "Tell me what they said of her."

"It was said she was a favorite of Empress Eugenie; that she had a somewhat colorful reputation; that she married her uncle, which made her grandfather also her father-in-law. I found that rather scandalous. Don't you?" she asked.

"My dear, that is not the half of it. Did they tell you about the duel?"

"No. Did someone duel over her?"

"Oh, no, much better than that. She challenged Countess Anastasia von Kielmannsegg to a sword duel. The two ladies stripped to the waist so as not to incur any infection should they be hurt. Or perhaps it was to save their dresses from the saber's edge. It was quite a scandal at the time. It is believed that the duel was over a disagreement supposedly stemming over a floral arrangement at the Vienna Musical and Theatre Exposition. Whether any of this is true is a matter of conjecture. She did, however, establish herself as a *femme de notoriété* in the Court of Napoleon. As a friend of Empress Eugenie, she attended every royal function as her guest. She was known to curse, smoke, and drink, all of which was overlooked by the empress but, unfortunately, not by others. She was generally disliked, but because of her high position within the court, she was protected and therefore not likely to be assailed for her bad manners."

Alexandrine asked what her relationship was with Richard Wagner. "I heard there was talk of her ambitions for Wagner in Paris. Evidently, she was much interested in art and music and wanted to influence Paris society to accept him. Is that true?" she asked him.

"That is true, of course, and she did," he answered. "However, because of her disfavor among the elite, they found an avenue through Wagner as a way to show their dislike for her. During his performances, the audience often hissed. So Wagner gained but also lost through his association with the princess. Berlioz, a contemporary of Wagner who admired him, said, 'The Parisian public is neither musical nor religious nor artistic; it merely wants to be amused.'"[10]

Alexandrine laughed as this is what she had thought all along of Parisian society.

Many more invitations to soireés followed. Most never lasted more than half an hour before their guests left for the next one until the evening was filled. Other times, they were invited to a dinner here, a ball there, or an evening of cards and conversations. It was a whirlwind of social events in what turned out to be the usual evenings for Paris society. After another round of parties, the season finally came to an end. Those who could left the city for the cooler, quieter countryside. Those who could not stayed in the sweltering heat and all the unpleasantness that comes with a city in the clutches of a steaming furnace.

Alexandrine stayed. There was little free time for Chlod-

---

10   Ernest Newman, *The Life of Wagner, Volume III* (Cassell and Company Ltd., 1945).

wig during his engagement in Paris. He was involved in endless meetings with other foreign ministers and trips to Berlin to report to Bismarck and Emperor Wilhelm. She saw little of him for weeks at a time. So she would not get bored, he assigned his attaché to chauffeur her around Paris to places she had not yet seen. On one of those outings, they spent the whole day at the Louvre standing in front of each painting, delighting in the finest art displayed there. The count thought himself quite an authority on art. Much as he annoyed Alexandrine with his constant chatter, she was very much in awe of his knowledge of the great masters.

After leaving the Louvre, he asked, "Who is your favorite artist?"

She thought about what she had seen that day. "Rembrandt and perhaps Rubens for his abounding love of the female figure. It was both pleasing and disturbing."

The count only laughed as he knew exactly what she meant.

On another outing, they visited the many parks in the city. The first park on their excursion was the one Napoleon III built and modeled after a visit to England's Hyde Park. Alexandrine, curious why Napoleon had built so many parks, asked the count, "Why would he undertake such a vast project?" The minute she asked, she regretted it as she knew he would expound on that subject until she nodded off with boredom. Nevertheless, she did not stop him.

With his vast knowledge of everything French, Count N explained to Alexandrine that Napoleon III spent years laying out plans for even larger parks—four in all at precise compass points around the city. For years, thousands of workers and gardeners were employed by the emperor to dig lakes, build water features and fountains, and plant lawns, flowerbeds, and trees. Within the parks would be chalets and grottos. They would be the envy of the world for their beauty and usefulness for the wealthiest of Paris to promenade, ride in open carriages around the many roads, or ride horseback through the woods. They became the center point in Paris to see and be seen.

"At least he gave work to those in need," she added.

Not wanting to stop there, the count continued. "The emperor, in addition to the four large parks, also refurbished and replanted the city's smaller parks. He then went to work planting twenty more parks and gardens so that every neighborhood in the city had one close by. One could be found less than a ten-minute walk from people's homes. The citizens of Paris praised him for these parks as it gave every class of people living in the city the opportunity to enjoy the 'flowering salons.' Napoleon in his later years was not only known for his parks but for social reforms he initiated for the working class."

"I know only a little about Napoleon III, but I believe he was a good emperor to the people," Alexandrine said.

"I believe he was," said the count. "Charles-Louis Napoleon Bonaparte III was the nephew of Napoleon Bonaparte I. A pamphlet written by Victor Hugo was widely circulated as a criticism of Napoleon III's rule and the Second French Empire. He called him 'Napoleon *le Petit.*' The name stuck. From the time he became emperor of France, Napoleon III spent much of his years until his death on efforts to restore Paris. During his entire reign, the city was under massive reconstruction. During his last years, he became ill and war-weary. The cost of rebuilding Paris, his lavish lifestyle, and wars depleted the coffers."

"Then why did he declare war on Prussia?" she asked.

"No one really understands what caused France to declare war on Prussia except that Otto von Bismarck, seeking German unification, somehow provoked France to declare war. France also wanted to reestablish its dominant position in Europe after the Prussian-Austrian war of 1866. He felt pressured by the people, so without allies and with inferior weapons and a weak military force, he made the greatest mistake in the summer of 1870 by declaring war on Prussia. Despite his declining health and because he was practically dying, Napoleon decided to go with the army to the front as commander in chief as he had done during the successful Italian campaign. The poorly disorganized French Army—outmanned, outnumbered, and facing superior logistics and leadership—was no match for the Prussian Army. The war was over in three months, and the emperor was a German prisoner of war. He died in exile in 1873. That is why there is now a Third Republic in France."

After listening to him talk, Alexandrine had a better understanding of why Chlodwig was appointed as ambassador of Paris. If he had been less of a politician, he would not have been selected by the emperor to go to Paris as Prussia's ambassador. At the time, the government in France was unstable. She knew he was the best choice to help stabilize the new regime. It was her understanding of the challenges of his position that influenced her decision to find her own course while in Paris so as not to interfere with his.

"Here, life is to be enjoyed, to savor life," Chlodwig often said. Alexandrine agreed with him, so she continued spending her days with the count.

He continued to call on Alexandrine to take her on tours of the city. There seemed to be no end of things to see around the city. One place he did not show her was the Left Bank, where the beggars were. He spared her from seeing the pitiful men without arms or legs squatting on the streets with a cap in their hands, begging for a franc or two, and the old women in tattered clothing with no one to support them, hoping for some change. He impressed upon her that Paris should be enjoyed with simple things like walks in the gardens or strolls down its broad avenues.

While Alexandrine spent most of her days touring the city, Chlodwig was facing major challenges. The French, still wounded by their loss to Prussia in the Franco-Prussian War, held many grudges against Prussia. France losing Alsace-Loraine to Germany was a major blow. Germany still saw France as the enemy, and Bismarck's solution was for Germany to form strong alliances with Austria, Russia, and Britain to keep France isolated diplomatically. Bismarck often expounded on what he called "iron and blood" to achieve his goals. Chlodwig was not always in agreement with Bismarck. He tried his best to keep the German-Prussian relationship on an even keel.

Chlodwig continued to confide in Alexandrine. He was inspired by her insight and advice. He asked her, "What do I do with unintelligent people who cannot express themselves? Must I be their psychologist? How do I retain my own character in the presence of a fool?"

She could tell he was under enormous stress over the recent political climate of France. The strain showed on his face and in his demeanor. She pleaded with him to find some relief from his duties. She could see him being swallowed up by all his cares and worries.

"A few days on the seashore would surely save you. Come, let's put politics aside and stay with me for a few days. The count can surely handle any emergency that comes up. Any letter from Bismarck can wait a day or two," she said while she took his hand and led him upstairs to the grand poster bed, where they had not so long ago loved each other after the last ball.

"You can rest a while at the seashore and need not so much as lift a finger," she said as she unbuttoned her bodice and let her dress and petticoats fall to the floor. He was exhausted but never too tired to look at her splendid naked pale body. Her vibrant vitality, which almost never stilled, glistened on her skin. She let down her hair and then smiled at him with a wicked smile. He knew what she wanted.

After breakfast, Gisela, laughing in her sweet childish way, came bouncing downstairs dressed in a pretty French frock covered in lace and ribbons; her hair in ringlets danced around her delicate little face. When she saw her father, she shouted, *"Papa, tu es à la maison."* Gisela learned French quickly, and the two of them spoke easily in French.

"Oui, mon cheri. I am home. Come to me."

She threw her arms around him and would not let go.

She was the happiest when he came to visit as she could sit on his lap, play with his mustache, and tease him. He stood up to leave, and Gisela begged him, "Do not go, Papa, *si'l vous plaît."*

"I will be back, *mon amour.* Your mama and I will take you to the seashore, where we can play all day. Would you like that?"

"Oui, oui," she cried out.

"The seashore? Oh, my dear, do you mean it? That would be so wonderful." At first, Alexandrine thought he was making fun until she realized he meant it.

On his way out, he told Alexandrine, "I will immediately

cable Emperor Wilhelm for permission for a short leave of absence."

As soon as he reached the embassy, he sent the telegraphed message to the emperor. While he was at the embassy waiting for the emperor's response, Alexandrine was making arrangements for a train. She told her maid to pack a suitcase for her and Gisela for a short trip to the south of France.

When he arrived back at the chateau with a downcast face, Alexandrine knew immediately there was bad news. He proceeded to explain to her that Emperor Wilhelm had refused his leave, citing that the situation in Paris was not stable. As anything could happen, he could not grant him leave even for one day.

The next morning, Alexandrine, not wishing to disappoint Gisela, set out with her little assembly and headed for the train station, leaving Chlodwig behind.

Alexandrine and Gisela traveled to Biarritz on the Bay of Biscay. Alexandrine, having a renewed interest in the places the former emperor spent his days, wanted to see the Villa Eugenie, where the royal couple spent their summers. After settling into a small tourist hotel, Alexandrine and Gisela took an open carriage and drove around the city, stopping at the villa. The large, impressive house was set on the main beach of the town. It was surrounded by gardens, woods, meadows, and a pond. It was said that Napoleon III chose this location for a summer retreat so his wife, who was Spanish, would feel closer to her home in Spain.

Alexandrine and Gisela spent several days exploring the rugged seashore, hunting seashells, and walking in the woods under the shadow of the Great Pyrenees. The days in the south of France on the seashore were idyllic but all too short.

When they returned to Paris, Chlodwig told Alexandrine that the political climate in France was slow to improve as Franco-German relations were still tentative. He could not find enough time to rest.

While Chlodwig busied himself with matters of state and forming a second parliamentary body, the French Senate, Alexandrine continued her pursuit of learning all she could about Paris and the French people. On a particularly clear and sunny day when there was not even a cloud to be seen, the attaché arrived in a phaeton, which was loaned to him by the *Duc* d'Monte. He was dressed in his German uniform with epaulets, tan breeches tucked into tall boots, which were polished to a high gloss. Alexandrine thought him quite handsome sitting in the phaeton with the reins in his hands behind a high-spirited black stallion.

"Come, madame. I shall take you to a place you've not been. Your carriage awaits."

She was clearly puzzled where that could be as they had already toured all of Paris. She grabbed her hat and parasol. He held her hand and helped her into the carriage and onto the seat next to him. He took the reins and slapped them at the horse. The stallion bolted forward, speeding down the avenue. Once out of the city proper, Alexandrine begged him to let her take the reins.

"You are a daring one, madam."

"Yes, Count, I have never shied away from any challenge. But I must tell you I have spent many a day maneuvering a carriage behind a horse," she replied as she took the reins. They drove down treelined boulevards that gave way to open farmland and, later, forests. After nineteen kilometers, before them stood the magnificence of Versailles, considered as the palace of the last emperors of France, unparalleled in all the world. Even King Ludwig II was inspired by the architecture of Versailles but could not completely bring it to the same ideal.

The count, again in control of the horse, guided them down the avenue toward the palace. It was now in the hands of the Third Republic Empire. "I've been here many times with the ambassador in meetings with foreign ministers and the like to discuss the future of France."

"Is there a future?" she asked.

"Yes, but not with the current provisional government."

"Why not?"

"I'm not at liberty to say, madam," he answered.

Alexandrine did not continue to press him for an answer as she understood his position. As Chlodwig's attaché, he could not. She knew she could ask Chlodwig the same question as he held her in his confidence and told her much about his role in assisting to establish a permanent government for France.

Even though the palace was not accessible, there were still the gardens to explore. The count circled the carriage around the Parterre d'Eau and the Parterre and Fountain of Latona closest to the palace, with pools that reflected its façade. Each fountain held a story. The count asked Alexandrine if she would like to hear them. She knew she could not stop him, so she said yes.

The count began, "The Latona Fountain down a stairway from Parterre d'Eau illustrates the story of Latona taken from the *Metamorphoses* of Ovid. According to the story, a peasant of Lycia insulted Latona, the mother of Apollo and Diana; the god Jupiter transformed the peasants into frogs. That is the reason for the figures of half-humans/half-frogs positioned around the fountain. Did you enjoy that story, madame?"

"Of course. You continue to amaze me with your knowledge," she said.

"Then I will tell you another when we get to the Basin of the Chariot of Apollo." He encouraged the horse on along a grassy lane to the basin. "Apollo, also known as the sun god, was the emblem of Louis XIV. The chariot that arises from the fountain symbolizes the rising of the sun. Let's keep going. There are many more fountains and gardens to see. If you are tired, madame, we do not need to go any further."

"Not at all, Count, I find it most interesting. Please go on," she said.

He stopped the carriage near the next formal garden with more fountains decorated with figures of Triton, sirens, dolphins, and nymphs. As morning had given way to afternoon, the count turned the carriage around into the forest that surrounds the palace. He found a small clearing and halted the horse.

"We are to have a picnic in the shadow of the palace," he said as he lifted out a large wicker basket from under the seat. He spread a blanket over the pine needles on the ground and opened the basket. Alexandrine was stunned by the preparations he had made. There was champagne, smoked salmon, cold duck, sliced peppered pork, fruits and vegetables of all kinds, several sticks of bread, an assortment of French cheese, and olives from Italy. Alexandrine and the count shared the food and champagne until they could eat no more. Alexandrine, relaxed and satisfied, sat up against the tree that had shaded them from the sun, when off in the distance, she saw a storm was birthing. The count, seeing the same ominous cloud approaching, quickly gathered up the blanket with everything inside, took Alexandrine's hand, and rushed toward a small pavilion. The rain had already started before they made it to their shelter just before the menacing clouds opened with a deluge.

Once inside, the count looked at Alexandrine and could not look away. Her arms were beaded with tiny rain droplets, making her skin sparkle as if diamonds dripped off it. Even though Alexandrine was eleven years his senior, he found her to be the most exciting woman he had ever seen with her disheveled hair and wet clothing. Alexandrine was shivering from the cold. He shook out the blanket and wrapped it around her shoulders to warm her. While holding her to keep her warm, he ever so lightly touched her neck, bringing himself close to her soft, curling lips. He stayed there for a moment, tempted to kiss her and declare his devotion. He was imagining how it would feel to kiss her soft lips, her eyelids, her neck; how his hands would caress her shoulders and her arms; loosening her dress and touching her naked breasts. Alexandrine, seeing the intensity in his blue eyes and sure of what he intended to do, raised her hand and gently placed it over his.

"My dear count," she said. "I am greatly indebted to you for all your kindnesses during the past months, and your companionship has kept me from my loneliness, but this cannot be. We cannot do anything that would cause us regret. Not going further would keep our friendship afloat as opposed to a complete shipwreck of both our lives."

The count withdrew his hand and leaned against the wall of the pavilion. "Forgive me, madame, for my impertinence. I should not have acted so. Your friendship means a great deal to me, and I should not be happy knowing I offended you."

As he finished apologizing, the sun again appeared. They returned to the carriage, which still had rainwater on its seats and on the floor. The count quickly dried everything the best he could. He took her hand and helped her into the carriage. They took one more lap around the three remaining fountains before heading back down the long avenue to the road leading back to Paris. The count said nothing more. Although she had a curious mind and enjoyed learning, she was glad not to receive any more history lessons or speak of what happened. He was a good companion and friend, but her love for Chlodwig was so great that she could not imagine betraying him even in the most innocent of circumstances.

～

Alexandrine's life continued as before except for the loss of the companionship of the young attaché. He requested to return to Germany to assist Bismarck. The dinner parties and balls continued as Paris society could not imagine a season without them. It was in their blood.

Chlodwig, too, held dinners at the Hotel Beauharnais, the official residence of the ambassador, where Alexandrine was his hostess. He undertook a series of extravagant ceremonies at his residence in the hope of establishing better relations so that Prussia and the newly formed French Senate could coexist. All of Paris society came to expect Alexandrine to be there. And when the matrons of the upper class held their parties, they invited Chlodwig and Alexandrine. Paris society was not one to judge who was or wasn't one's wife. Unlike in Munich, there was no talk of scandal for a man to have a wife secured somewhere and a mistress by his side.

Evening followed evening until everyone in Paris's noble class had at least one formal dinner or a ball before the end of the season. Alexandrine received almost daily invitations. One such came from Duchesse L'Ambrose, whom Alexandrine had met at one of the balls given in honor of the new ambassador to Paris. On that day, Alexandrine dressed in a royal-blue fitted jacket over a slim skirt. A hat in the newest French fashion sat coquettishly tilted to one side on her head. She was welcomed most warmly by the *duchesse,* who, quite advanced in age, was still elegant and composed. Her hair was still black with only a few traces of gray. She was dressed in a black fitted dress as she still was in mourning over the death of her husband, the *duc,* the last year. Shortly after Alexandrine's arrival, the butler and a maid brought in trays of coffee and orange cakes.

"Tell me, my dear, what have you seen so far in Paris?"

Alexandrine told her of the many trips and tours she made around the city and countryside, including the gardens of Versailles. She also said she saw the ruins of the Tuileries Palace when she passed through the Arc de Triomphe. "How sad that looked," she said.

"Yes, it is a truly sad part of Paris. Were it not for the recent war with Prussia and the overthrow of the French Empire at the hands of the communards, the palace would not have been set afire. But let us not speak of politics; there has been too much of that already. I would rather tell you of what Paris was like before the war, when Louis Napoleon III still lived there."

"I would like to hear more, madame, if you care to tell me," Alexandrine said, putting her coffee down and looking at the *duchesse* with new interest.

"I know only a little, but I can tell you it was a glorious time," she said. The *duchesse* went on. "The palace was the home of most of the French monarchs including all the Louises and, of course, Napoleon Bonaparte I. One end included the Louvre, which, as you saw, was partly destroyed during the fire. The Arc de Triomphe was the entrance to the palace, where parades of horses, carriages, and armies marched down the Champs Elysées to enter the palace courtyard. Gala parties and balls were frequent. At the end of the season, there were usually over six hundred invitations. The palace was a true work of art. The emperor's rooms were on the ground floor, and the rooms on the second floor were for the empress. I had occasion to receive an invitation from Empress Eugenie on numerous occasions to visit her in her suite. I remember it to be highly decorated in the style of Louis XVI with salons of different colors: one pink, one green, and another blue. Unlike her apartments in Versailles, hers in Tuileries were just as grand as the emperor's."

By this time, Alexandrine was imagining herself walking through the corridors of the palace that the *duchesse* was describing in such great detail. She was, however, saddened at its destruction. "Do you think it will ever be rebuilt?" she asked.

"*Non, mon cher.* It is not likely. The new regime cares not for beauty or history. Much of Paris had already been destroyed during the Revolution of 1789. Emperor Louis Napoleon spent much of his reign and money rebuilding Paris to its former glory. But when the war with Prussia started, he could not continue. He led his troops into war and, as you know, was captured by the Prussian Army. The poor emperor died in exile. The empire is no more. Since then, France has gone through one provisional government after another. What's to become of France, I do not know. Perhaps the new Prussian ambassador to Paris can enlighten us."

With no more to discuss, Alexandrine said goodbye to her hostess, knowing that this invitation was not so much a social call but rather a means to perhaps influence Chlodwig's political stand through her.

At the end of another social season, which was signaled by the approaching days of summer and the oppressive city heat that came with it, Paris's advantaged again left the city for milder climates. Once again, Alexandrine chose to stay in Paris with Chlodwig.

During those long summer months, Alexandrine sought to keep herself occupied, besides touring more of the city. She wanted something to do that would satisfy her inner need to be useful. She remembered traveling with the nuns on her way to Jerusalem many years ago. She remembered they were the Société Française de Secours. Surely, they could use some help, she thought. The Reverend Mother welcomed Alexandrine with open arms even though she had no experience nursing the invalids other than emptying the buckets of vomit of the seasick nuns on the ship to the Holy Land. She viewed Alexandrine as a welcome benefactress to their plight.

Alexandrine asked about Sister Maria Louise as she remembered the young nun from her voyage to the Holy Land a few years ago.

"Sister Louise is no longer at de Secours. She has been sent to the French colony of Guiana. She is working at the penal colony's mission. I am afraid she is finding it difficult in this inhospitable place but is finding her reward doing the Lord's work."

"Thank you, Reverend Mother. I had hoped to see her again."

There were never enough funds to pay for all the bandages, medicines, or linens they needed. When Alexandrine told

Chlodwig of her desire to assist the nuns at *de Secour* and how serious she was in her efforts to help, he happily subsidized them in their charity work.

Alexandrine was given other work to do and was asked to visit the city's poor. She had not been to the slums of Paris. She had not seen the poverty, the unsanitary conditions, the filth in the streets, the children begging for any morsel of food. Riding in her carriage through these streets, she saw rowhouses in disgraceful disrepair and horses without spirit hanging their heads, with ribs showing under their matted coats, pulling wagons laden with food that smelled of rot. There were no fine street shops, only dilapidated wooden-framed stalls. Children dressed in ragged clothes ran barefoot in the filthy streets, and rag pickers searched piles of garbage for anything they could use or sell.

Returning to the mother house, Alexandrine could not hold back her tears. The Reverend Mother told her of the extreme poverty that had engulfed Paris during the last war and the following depression. "Sadly, it lingers today," she said. "It was said during the past years, people were so despairing they would eat anything they could, even birds and rats. Some said that toward the end, when everything else was gone, they were butchering the zoo animals for food."

Alexandrine found this so disturbing, she asked the nun, "How can this be when I have seen so much plenty among the wealthy?"

The nun replied, "The nobility has its ways of protecting itself. Only a few of them concern themselves with the poor. It is the French way. We do what we can, but it is never enough."

With a heavy heart, Alexandrine returned home. She confided in Chlodwig of her visit to the city's slums. His sensitive heart agreed with her that such degradation should not befall any city. However, it was not within his power to change it. She felt hopeless and saddened but continued to help at *Société Français de Secours*.

It was during this time that Alexandrine, brought up Evangelical, as was her mother, decided to embrace Catholicism. Working with the religious society had made an impression on her regarding the goodness of the Church and how they cared for the poor. Attending Mass with the nuns, she admired the ceremonial rituals and what seemed to her a mysticism. She knew nothing of the sacraments of the Catholic Church, but it inspired her imagination. While with the sisters at *de Secours*, she visited the convent, watching them praying together in the little chapel. Other nuns were singing softly in a quiet chant. It stirred her deeply. To her, it seemed to be such a peaceful life devoting themselves to God in every way. Until then, Alexandrine only knew the austere and pragmatic Protestantism of her former belief. However, a conversion to the Catholic faith was not a decision she could make lightly, and she pondered it for several more years.

28

Cholera

Having been in Paris for three years, Alexandrine longed to see her son Hermann and also her children in Augsburg. It was while she was making preparations to leave Paris that she received an urgent dispatch from a friend in Munich that her faithful cook was ill and requested she come at once. "I must go immediately," she told Chlodwig. He did not stand in her way, fully understanding her devotion but nevertheless saddened by her departure.

When she arrived at her house on Karlstrasse, she found the cook ill with cholera. The doctor came but told her that the woman was beyond help. Still, Alexandrine nursed Lisel as best she could. She sponged her brow with cool water to ease her fever and spooned soup over her blue, cracked lips. Her bulging eyes looked at Alexandrine in terror. Sadly, in a few days, the poor, sickly cook died, not having enough strength to recover.

Soon after, Alexandrine was seized by violent cramping, vomiting, convulsions, and finally uncontrollable diarrhea. The disease struck her with ferocity. She took to her bed. She was alone until her son came to see her. In her delirium, she thought she heard him say, "Please don't die, Mother, but if you will, then take me with you." She whispered, "Let Chlodwig know but do not let him come."

Hermann called for the doctor. It seemed that all of Munich was infected with cholera. However, it was only a small part of the city, which happened to include Karlstrasse. When the doctor came, he brought along a priest as he only had time to see the most severe cases so he could give them a priest's blessing. The doctor looked at Alexandrine's swollen eyes ravaged by fever and nodded at the priest. It could only mean one thing. The priest took his stole, put it around his neck, and let the two ends hang down over his white tunic. An embroidered cross decorated the ends, which he put to his lips and kissed before making the sign of the cross over Alexandrine's languid body.

The priest prayed over her. Her red eyes could barely open. But she saw the priest as he asked her, "Do you, my daughter, embrace the Lord Jesus and the Catholic faith to restore you to health and the love of God?"

In a feeble voice, she said, "I do, Father."

After several more weeks of fever, she slowly regained her strength until she made a full recovery. It was the Scheffers and Hermann who sat by her side and tended to her. At last, she felt she could write to Chlodwig that she was well again and would soon be restored to good enough health to travel and return to Paris.

He immediately sent a telegram: "It is I whose life is restored."

Alexandrine spent several more weeks in Munich with Hermann. He was growing into a handsome young man full of dreams and ambitions. After she recovered, he returned to school as he had several more years before he would matriculate.

Chlodwig missed Alexandrine greatly. In a short note to her, he wrote, "My duties give me no repose. People are mere passing ghosts of no interest to me. I miss our tranquil evenings together. Return soon. Your faithful friend."

Before returning to Paris, Alexandrine made one more trip to Augsburg in an attempt to see her children. It was without success as Erzberger once again prevented it. She begged and pleaded with him to no avail. His heart turned to stone at her pleas once again.

Saddened but resolute to keep trying to bend her former husband to her will, she decided to return to Paris. The city had a hold on her. *"What is the allure?"* she wondered. *"Is it the art, architecture, or the people? It is all of it that cultivates the soul,"* she told herself. But it was Chlodwig and Gisela who held her heart.

After her spiritual awakening when the priest prayed over her during her illness, Alexandrine returned to the sisters of Secour. During that time, she felt a need to grow her spiritual life. Mother Superior advised her to devote herself to her mission to help the sick and the poor. "You will be doing God's work, and in doing so, you will find the true meaning of charity. God will show you the way."

When, after much thought and searching her spiritual soul, she decided to take the final leap into this new faith, she sent a letter to Dean Mayer in Augsburg to request her withdrawal from the Protestant Church. In her letter, she wrote that she wanted to devote the rest of her life to the Catholic

Church and sought his permission to do so. Weeks of waiting followed. No letter came.

She was determined to not let anything stand in her way. There was another solution. She decided to travel to Salzburg to see her old friend Elisabeth and ask her for advice. When she arrived, Elisabeth was delighted to see her friend. After telling Elisabeth of her intention to renounce her Episcopalian faith, Alexandrine explained her plight that she had not heard anything from Dean Mayer regarding her request to withdraw from the Protestant Church. At the urging of Elisabeth, she wrote another letter to Dean Mayer. This time, the letter included an appeal from Baroness Elisabeth herself on behalf of her friend. After another week went by, the sought-after letter arrived, granting her release from the Protestant Church. Elisabeth arranged for Alexandrine to meet with Cardinal von Tarnosci, who instructed her on catechisms and tenets of the Catholic faith. The cardinal arranged for her to be admitted to the Catholic Church in the Chapel of St. Hubert in Salzburg once her lessons were completed.

She immediately wrote to Chlodwig, a devout Roman Catholic himself, who was happy to hear her news. He left Paris, arriving in Salzburg the next day to be at her side when she made her profession of faith to the Catholic Church. They kneeled together in the little church for their first Mass together, receiving communion side by side. As he could not stay any longer, he boarded a train to return to Paris. Alexandrine decided to return to Munich.

Before leaving, she was given a letter of introduction by Cardinal von Tarnosci of Salzburg to present to Canon Obercamp, a Jesuit priest in Munich. Over the next weeks, her instructional guide and mentor, Canon Obercamp, guided her in pursuit of her new faith. As a result, she shared a particularly resolute relationship with him. Her friends could not believe how much influence this Jesuit had on her. It was as if his power over her made her so devoutly obedient to him that they thought it against her nature. As a result of that first meeting with this Jesuit, the priest became her confessor for the next twenty years. It was a turning point in her life. Her blind obedience to the Catholic Church would result in an unexpected fatal step some years later that would change her life in the most unforgiving way.

When Chlodwig heard of her devotion to Canon Obercamp, realizing his influence over her, he became angry as he had more than once argued against the Jesuit's authority in Germany. He wrote to her:

> I am not opposed to the individual who is a Jesuit priest but with the Order itself. I have supported Bismarck's anti-papal policies with regards to the Jesuits. There has been a distinct declaration of war by the Society of Jesus against the foundation of our life as a State. I have spent years arguing for the prohibition of the Society of Jesus. They are against freedom of education, religious tolerance and the freedom of conscience. When I was a member of Parliament, I presented a Bill to the House that simply forbade the Jesuit order, much like Switzerland had already done. I cannot condone your continued endorsement of this Jesuit.

As it happened, the two large German states failed to endorse his bill, which would have forbidden the Jesuit Society to continue in Germany had it passed.

After reading his letter on his views of the Jesuits, Alexandrine could no longer keep quiet. She vehemently held to her belief. She wrote him that she would continue with her mentorship with the Jesuit priest and would not be persuaded otherwise. It was one of the few times in all the years they had been together that she did not agree with him. This argument over her relationship with Canon Obercamp caused a chasm between them. In the past when they disagreed, they could quickly heal the wounds it caused because of their love for each other. She hoped that this new division between them would also heal in time. At least it was put aside for the time being. But she did not return to Paris.

29

Hermann

Hermann was now finished with his schooling. He lived with his mother until he could decide what kind of a life he wanted. One day, his father called on Alexandrine in Munich. Scheffer had served in the Bavarian Army during the Austro-Prussian War and had been promoted to major. It was during that conflict when he was severely wounded by a bullet that lodged in his hip. It was successfully removed but caused him to limp. He was still in the army, stationed in Bayreuth, when he made the decision to go to Munich to see Alexandrine.

They had not seen each other for over ten years. He admitted he failed his son as a father as he knew little of him, nor did he spend enough time with him. Hermann was away at school for the last six years, and in all that time, his father did not visit him. Now that Hermann was seventeen, he wanted his son to live with him in Bayreuth.

"I intend to adopt Hermann," he said.

"Why now?" she asked a little spitefully.

"I want to get to know Hermann better, and besides, he

should know his brother." Scheffer married soon after leaving Alexandrine and had a son, who was only a few years younger than Hermann. "It is also my intent that he should benefit from my inheritance as my son."

"Let us see what he decides after living with you for a short while in Bayreuth," she said. "He is old enough to make his own decisions, and I will not stand in his way."

Any feelings she once had for Scheffer had long vanished and were buried with the other memories of her youth. He was older now with sharp lines carved into his cheeks. His golden hair was speckled with gray. As he looked at her with his soft blue eyes, she had not even an inkling of worry as she knew he was an honest and good man and would treat Hermann well.

Hermann stayed with his father and stepmother for a month before returning to Munich. Alexandrine threw her arms around him. Secretly she knew he would leave her again and possibly forever. The pain of that was no less than the pain she felt when she lost her other children to her husband.

Hermann, understating her apprehensions, said, "Do not concern yourself, Mother. No one will replace you in my heart. Bayreuth is not so far away. The main railway line that used to go from Nuremberg to Hof and past Bayreuth has been improved with a connection by way of the Bayreuth-Neuenmarkt Railway. We can visit often."

She knew in her own heart that he meant it. During those few short days with her, he often talked about his father. But, more often, he talked about Scheffer's wife, Sibelia. "She is a person of high intellect with a sweet and giving nature. I am sure, Mother, you would like her if you could someday meet," he would say.

"I have no doubt as your father, being a person of high integrity, would search for a wife equal to him."

After a few weeks, Hermann returned to Bayreuth. Several years later, she received a letter from him that his father had died. He had been sick for several years but never confided in Hermann about his illness. When she received the news, she went to Bayreuth to be with Hermann. While there, she had occasion to spend a little time with Sibelia. Alexandrine, not very tall herself, towered over this much shorter woman, who was somewhat plump. However, it is not that but her happy face with a ready smile that one sees first. When she laughed, it rang throughout the house with a gaiety not often heard. She saw in her an easygoing nature, which made her feel immediately at ease.

Alexandrine was happy that Scheffer's wife was a good and loving second mother to Hermann. Even their young son was like a brother and friend to him. She thought about how Hermann described Sibelia and how right he was. She saw a woman with goodness and sound judgment. It was clear that Scheffer loved her and was happy to have someone so moderate in nature. Alexandrine knew that she could never have succumbed to be such a tame creature as his wife was. Her wild nature would not allow it. In her heart, she knew that Scheffer could never have had the tranquility in his life with her that he enjoyed with his wife. Chlodwig often called Alexandrine a "tiger who could not be tamed."

After her visit with Sibelia, Alexandrine confided in Chlodwig that, in a way, she was envious of the happy life they had. He agreed with her that a loving home is every man's desire, but there is more to it than pleasantness. He explained in all sincerity, "Love is not always perfect but should be a harmonious union between two people who can express themselves perfectly through diverse emotions. That is the ideal." She knew what he meant. She often felt that way with him.

After Scheffer died, Hermann made the decision to join the army and, like his father, became an officer. But he did not stay. He had other interests more to his liking and talents.

30

A Commission in Berlin

*I*n 1880, at the death of the German Secretary of State for Foreign Affairs, Bernhard Ernst von Bülow, Chlodwig was called to Berlin by Bismarck. Bismarck was also head of both the Imperial and Prussian Offices of Foreign Affairs, which meant he had complete control over domestic and foreign policy. He would not accept any opinions contrary to his own and demanded truth above all else. Bismarck wanted Prince Chlodwig to temporarily assume the position of German Secretary of State of the Foreign Office. Bismarck was ill at the time and chose him as he knew him to be of honest character as well as a diplomat of integrity. The Foreign Office, located in Berlin, was first established in 1870 to form the foreign policy of the North German Confederation and then, in 1871, of the newly formed German Empire.

Bismarck suffered several illnesses during those times and was often confined to bed. He only appointed people he trusted. It was a logical choice to select the prince to represent him during his absences.

Receiving his new commission as German Secretary of

State, Chlodwig left Paris immediately for Berlin. Now in his sixty-first year, he was still in good health and vitality. Alexandrine and Gisela, who were once again in Paris, said goodbye as he took the train to Berlin. They both stood on the station platform with white handkerchiefs, taking turns waving them and drying their tears. For Alexandrine, his leaving was especially hard as in the past months their days together were so constant. They both felt the pain of loneliness that would surely come as he made his home in Berlin.

As his train pulled out of the station, Alexandrine and her daughter boarded another train. Gisela was now ten years old. Her tutors were no longer needed as she could learn no more from them. It was decided that she should return to Pasing to the school there for further studies. Alexandrine accompanied Gisela there to meet with the family that would care for her while she was in school. Then she returned to Karlstrasse. Once again, she was alone but richer for her experiences in Paris.

All the past restless years subsided and gave way to contentment again. A fair wind blew once more as the threatening clouds of the French political climate had lifted with their departure. Chlodwig was still the cornerstone of her life. He, too, found the darkness lifting and looked forward to a new serenity. His new residency in Berlin did not stand in their way. Alexandrine stayed with him in Berlin when he was there. His position as secretary of state often took him on missions to other countries for meetings with a Turkish sultan, a foreign ambassador, or the Russian Czar Nicolas. During those times, she would go back to Munich.

A year after Chlodwig's appointment, she noticed his inner joy decreasing in frequency the more he was away. His furrowed brow became more prominent, and he had the walk of a tired man.

After a particularly long stay in Russia, he returned to Munich and Alexandrine. "I have escaped," he would say. "It is with you that I find repose so that I can again return to the constant demands made upon me and all the official ceremonies that I am forced to attend. My spirit is renewed by looking into your soft and loving eyes. You are the only one who gives me solace and the strength to carry on."

He longed to stay in her comfortable house longer with each visit but could not. She wished it, too, as she felt the separation from him more deeply each time he left. "I cannot bear it when you leave. Each time it crushes my heart until you come again to restore it," she would say to him.

Shortly after he left on another mission, she received a note written from the Munich train station:

> *I will not leave here without telling you that you are a dear, lovely, splendid child. For that wish of yours yesterday is a young wish and it has cheered me through and through. I remain some days at Nürnberg. If you will write me there, and tell me . . . I shall be sure to get the letter. Your truest friend.*

Spending summers in Altaussee became somewhat of a routine. The summer there was a time when the rest of the world was far away, where the silent woods held their secrets to release them only with the rustling of leaves. The only other sounds that could be heard were the sweet chirping of birds. It was a place where wild nature and loveliness were in harmony. Such peacefulness in nature, such wonder, nurtured Chlodwig's heart and mind. It was the force behind his poetry, inspiring him to write often about moonlight and the light that falls in ribbons over the rivers and lakes, the sun's brilliance, and golden rays nourishing the fields, bringing forth life upon the earth. It was why he built Altaussee, his haven away from the cares of the world, perfectly set in nature.

When Alexandrine could not accompany him because her health did not allow her to travel, he would go without her. After leaving Altaussee, he wrote:

> *I am beginning a letter to you, dear Alex, though the longed-for Monday on which your promised word is to come, is still in the future. But fate has spoilt me this summer by granting me the boon of seeing you and talking with you almost daily. And so, I find it hard to get used to being parted from you again for weeks and months. I often ride past your windows,[11] where a dismal notice announces that there are rooms to let, and spoils my attempt to deceive myself into thinking that your sweet startled eyes are looking through the iron railings. Those six weeks from July 13 were a beautiful time. Now I wander about aimless and lonely, without that magnetic spell to draw me on the familiar way to The Market. My friend Kels whom I often meet looks at me with compassionate smiling eyes, as though he would say: "I know she's gone."*
>
> *I positively dislike it now when I have time and leisure to go into the garden-street. What good is leisure to ME? I*

---

11 At the inn in Altaussee where Alexandrine stayed while they were there.

employ it solely in reading, writing letters, and putting my
domestic affairs in order.
    As always, Your faithful friend.

He spent those summers nurturing his passion for writing poetry, which grew stronger as he aged. He would spend
an entire day writing on those long and stormy summer days
when he could not go outside. Ever young at heart, he wrote
poems even to his last days. To Alexandrine, he wrote:

> *To keep the heart of youth undimmed within*
> *Though time has bleached the hair to chilly gray*
> *This what all desire, yet few can win*
> *For only to the blessed shows that way.*
> *And some will mock the hours with laughter thin,*
> *And some will dully creep through day by day*
> *But whether in the breast be calm or die*
> *Each heart must surely turn to ice, men say.*
> *Yet when I saw thee, all my fearing died*
> *For the world's strife had left their head unbowed*
> *Thou of thy strength, hadst flung old age aside*
> *And he who in such conflict holds him proud,*
> *Shines though his heart may slowly pulse with wide*
> *Clear beams of youth that break through age's cloud.*

When Chlodwig's political life interfered, Alexandrine
went without him to Altaussee, taking Gisela with her to explore this natural world of his. It was a happy change from
the smoke-choked cities, the clamoring noise of the people,
horses drawing carts laden with rank-smelling refuse, house
upon house with no place between for children to play. Here

they found woods, fields, lakes, rivers, which all beckoned to explore their mysteries. From dawn to dusk, Gisela played outside, only coming inside when called to dinner.

Alexandrine, too, felt her spirit renewed among the trees and sun-kissed meadows. She could ride her horse with abandon through the fields and forests with no one to fear for her. Some days, she walked to the village market, bringing home bushels of apples, pears, and plums. Gisela would grab a pear or plum from the basket and eat it with delight, letting the nectar dribble down her chin. Alexandrine left the basket of fruit with Frau Kels, who owned the inn where she stayed, so she could prepare either a fruit tart made from the plums or applesauce from the apples.

On one exceptionally sunny day with the bluest of skies, Alexandrine took Gisela by the hand and walked the now-familiar path to the village. There, she took another path around the lake, which wound through the woods and then opened to a clearing filled with wildflowers. She let Gisela run free among the flowers kissed by butterflies flittering from one to the other. Her merry laughter, chasing butterflies or rolling around amid the daisies, filled her mother's heart with joy. Alexandrine remembered her own youthful days playing hide and seek with her sisters in the meadows around the castle in Silesia. Those times were the most joyful days of all when her childish heart could be free of care. Seeing Gisela do the same gave her such happiness.

From the balcony of the inn, Alexandrine could see the village below. That day, the church bells pealed wildly. She heard them many times before, but today they seemed louder and brighter than ever. Soon she learned why. The people of the village were gathered around the church, chattering happily as a wedding party emerged from inside. There was a cacophony of well wishes, whistles, and clapping as this was a special day. The clockmaker's daughter, Ilsa, known in the village for her well-endowed figure, welcome smile, and long flaxen hair, married Joseph, the only son of Kurt Kessler, who owned the butcher shop. Laughter, singing, and dancing broke out as someone picked up a fiddle and started to play. Alexandrine and Gisela, having heard the commotion, walked into the village for the revelry. They joined hands with the other villagers making a large circle to dance in the street. In the middle of the circle, the bride twirled in the arms of her husband, only to be swept away by another, and Joseph was captured by one of the women as more and more of the villagers joined in the dance. Another man took out his fiddle, which, in an instant, turned into a contest between the two. They played faster and faster until everyone was laughing so hard their sides ached. Alexandrine and Gisela were cheering them on until both fiddlers became exhausted and the strings of the violins were in shreds. The merriment continued while the butcher brought out several trays of sliced meats and strings of sausages. Someone else brought a variety of large rounds of cheeses, boiled potatoes, sauerkraut, red cabbage, and loaves of bread for a feast. Beer flowed like water until only half of the men were able to stand up.

The customary horse-drawn wagons laden with the wedding furniture as a gift from the bride's family made their way slowly through the crowd. The bride and groom, sitting together atop the marital bed on one of the wagons, were cheered on. A few of the men, drunk with too much beer, staggered over to the bride and groom's wagon, shouting what they called "advice" for Joseph on the wedding night. Alexandrine and other mothers covered their children's ears. The local priest, hearing what he wished not to, came upside the men. Father Peter, who was clearly much larger in girth than the men, grabbed them both by the collar and abruptly pulled them aside. In a loud, booming voice, he chastised them. "I'll see you in confession come Sunday. Now go home, you drunkards," he shouted at them.

After everyone had eaten their fill and the musicians were exhausted, the villagers slowly drifted away to their homes. The sky now deepened to azure as the sun began to hide behind the mountains. A tiny breeze rustled through the leaves, and the flowers in the field would soon nod their heads to sleep. Alexandrine and Gisela also turned up the path toward the inn. They were still in a happy mood but tired when they entered their room. Gisela threw herself on the bed and went to sleep. Alexandrine, not ready to go to bed, wrote a letter to Chlodwig about their fine adventure in the village:

> *My dear friend. Today Gisela and I ventured into the village where there was a wedding party for two young people. We had the most delightful time dancing and laughing with the people of the village. Gisela is growing into the fairest girl with great blue eyes and her golden hair framing her radiant face. I delight so much seeing her here in the countryside so happy, smiling at me from behind her curls. I can see the gentleness and loving nature, her tranquil sweetness, the beneficent calm of her father in her. We both miss you. Come soon if you can.*
>
> *Your devoted, Alex*

In 1885, Bismarck chose the ever-faithful and trustworthy

prince to assume the position of governor of Alsace-Lorraine. He was given the task of carrying out coercive measures introduced by Bismarck. Even though Chlodwig disapproved of these measures, he managed to reconcile Alsace-Lorraine to German rule. Since he would no longer have a reason to travel to Munich, he asked Alexandrine to stay with him in Strasburg. Even though they could not live together, he would secure her a location nearby. After giving this much consideration, Alexandrine thought it best to remain in Munich. He sent her a telegram: "I arrive in Munich tomorrow morning." Never before had such a brief message from him arrived without at least a few words of endearment.

He did indeed arrive the next morning with the intent to discuss the matter of her reluctance to join him in Strasburg. Alexandrine, ever mindful of the gossip that could so easily erupt, continued in her attempt to dissuade him.

"Chlodwig, you are in the public eye more than ever. I only want to shield you from those who would declare war on you and your policies. If I go with you, I will not be able to avert any scandal. I do not want to give anyone cause to harm you or jeopardize your political career. Living in Strasburg would surely open the flood gates and possibly ruin your long-held reputation as one of Germany's greatest statesmen."

Not being with her truest friend and not giving in to his desire cost her dearly, but she remained resolute.

My dear Alex, you concern yourself with too much. I know Strasburg is not like Paris, but it matters to me not what is said. My position is secure. When you change your mind, I will welcome you with open arms.

After some time, she could no longer stay away. She followed him to Strasburg, or Berlin, or wherever he might be. No distance, or time, could diminish her love and desire for him. She could not bear to be without his friendship. He, too, always found time, no matter the burden of his office, to be with her just for a few moments. When she was not there, he wrote her letters filled with poetic words of love that came from within his soul. "You are my oasis," he would often say. And at another time he wrote, "My heart sings when I see you, you give me light, the dreams of youth. You are my fairest world, my peace on earth."

Every year after that brought them together in this way, without, however, making any change in each other's mode of living arrangement. On his trips to Vienna, St. Petersburg, Rome, Paris, or Berlin, Alexandrine accompanied him whenever she could but often stayed apart from him. Other times, she would stay in Munich or visit Gisela in Pasing. Some summers, when Chlodwig could, they all spent their days together in Altaussee. At summer's end, Alexandrine returned to Munich; Gisela returned to school in Pasing.

Feeling the pain of being alone without her three children, Alexandrine made one last plea to her former husband to allow them to spend a few months with her. They were almost grown now, and she had not seen them for ten years. Her pleas went unanswered. This grieved her unconsolably. She decided to travel to Augsburg to face her former husband. She was older now. She had braced the chilling wind and stood tall against the gale of misfortune in her past, so she could face Erzberger with a new confidence and strength. She failed.

Once more, he stood firm. He could not grasp her maternal longing for her children; he had no understanding of a mother's love as his own mother was cold and uncaring toward him. While they were married, he never understood her greater view of life and love. Even now, he could not. She went away dejected and saddened once again with no hope of ever attaining what she wanted most in life: all her children by her side.

In those times of despair, she felt secure in Chlodwig's love for her, which she used as a shield to protect herself from this latest punishment inflicted on her by her former husband. She was sure that their love for each other was not just a pleasant interlude. She believed that she and Chlodwig were bound together as two souls so alike in feeling and emotion, which could only grow stronger with each year. This was never more evident than when he would arrive at her house, exhausted from his lengthy journeys, conferences, and diplomatic duties. He sought repose and the security of her love to give him solace and renewal to face the next days of the same. She, in the same manner, sought him to comfort her during her dark days. It was a perfect union. It was a union as strong as any marriage could be.

During the next year, Alexandrine became equally involved in his political career. He often talked openly to her of his affairs and asked for her opinion on matters of state, trusting her implicitly. He referred to her as "diplomat and statesman" in jest but more often told her how fortunate he was to have her in his life with her keen insight into politics. Later in life, her children often remarked how much she contributed to his career. Whether anyone else knew of this, she never disclosed.

Opportunities presented themselves in a way that Alexandrine could, through her contacts in Austria, be useful to Chlodwig in obtaining information on Austria-Hungary's role in joining the mutual defense treaty with Germany and Italy. With the blessing of Bismarck, she would travel to Vienna in the company of the publisher of the Augsburg *Algemeiner Zeitung*, who was nominated as a member of the official council in Vienna. She would refer to him only as "O" so as not to divulge any political secrets in her connection with him. Her mission was to offer "O", under certain conditions, the Bavarian Home Office if he would use his contacts to obtain information for Germany. He was not inclined to accept all the conditions— and those he did, did not satisfy her or the goals set by the mission. She reported this to Chlodwig, who expected this and sent her on another mission to gather information from the Austrian Council. This time, she went alone.

After that, she made several more trips to Austria, resorting often to diplomatic tricks to obtain information. When that didn't get her what she wanted, she used her feminine wiles. As a result, she often exposed herself to danger, having to secretly flee Vienna at least twice to seek refuge in Salzburg with friends until she could hand the information she obtained over to Chlodwig. She was so successful that Bismarck, on at least one occasion, expressed his most cordial and personal thanks for her efforts.

After she returned from those daring trips and was once again with Chlodwig, she put aside her political nature, replacing it with her feminine one, which was more to her true nature. In that way, they could once again enjoy their days together in loving words, caresses, and laughter without the burden of politics.

It was not much later that Chlodwig's open Prussian tendencies came into conflict with his colleagues in the Foreign Office. An incident early on may have led to his early resignation as head of Foreign Affairs, a position he continued to hold. It had to do with a meeting with King Ludwig II of Bavaria regarding an alliance with Prussia. He remarked to the king that other ministers were opposed to such an alliance with Prussia. The king replied he had no concern with what other ministers had to say as it was he, Prince Hohenlohe, who was in charge of Foreign Affairs. In the next presidential election, the Ultramontane Party won. As a result, in the next Cabinet meeting, options were so divided on the question of a partial or complete resignation of the ministry that the whole crisis was blamed on the prince, which resulted in the other ministers rallying against him.

In 1886, Chlodwig was sitting comfortably in his high-back leather chair at his residence in Strasburg, enjoying his cigar and drinking Vichy water, when a messenger arrived with a letter. It merely said that King Ludwig II was dead. This bothered the prince greatly as Ludwig admired and supported him throughout his career. He took the first train to Munich and went immediately to the Upper House, where he was asked to participate in the investigation into the circumstances of the king's death.

What he learned was that Ludwig had fled the Castle at Tegernsee with Dr. Gudden in a small boat. The king was found drowned the next morning, and Dr. Gudden had been shot. There had been talk over the past years of Ludwig's inability to govern, and he had increasingly acted in a manner that some considered a mental malady. Some ministers thought he was insane, while others thought him to be only eccentric. Moreover, his incessant passion to build even more elaborate castles throughout Bavaria, each one costlier than the last, was draining the coffers.

Chlodwig was put in charge of finding the true cause of Ludwig's death as it was generally thought the circumstances seemed somewhat mysterious. The ministers thought Ludwig committed suicide and drowned, although there was no evidence of water in his lungs. Others believed he was murdered while trying to escape during the time he was being held captive as his uncle Luitpold was attempting to take over the government. Many of the documents or statements regarding Ludwig's death were conveniently "unavailable." In the end, after many meetings and reviews of the facts of Ludwig's demise, no conclusion could be rendered. There was nothing more to find other than the king drowned. All thought conclusively that Ludwig's reign ending was in the best interest of the country.

Ludwig's younger brother, Otto, was declared king of Bavaria. However, it was well known that, since birth, Otto had a diminished capacity and was therefore declared incompetent. A regent was appointed.

~

In 1888, Princess Gisela von Hohenlohe married Baron Oswald Carl Hans von Hornstein-Bietingen, who was eight years older than she. Oswald was a handsome and wealthy aristocrat in a very important position as captain of the Imperial Horse Calvary. The marriage ceremony was a magnificent event in the neo-gothic Konstanz Minster in the city of Konstanz. Alexandrine and Chlodwig watched as their daughter walked down the long red-carpeted aisle to meet who she referred to as "her prince." Alexandrine could not help shedding tears of joy looking at her "love child" in a silk gown. In her delicate gloved hands, she held a large bouquet of red roses, signifying love and beauty, together with lilies of the valley and sweet-smelling daisies as a symbol of innocence.

Alexandrine recalled her own wedding so many years ago when she stepped on a thorn. There were no thorns today. It was a glorious April day with shafts of sunlight cutting through the intricate stained-glass windows, casting rainbows of colors all around. She loved the smell of incense wafting through the church as the wedding vows were read. *There is nothing more ritualistic than a Catholic wedding ceremony in an ancient cathedral*, she thought.

Gisela and Oswald enjoyed traveling, and it was on one such trip to Bolsteg, Switzerland, that Gisela gave birth to their first child, Ludwig Chlodwig Alexander Feodor. Soon after they settled in Villa Geyerberg in southern Germany, two more children followed: Gisela Karolina Anna in 1891 and Klara in 1892. It was during these years that Alexandrine spent most of her time in Villa Geyerberg with Gisela and her grandchildren.

Chlodwig stayed in Strasburg until 1894, governing Alsace-Lorraine under German rule. During that time, much had changed in Prussia. Emperor Wilhelm I died in 1888, succeeded by his son Frederick III, who at the time was already dying of cancer. He reigned for only ninety-nine days. Following Frederick's death, Wilhelm II was made emperor at age twenty-nine. He opposed Bismarck's carefully laid out foreign policy, preferring vigorous and rapid expansion to enlarge Germany's "place in the sun" as he called it. Bismarck, the mastermind of German unification, feeling pressured and unappreciated by the emperor, resigned in March of 1890 at the urging of Wilhelm, who had lost all confidence in him. Thus ended an illustrious public career of twenty years for this dedicated servant of the German people.

Otto von Bismarck was succeeded by Count Georg Leo von Caprivi, who served for four years. Bismarck, at age seventy-five, went into a restful retirement until his death in July of 1898. A story circulating at the time was that before his death, he warned the German people of many troubling things that would occur over the next twenty years. One was his prediction that a great European war would break out in the Balkans. Of course, no one believed this old man, and so he died not knowing how right he was.

In 1894, Emperor Wilhelm II summoned Prince von Hohenlohe-Schillingsfürst to succeed Caprivi as the third Imperial Chancellor of the German Empire.

As third chancellor, Chlodwig, at age seventy-five, had achieved the height of his diplomatic career. However, his good health was waning during the years of his chancellorship. He became less and less conspicuous in public affairs and seldom appeared in sessions of Prussian and German Parliaments. Whether it was his age or his growing disinterest in politics is not known. It was during this time that he spent even more time at his estate in Schillingsfürst. No longer feeling young and vigorous, he sought the peacefulness of his home. Nature called him forth again to the forests and meadows there.

To Princess Marie, he remarked, "I have no feeling other than a joyous happiness at Schillingsfürst when I lie under a leafy tree and watch the clouds drift over the blue sky. I am content now and my heart is filled with gratitude to God who has guided and blessed me."

During those years, Princess Marie became ill. She was

no longer the elegant aristocrat but was in frail health in her sixty-eighth year. Their remaining children were now grown. She, like Chlodwig, was moving closer to a peace of mind that only the quiet of her home could provide. During these years together, he and Marie found themselves in conversation, speaking more candidly of their life together than in all the past years.

"I have only one regret in life," he said to Marie.

She asked, "What regrets do you have, my dearest? You have achieved all you could achieve in your life. No one has achieved more."

"My regret, Marie, is that my duties did not allow more time to be with my children. I have failed them."

"You did not fail them, Chlodwig. They know of the fatherly devotion you had for them, and they love you."

Another time, sitting by the window, watching the cold dark gloom at day's end fall over the meadows and forests, he reminisced, "I have attained all that I set out to do, but when I was called to the greatest position of all, I have nothing more to do but keep what was already done in working order. I am tired and can do no more."

"History will tell a different tale, Chlodwig," Marie replied. "You must gather your notes and letters which you have kept all these years and write your memoir. You have devoted your life to your country and done more than anyone in your time. Do this for your children, for the country, and for history."

In 1897, Princess Marie of Sayn-Wittgenstein-Sayn died a peaceful death in her home with Chlodwig and their children at her side.

After Marie's death, this great man, a public servant who was a loyal statesman and pioneer in the unification of Germany, still felt he did nothing noteworthy. It was then he remembered his wife's words. He decided to pen his autobiography to put into writing all the accomplishments and mistakes of his political career according to his own views. He spent many days gathering up his letters, notes, and papers he had accumulated throughout his career. He intended to start his memoirs, when fate intervened.

31

A Painful Decision

Alexandrine, at age sixty-four, was no longer the youthful beauty who captured the imagination and hearts of so many men. Her former beauty, however, could still be seen through extra lines on her once-youthful face. Her skin, still soft and porcelain, did not diminish with age. Her violet eyes still held a fascination and told much. Her auburn hair, which she continued to braid and pin around her head, showed only a little gray.

Chlodwig, well advanced in years, now looked old as his hair turned gray and continued to recede. His countenance, from years of stress and strain, showed a man no longer young with carefree laughter but in a serious mood. It was in this mood that, at the age of eighty, he declared his desire to have his faithful friend and companion by his side until the end of his days. After his wife's death, he made his intentions known to his children, who did not approve of his marrying a woman who was not born into a princely class. Despite all their opposition, he was determined to let nothing stand in the way of his intended union with the woman he had loved for the past thirty years.

On an evening in the house where they first met almost thirty years earlier, while he was sitting in his favorite comfortable chair by a warm, bright fire, he took her hand most lovingly, looked into her eyes, and said, "Alex, my dearest friend, you have been my companion throughout our thirty years together. You have stood by my side during hardships and strife. I have loved you with a passion I never knew. I wish to finally make you my own. I cannot live the rest of my days without you by my side as my wife."

The rush of her emotions as he said these words gave way to a pain in her heart so deep that she could not breathe. She looked at his dear, sweet face and could not speak. The prospect of the happiness she must refuse made her eyes wrench with tears.

She said nothing of the letter she had recently received from Prince Alexander, Chlodwig's son, who wrote that he and his brothers and sisters did not wish her to marry their father. "I beg of you, you must promise that you will not marry our father," he wrote.

There was an even greater reason she would refuse him. While her heart was breaking, she told her truest and most devoted friend, "I have embraced the Catholic Church with all my heart, and for the salvation of my soul, I cannot marry you."

His face red with anger, he railed against her. "It's that Jesuit! It is not within my comprehension how that Jesuit has managed to make you—the born intransigent—into his creature."

Chlodwig was a forgiving person, and in all the years they

were together in body and soul, he always forgave her without malice or anger for whatever indiscretions she extracted. This time, he could not forgive her.

"How can you refuse me now? I have devoted my life to you. I gave you my heart and love all these years. If I cannot share my last days with you, let us break now, forever." He spat out the words.

Her heart shattered as she listened to his reproach. She had never heard him speak with such malice. It was as if a huge rock hovering over her had, in an instant, descended and crushed her. Tears flooded her eyes and ran down her cheeks in waves. His expression was not the face of the man she loved. This was something she had never seen before.

Seeing him with his eyes narrowed and his forehead furrowed, she knew that all was gone. She played the words "Let us break now, forever" over and over again in her mind. Those words cut so deep.

She blurted out, "Our youth is spent, and the years we still have together grow shorter. How can you abandon me now?"

Chlodwig sat bent over with his head in his hands, not believing that she had refused him. The cruel blow of her rejection descended on him like a thick black cloud that could not be lifted. All the joy he felt when he came to her left him.

He asked himself, "How could one's deepest security in the love of another give way to such despair in an instant? I sit in the twilight of my years and shiver with disappointment. It cannot be!"

Alexandrine, in her pain, ran out into the street, broken and wretched. She did not know where she was going as a blinding craziness overcame her. She forgot everything: love, friendship, motherhood, God. His cruel words played over and over again in her mind: *"let us break now, forever."* Nothing else mattered.

She stopped running when she came to the bridge over the Isar River. She bent over the stone wall, looking down into the swirling, muddy water below. She was sure that her life was no longer worth living without the man she loved and to whom she had devoted herself with a willing heart for the past thirty years. Without him by her side, there would be nothing more to live for. She stared blankly into the water below and, with a heavy heart, stepped onto the wall. In an instant, she threw herself into the river below.

Someone else was walking on the bridge that fateful night. The man saw the distraught Alexandrine throw herself into the river and, without a moment's hesitation, jumped in after her. He did not know who she was but carried her unconscious, limp body from the river onto the bank.

Chlodwig, distraught, eyes blurred with tears, watched Alexandrine run out the door and into the street. When she did not return that evening, he sent a telegram to Hermann to help find her. In the dark of night, Hermann searched for his mother. He walked the streets and alleys and found nothing. He returned to Karlstrasse and waited.

Several days later, Friedrich Bodenstedt was visiting a friend in the Münchner Klinik when he happened to see Alexandrine in one of the beds.

"What has happened to you?" he asked.

Alexandrine, still in despair and shock, said nothing.

Bodenstedt no longer lived in Munich but remembered that Chlodwig often stayed with Alexandrine. He took a carriage to Karlstrasse in the hope of finding him there. As he approached the house, he could see lights through the windows. Chlodwig, in despair, had not left the house, hoping she would return.

Bodenstedt ran up the steps and burst inside. He saw Chlodwig sitting hunched over next to the fire, obviously distraught, looking pale and tired. He ran to him and asked, "What has happened to Alexandrine? I saw her in the Klinik in the most distressful condition."

"You have found her, my friend! Thank you."

"But what is she doing in the Klinik?" he asked.

Chlodwig told him, "I wanted her to marry me so we could spend the rest of our years together as man and wife."

"What did she say?"

"Alex told me that she could not. It is the Church that would not allow it."

Bodenstedt listened to him but thought there must be more.

"I told her if she would not marry me, we will part. She became angry and ran out of the house and did not return. Hermann and I looked everywhere over the past four days but could not find her. I have not slept since she ran away."

Bodenstedt, ever the friend, said, "Let me take you to the Klinik. She will surely be gladdened by your visit."

Chlodwig thanked his friend but said he would call for his coachman to prepare his carriage. He instructed his driver to make all haste to the hospital. When he arrived, the sister took him into the ward and pointed to the bed where Alexandrine lay.

He was overcome with the greatest sorrow to see her lying on the bed. She was as white as the sheet that covered her, a frail shadow of her former self with her eyes closed. The nun told him what had happened. "It was a young man who brought her here. He rescued her from the river. She has not been awake since."

He could not have imagined that she would do such a thing. He sat with her every day until she finally opened her eyes and looked at him with a painful sadness.

"Why, why?" he asked with sadness in his voice.

"I could not bear to be without you, my dear friend," she whispered.

With a heavy heart, he thought of the circumstances that brought her here. "It is my fault," he said to himself. "I should not have been angry with her. If she dies, I will die too."

Her body was so ravaged and fragile from the event that Chlodwig made arrangements to send her to Nervi in the Cote de Azur to recover. While she was there, her mind argued over her sad and hopeless fate. *"My life with him is at an end, kept apart by both man and God,"* she would say to herself. Her grief was profound.

When she was fully recovered several months later, she returned to Munich not knowing what lay ahead. She was back in the house on Karlstrasse, where so much had happened. A brooding kind of peace now found her. She reminded herself that she had the greatest joy of loving this great man, to whom she devoted herself for so many years.

"Perhaps it was too great a love," she thought to herself. She did not know if he would return, and that saddened her even more.

Hermann and Gisela came often to comfort her. Gisela brought her children, whom Alexandrine adored. Ever so slowly, the confusion of the past eased, and she came to a peaceful readjustment of her life.

Some weeks later, when Chlodwig heard she was back

in Munich, he came to see her. When she heard the clattering of carriage wheels stop at the front of her house, for one wild moment she thought he had returned to her. When he approached, the prospect of happiness vanished like a wishful fantasy. He had much changed during the months she was away. He had suffered from asthma for years, which had suddenly become worse. She noticed a marked increase in his deafness. When he walked, he shuffled along at a slow pace unlike his youthful exuberant stride. He was still the same man she loved, and the change in him gave her concern.

Distressed at his poor health, she was not sure what care he needed. She called on her physician friend in Tyrol, who, with her insistence, came immediately to offer what help he could. He advised the prince to find immediate relief from his duties and seek complete rest. Chlodwig, understanding his deteriorating condition, knew what he must do.

32

Twilight

*I*n November of 1900, Prince Chlodwig resigned as chancellor. He cited in the request to Emperor Wilhelm his increasing age and poor health as his reasons for wanting to retire. Much to his relief, the emperor of all Prussia accepted his request. Soon after, Prince Chlodwig was conferred the Order of the Black Eagle as one of the highest honors for his past years of dedicated service to Prussia.

In January 1901, Queen Victoria of England died. Chlodwig wrote to his sister Princess Elise. In the letter, he stated how much he mourned the death of Queen Victoria as she was a gracious friend to him. Shortly before her death, Queen Victoria asked him to visit her. He unhappily declined as his own health prevented it. He went on to say that after she had lost all her old friends, he was happy and honored that she still remembered him.

In the same year, he complained of not feeling well. He had been in Paris when an ailment attacked him, which severely diminished his strength. In May, he was still not feeling well when he visited his sister Elise in Berlin. After a few pleasant days together, they traveled to Corvey, their childhood home.

"Look, Chlodwig, people are coming with bouquets of red roses for you," she remarked as they walked from the castle down a pleasant treelined path to the chapel that was built over the family vaults. He walked as if he was tired. Elise, holding his arm, opened the door to the vault. Inside lay their father and mother.

Chlodwig, laying a wreath of white carnations on the coffins, remarked, "It has been sixty years since our father died."

They both stayed and prayed over the two coffins. On the way back, he reflected on his views on eternity, saying, "I have recently been overwhelmed by the concept of eternity. It is appalling in its inconceivable nature. Time and space are not only inconceivable but unthinkable."

To which Elise answered, "Here, faith alone can help us."

He made no comment but lapsed into a long pause as it required no response. Walking back down the path, he asked Elise, "Do you remember the time we were walking through the Hohenlohe cemetery long ago? We came upon a headstone that was engraved with 'Learn to Die!' We learn to live, but how little we think of death."

"Yes, Chlodwig, we must all learn to die," she answered.

This was not the first time he thought about these concepts. It bothered him a great deal toward the end of his days as he turned more toward God and his faith. Upon leaving his sister, he said, as if a premonition had come to him, "It is at an end. I am going away."

After leaving Corvey, he wanted to travel to Bad Ragatz, Switzerland, in the hope of recovering. On the way, he stopped first in Colmar to spend a few days with his son Prince Alexander. Alexander begged him to stay as he thought his father was too ill to travel so far. But Chlodwig insisted on continuing his journey to Bad Ragatz for rest and recovery. Before leaving, he wrote a short letter to Alexandrine. He wanted to tell her about his sudden illness and that he would write again upon his arrival in Ragatz. He was certain that after some rest and time away from his worries, he would soon recover. She, in all goodness of thought, sent him a priest to hear his confession as he had not gone to confession in all the years of their time together. He had ample opportunities to confess on his many trips to Rome in the pope's private chapel. He never did.

As promised, she received a letter from him soon after his arrival telling her that even though the trip was tiresome, he felt much better. Her heart was full of hope with this news.

My dear friend, my health has not improved and I spend my days sitting here with nothing to do finding no comfort or companionship. I hope to be better soon and return to you. Your friend.

Alexandrine hoped for another letter soon with better news. It did not come. One day, after she returned from a little excursion into the city, she was met by Gisela standing outside her door, sobbing uncontrollably. "Papa has died," she said through her tears. "It was in the newspaper."

Chlodwig died in Bad Ragatz, Switzerland, in 1901 at eighty-two years of age.

Alexandrine, overcome by the news, collapsed in Gisela's arms. Gisela held on to her mother, walking her inside. She handed her a copy of the newspaper, which, of course, extolled Prince Chlodwig's achievements through his long career as a diplomat, calling him the pioneer of the reunification of Germany, doing his duty to king and country throughout his long life, fighting and struggling to make the impossible possible. History would shed a golden light on this remarkable man.

After she read it, Alexandrine wept, unable to stop the flow of tears. Strange as it seemed to her, she wept not just for herself but also for his children, who had lost their father. Even though she knew of his illness and accepted the fact that he may one day die, she could not stop the pain when it finally came. Her love for Chlodwig was true to the end. And she was comforted by the knowledge that, throughout their years together, he loved her.

All the memories of their thirty years together flooded her thoughts, blocking out all else. Then she remembered Gisela was sitting there with her arms around her, crying bitterly. "Your papa loved you beyond measure," she said. "You were the sun that shone on his world."

Alexandrine woke the next morning with a cold, numb heaviness in her heart. The sun was up, and she leaned against the window, looking down below at the steps he had frequented so often. She knew that her memories would not fade but stay her constant companion throughout her days. She dried her tears and put on a cheerful face as Gisela was waiting for her downstairs.

She entered the drawing room, embraced her daughter, and sat down with a cup of coffee. Alexandrine, visibly pale from lack of sleep, tried to be cheerful in front of Gisela. It did not last long. She confessed to her daughter, "Today I am unable to find any happiness. I am frozen in grief. When we were together, I was as happy as I could ever be. Maybe I had no right to be."

"Will you go to his funeral?" Gisela asked.

"No, I will not go. My choices in life have made me an outsider. I would be an unwelcome mourner. I am a widow yet not a widow. I shall grieve alone here in the house where we were together, breathing the same air, feeling as one. His death will not take away any of those memories."

Chlodwig was laid to rest in the place he sought nature and refuge from the cares of the world. In the crypt at Schillingsfürst, his coffin was covered with red roses. An honor guard of the Order of Black Eagles stood at attention while a steady procession of people from all walks of life paid their respects. The funeral was attended by dignitaries from Europe, Asia, and beyond. Foreign ambassadors, past and present ministers, princes, monarchs, family, and friends came in carriages and new gas-powered automobiles. Even the emperor postponed a trip to pay his respect to the man he admired. His funeral was befitting this great German statesman's life.

A few weeks later, Alexandrine, despondent, joined a pilgrimage to Jerusalem to ease the burden of her unending grief. Since her conversion to the Catholic faith, she had the desire to return to the Holy Land. This second trip made a different impression on her as she beheld it in a more religious light than her first trip. Father Obercamp's teachings gave her a new perspective on where Jesus lived and what He taught his people. Taking the steps where Christ once walked, she found a glorious renewal of her newfound faith.

The trip to the Holy Land, although a respite from her sorrow upon losing her friend and companion, did not last. Even though it renewed her deepest religious emotions, she returned to Munich even lonelier and more inconsolable than before. Her children were married and living their own lives.

Munich seemed empty and barren without them. The rooms in the house where she and Chlodwig had spent so many days and evenings conversing and planning his next political maneuver were now quiet. The quiet, so dark and unforgiving, made her feel alone and forsaken. It had an emptiness with no consolation. As she sat by the fire, she watched the glow of the coals as she had done for so many years. And just as the coals would die, she knew that every human life had a limit and no one could reach beyond the grave.

33

Finding Solace

Alexandrine could find no more happiness in Munich. The burden of an empty house became more unbearable each passing day. When she received a letter from her friend Elisabeth in Salzburg, after hearing of Chlodwig's death, she wrote back:

> *My dear friend, your letter finds me still in grief over the loss of my dearest friend. You might ask me what was it like to love and be loved by this great man. I can only tell you that it was the happiest time of all my life. We had the music, the loveliest of melodies. Now our symphony has ended. I will remember my friend as he was: holding my hand in his; caressing me so lovingly; speaking softly to me as his warm body lay next to mine. From the beginning, he belonged to me. We lived within each other's mind and heart.*
>
> *Now, I only look for solace in my remaining years. I will close the doors on Karlstrasse forever as it seems so empty now. Even though Chlodwig had only a few hours*

289

at a time to spend there with me, he possessed every corner, every breath of air, every light therein. His voice echoes through the walls, and I still hear his footsteps on the stone steps. I will let those remain there as I have my memories. Those will never be left behind.

I plan to make a new home in Bruck for as long as I am able. Gisela is nearby as are my grandchildren. My joy will be to see them often. They will give me comfort. To you, my friend, I leave you with fondest remembrances,

Your friend, Alex

In 1902, she moved to Bruck, where she made her home, finding new friends and being surrounded by her children Hermann and Gisela. Still mourning the loss of her dear friend, she kept herself busy volunteering through her church, helping the poor and unfortunate.

Gisela, Hermann, and her friends heaped mountains of affection upon her to make her days easier. Her children, as adults, found a friend in her to whom they could confide their innermost fears, thoughts, griefs, and joys.

On one of those occasions, Gisela confided in her mother that not all was happy in her marriage to Oswald. "I was young and naïve when I married. I knew nothing of his family and found them unwelcoming. His brothers Alfred and Idei come to visit often but offer no warmth. They would spend hours talking with Oswald about their individual properties, politics, and social reforms. Their conversations are completely devoid of any of the finer things like music, art, or literature."

"My dear child, how lonely you must be."

"Yes, Mama. But at least I have my children." Gisela started to cry. "He is often gone on trips. I do not know where.

When he returns, he does not concern himself with me or the children."

Alexandrine was saddened by Gisela's unhappiness as she herself had found so much love, and her beautiful child had found none. She was at least happy that Hermann had found a passion, not with a wife but in the arts. In his early youth, Hermann dreamed of a career in the army but instead was lured away by such artists as Possart and Christen, who saw in him a promising talent on the stage. Hermann was a great success, receiving countless accolades for his performances. Alexandrine took every opportunity to see him perform when he was nearby and gleamed with pride when she saw him.

Her only regret in life was never having the chance to be reunited with her children from her marriage to Erzberger. Even though those days were gone and could never be reclaimed, deep within her soul there still lived a motherly passion. It intensified over the years, perhaps as a result of her own childhood in a motherless, ruthless world, and she was at least able to lavish it on Gisela and Hermann. In all the years, neither Erzberger nor his family made any concession to her many pleas to see her children or told her anything about them. It was only recently through a mutual friend that she heard any news at all. Her son Egon had an illustrious career as an artist. Claire, still living in Augsburg, was married to a government director, who, coincidently, had been acquainted with Prince Chlodwig in the past, and they had formed a particular friendship. Alexandrine at least could take comfort in knowing they were happy and well. She never found out what happened to her firstborn child, Carl.

As she thought back on her life, she came to the realization that there was a constant ebb and flow. She would ascend from the serenity of a placid pool to the highest pinnacle and then suddenly plunge helplessly into dangerous raging waters below. Only Chlodwig could still the turbulence with his goodness and bring her back to a peaceful place. They often talked and argued enthusiastically about art, literature, and politics, and after the stormy waters always came the cool and tranquil seas in which their love sailed forth again. With him gone, those turbulent but not unhappy times were safely stored away in her memory.

During the next years, sweeter memories found a home within her. Her lovely daughter, unshackled from an unhappy marriage, found, in time, another man to love. Thoughts of Gisela surrounded her with unparalleled joy as she mused over her daughter's tranquil sweetness and goodness, which reminded her of Chlodwig. Gisela came often with Ludwig, Gisela Karolina, and Klara. Their grandmother doted on the three grandchildren, telling them stories of her own young life. Not the tragedies or the disappointments but the times she was happiest. Those stories of her riding through the forests of Silesia like a wild spirit on a horse flying across the steppes delighted the children. They screamed with joy, asking for more with each telling.

Late in her life, when Alexandrine brooded over some worthless, unhappy memory, Gisela clasped her mother to her and said, "You were the most devoted person, sacrificing all to my dear papa. You are the most beautiful and noble being, a poet and maker of happiness. You have blessed all who knew you."

Alexandrine would say to her, "I dwell among happy memories which outshine the sad ones. My life was rich in joy,

and today I want for nothing more than what my present circumstances cannot offer me."

Both Hermann and Gisela often urged her to write down
what she remembered from her life and the years she was with
the prince. They thought her time with this great man should
not be forgotten. "I will see," she replied at each asking.

Epilogue

$\mathcal{A}$lexandrine von Hedemann died in 1913, shortly after publishing her memoir in 1912. She wrote a poignant autobiography of her life with Prince Chlodwig.

When Gisela married Baron Oswald von Hornstein in 1888, her father, Prince Chlodwig von Hohenlohe, gave him Villa Geyerberg and 100,000 goldmarks as a dowry. Oswald and Gisela lived at Geyerberg, where Gisela Karolina and Klara were born.

Gisela married into a family whose history spans twenty-two generations dating back to 1247 AD. Over the centuries, the von Hornstein family divided itself into a dozen or more family seats owning properties throughout southern Bavaria. The first Hornstein Castle, built in 1359, is in ruins today, but a thriving effort is underway to restore at least part of it.

In the years following World War I, titles of the nobility in Germany and Austria ceased to exist. On August 11, 1919, the Weimer Constitution declared that all Germans were equal under the law, which eliminated the nobility as a class and, with it, all noble privileges. Although the noble class is no longer recognized in Germany, the German Commission on Nobility Law can decide matters such as lineage, legitimacy, and a person's right to bear a name of nobility as it existed prior to 1818. At the end of World War II, all properties belonging to the German nobility were confiscated by the Allied forces. Only a few properties were reinstated over time. One was Castle Schillingsfürst, located twelve kilometers southeast of Rothenburg ob Der Tauber in Bavaria. It remains in the Hohenlohe family.

Most of the von Hornstein properties were confiscated during World War II and either sold or destroyed. Only a few that remained were returned to the surviving von Hornstein family members, some of whom continue to live there today.

Gisela and Oswald divorced when he took a mistress. As with Alexandrine, Gisela was deprived of her children. When they divorced, the children remained with their father, as was the custom. Before WWI their birthright entitled them to their father's title, and the sons would inherit the von Hornstein estates. While growing up, the three children—Ludwig, Gisela Karolina, and Klara—were sent away to schools or lived with other relatives. They had very little contact with their mother. Oswald died on March 7, 1945, after a serious fall at the Rosenheim, Germany, train station.

It is believed Gisela later married Arnold Gottlieb Benedikt Brinz. She died on April 1, 1933, in Munich, Germany.

What became of Hermann von Hedemann is not known.

At the age of eighty-two, Prince Chlodwig von Hohenlohe asked the writer Friedrich Curtius to help him write his memoirs. From 1866, the prince kept a continuous record of his experiences during his political years from the time he was appointed minister-president of Bavaria to his greatest political position, Imperial Chancellor of the German Empire. He proposed to send all his journals, papers, and letters to Schillingsfürst so that they could be arranged and prepared for the publication of his memoirs. He invited Curtius to Schillingsfürst to work with him to get the papers in order and, together, plan how the book would be compiled. Before this could be accomplished, Prince Chlodwig died.

After his death, Curtius felt an obligation to continue with the task of putting his copious notes together to fulfill the prince's last wish. Prince Alexander, Chlodwig's youngest son, published the book together with Curtius. Unfortunately, Prince Chlodwig was denied the pleasure of beginning his memoir and the opportunity to add to it from his personal recollections.

Memoirs of Prince Chlodwig of Hohenlohe Schillingsfürst Volumes One and Two were published in 1906, five years after the prince's death. Both volumes were translated into English from the first German edition by George W. Chrystal, BA. The memoirs provide an intimate view of Chlodwig's life growing up, his love for his family, and his close relationship with his sister Amalie, with whom he shared his innermost thoughts. Beyond that, the memoirs depict a close and first-hand account of German politics of the time and the role the prince played. They also minutely detail points of German constitutional history that, even today, are of interest to students of politics. But mostly his memoirs provide a thorough insight into this exemplary statesman and his valuable contributions to Germany from 1848 until his death in 1906.

Becoming a member of the Upper House of the Bavarian Reichsrat (government) in 1846 was the beginning of his entry into the political arena. It afforded him experience in the practical affairs of government and insight into the strengths and weaknesses of the Prussian system of government at the time.

As a liberal, his views often clashed with the conservatives, but he persevered. He was well liked and admired by Otto von Bismarck, King Wilhelm I of Prussia, King Ludwig II of Bavaria, Emperor Wilhelm II of Prussia, Czar Nicholas II of Russia, sultans of Turkey, and numerous foreign ambassadors, ministers, kings, queens, and princes. His sphere of influence spread from Europe to Russia, China, Turkey, and Egypt. There is no doubt that Prince Chlodwig von Hohenlohe-Schillingsfürst was one of Germany's greatest statesmen.

1846–1866	Member of the Bavarian Reichsrat (government)
1866–1870	Nineteenth Minister-President of Bavaria
1873–1885	German Ambassador to Paris
1879–1880	Temporary Secretary of State of Foreign Affairs
1885–1894	Imperial Governor of Alsace-Loraine
1894–1900	Fourteenth Minister-President of Prussia
1894–1900	Third Chancellor of the Germany Empire

Poems by Prince Chlodwig von Hohenlohe

From Chlodwig's earliest years, he found within himself the heart of a poet. A few of his many poems were preserved by Alexandrine. These three poems were written during his first winter and spring at Schillingsfürst:

You asked me why, thou erst so cold,
I now breathe warmth and joy;
You asked me why, though erst so old,
I caught like any boy.

You are my spring, my sunlight clear,
Your eyes have warmed me through—
Broken the ice about me, dear,
Brought back my boyhood too.

Alexandrine

Once again spring-sun is beaming
In the streets all gay and bright;
And my heart is set a-dreaming,
Heart so long denied the light.

Like the trees now gladly breaking
Into April beauty—see!
Budding, whispering, awaking,
So today, in poet fashion,
I go rhyming, chiming these—
Tis the spring, the vernal passion,
Budding, like the old young trees.

~

In the sky, dark clouds are heaping,
On the set, sweet flowers are sleeping,
And the waves are flowing dully,
And a stillness strange is creeping
O'er the pasture lands so thirsty.
Ah, like such storm-warnings stealing
In the sultry days of summer,
Are the hours when, dimly feeling
All its need, the heart imploreth
Tears, quick tears, for sorrow's healing!

~

Chlodwig wrote this poem after the tragic death of his beloved
daughter, Stephanie. He sent it to Alexandrine.

You were carried to rest in flowers
The breaths of flowers drifts across your chest

Poems by Prince Chlodwig von Hohenlohe

You were like spring and the scent of spring yourself
Like sunshine on bloom filled days
And when you came, there was joy, there was comfort
In every heart as if in the spring air
The young green buds call for new life
And gently sing the nightingales in the grove.
Now what makes us so happy is over
It broke our eye's brilliant shine
The cheerful smile on your lips has disappeared.

~

At the age of seventy, he wrote this poem to Alexandrine:

To preserve the joyful sense of youth,
Even if old age has already bleached the loden
This is what everyone wants, but difficult to reach
Because it is reserved for the happy only.
Whether we switch happily with the hours
Whether you creep through the days phlegmatically
And whether it storms in the bosom or is silent,
The heart must gradually unfold.
But when I see you all my sayings vanish
Because unbowed in battle with the world,
Did you keep old age out of the way?
Whoever keeps the courage in this fight,
He stays, even if his heart beats quieter,
Sunshine lit by eternal youth.

~

From a letter to Alexandrine while at Altaussee:

> Even when comes the morning,
> It does not go away
> So, in my heart I bear it,
> Through all the live-long day.

~

The following poems were written while spending what he called a "terrible winter, which however, had its good side; man can bear everything if he only will." They were included in *Memoirs of Prince Chlodwig von Hohenlohe-Schillingsfürst, Volume One.* From the context, the first one seemed to have been written after the death of his brother, Prince Philipp Ernst.

> From the castle's rocky height,
> Clear beneath the winter moon,
> See the valley decked in light,
> See the church and see the tomb!
> There they laid thee in the grave,
> Warm and loving friends we were:
> Thou wert loyal, strong and brave;
> None with thee shall e'er compare.
> Many a bitter tear they shed,
> Standing round that holy spot.
> But their sorrows now are fled,
> For, alas, they know thee not.
> But my tears shall ever flow
> As upon that gloomy morn.
> When I made thy grave below,
> Broken hearted and forlorn.

O'er the valleys and the hills
I would be a wanderer bold;
Though the cruel winter storms,
Thunder round our castle hold.

I would be a mariner
Boldly sail the waters dark.
Though the fury of the wave,
Bode destruction to my lark.

With the children of the South
Through the palm groves I would haste.
And upon an Arab steed,
Scout the desert's burning waste.

With the sword for freedom's cause
I would smite the enemy.
And the triumph of my land
With my dying gaze decry.

Anything were better than
Thus o'er musty deeds to frown;
Yawning sharpening a pen,
Slippered, in a dressing gown.

Alexandrine

Clouds o'ercast with gloom the sky,
Wilted blossoms droop the head;
Waters cease their lullaby.
Comes a bonding hush of dread
O'er the parching face of earth
Ah, the signs of thunder-shower
In the sultry summer days
Oft recall each weary hour
When the worn, long hardened heart
Yearns for tear-drops' softening power.

Sources

Hedemann, Alexandrine von. *My Friendship with Prince Hohenlohe.* New York and London: G. P. Putman's Sons and Knickerbocker Press, 1912.

Hohenlohe-Schillingsfürst, Chlodwig von. *The Memoirs of Prince Chlodwig of Hohenlohe-Schillingsfürst Volumes I & II.* Translated from the first German edition by George W. Chrystal, BA. Edited by Friedrich Curtius for Prince Alexander von Hohenlohe-Schillingsfürst. London: William Heinemann, 1906.

Newman, Ernest. *The Life of Richard Wagner, Vol. III 1859–1866.* London: Cassell and Company Limited, 1945.

Made in the USA
Las Vegas, NV
07 July 2022